MCPD 70-519
Exam Ref:

Designing and Developing Web
Applications Using Microsoft® .NET
Framework 4

Tony Northrup

D1315971

Published with the authorization of Microsoft Corporation by:

O'Reilly Media, Inc.
1005 Gravenstein Highway North
Sebastopol, California 95472

ISBN: 978-0-7356-5726-7

1 2 3 4 5 6 7 8 9 QG 6 5 4 3 2 1

Printed and bound in the United States of America.

Microsoft Press books are available through booksellers and distributors worldwide. If you need support related to this book, email Microsoft Press Book Support at *mspinput@microsoft.com*. Please tell us what you think of this book at *http://www.microsoft.com/learning/booksurvey*.

Acquisitions and Developmental Editor: Ken Jones
Production Editor: Adam Zaremba
Editorial Production: Octal Publishing, Inc.
Technical Reviewer: Bill Chapman
Copyeditor: Roger LeBlanc
Indexer: Denise Getz
Cover Composition: Karen Montgomery
Illustrator: Robert Romano

For my favorite nephews and niece: Tyler, Austin, and Mya Rheaume

Contents at a Glance

Contents

What do you think of this book? We want to hear from you!

Microsoft is interested in hearing your feedback so we can continually improve our
books and learning resources for you. To participate in a brief online survey, please visit:

www.microsoft.com/learning/booksurvey/

What do you think of this book? We want to hear from you!

Microsoft is interested in hearing your feedback so we can continually improve our books and learning resources for you. To participate in a brief online survey, please visit:

www.microsoft.com/learning/booksurvey/

Introduction

Most development books take a very low-level approach, teaching you how to use individual classes and accomplish fine-grained tasks. Like the Microsoft 70-519 certification exam, this book takes a high-level approach, building on your lower-level web development knowledge and extending it into application design. Both the exam and the book are so high-level that there is very little coding involved. In fact, most of the code samples this book provides simply illustrate higher-level concepts.

The 70-519 certification exam tests your knowledge of designing and developing web applications. By passing the exam, you will prove that you have the knowledge and experience to design complex web applications using Microsoft technologies. This book will review every concept described in the exam objective domains:

- Design application architectures
- Design the user experience
- Design data strategies and structures
- Design a security architecture and implementation
- Prepare for and investigate application issues
- Design a deployment strategy

This book covers every exam objective, but it does not necessarily cover every exam question. Microsoft regularly adds new questions to the exam, making it impossible for this (or any) book to provide every answer. Instead, this book is designed to supplement your relevant independent study and real-world experience. If you encounter a topic in this book that you do not feel completely comfortable with, you should spend several hours researching the topic further using MSDN, blogs, and support forums. Ideally, you should also create a practical application with the technology to gain hands-on experience.

Microsoft Certified Professional Program

Microsoft certifications provide the best method for proving your command of current Microsoft products and technologies. The exams and corresponding certifications are developed to validate your mastery of critical competencies as you design and develop, or implement and support, solutions with Microsoft products and technologies. Computer professionals who become Microsoft certified are recognized as experts and are sought after industry-wide. Certification brings a variety of benefits to the individual and to employers and organizations.

> **MORE INFO** **OTHER MICROSOFT CERTIFICATIONS**
>
> For a full list of Microsoft certifications, go to *www.microsoft.com/learning/mcp/default.asp.*

Acknowledgments

First and foremost, I'd like to thank Ken Jones at O'Reilly for his work in designing the Microsoft Press Exam Ref book series, for choosing me (once again) as an author, and for his work as an editor. It's been great to work with you, as always, Ken!

I'd also like to thank Bill Chapman, the Technical Editor, Adam Zaremba, the Production Editor, Dan Fauxsmith, the Production Manager, and Roger LeBlanc, the Copy Editor.

Finally, I must thank my friends and family for their support, especially Eddie and Christine Mercado (for letting me use of their home after hurricane Irene), Brian and Melissa Rheaume (for taking me to Greenport on their boat), Jose and Kristin Gonzales (for the many laughs), Chelsea and Madelyn Knowles (for their patience while I worked too much during the Summer), and Papa Jose and Nana Lucy (for the meat pies).

Support & Feedback

The following sections provide information on errata, book support, feedback, and contact information.

Errata

We've made every effort to ensure the accuracy of this book and its companion content. Any errors that have been reported since this book was published are listed on our Microsoft Press site at oreilly.com:

> *http://go.microsoft.com/FWLink/?Linkid=229774*

If you find an error that is not already listed, you can report it to us through the same page.

If you need additional support, email Microsoft Press Book Support at *mspinput@ microsoft.com*.

Please note that product support for Microsoft software is not offered through the addresses above.

We Want to Hear from You

At Microsoft Press, your satisfaction is our top priority, and your feedback our most valuable asset. Please tell us what you think of this book at:

> *http://www.microsoft.com/learning/booksurvey*

The survey is short, and we read every one of your comments and ideas. Thanks in advance for your input!

Stay in Touch

Let's keep the conversation going! We're on Twitter: *http://twitter.com/MicrosoftPress*

Preparing for the Exam

Microsoft certification exams are a great way to build your resume and let the world know about your level of expertise. Certification exams validate your on-the-job experience and product knowledge. Although there is no substitute for on-the-job experience, preparation through study and hands-on practice can help you prepare for the exam. We recommend that you augment your exam preparation plan by using a combination of available study materials and courses. For example, you might use the Exam Ref and another study guide for your "at home" preparation, and take a Microsoft Official Curriculum course for the classroom experience. Choose the combination that you think works best for you.

CHAPTER 1

Designing the Application Architecture

The highest level aspect of the design process is also the most exciting: designing the application architecture. In this stage, the application begins to come to life, and you are not getting bogged down in technical details. You create a logical design for your application and then map the logical layers to physical servers. After you determine the physical layout, you can choose interapplication communication mechanisms and plan for cross-cutting concerns, such as systems administration.

> **IMPORTANT**
>
> ***Have you read page xix?***
>
> It contains valuable information regarding the skills you need to pass the exam.

Further into the design process, you choose how presentation logic will be divided between the client and server. For client-side components, you will need to decide between basic JavaScript, jQuery, Microsoft AJAX, and Microsoft Silverlight. For server-side components, you will need to choose between HTML controls, server controls, user controls, and Web Parts.

Finally, you will need to decide how to implement various state-management tasks. The Microsoft .NET Framework provides a wide variety of technologies, including application state, session state, view state, cookies, and caching.

Objectives in this chapter:

- Objective 1.1: Plan the division of application logic
- Objective 1.2: Analyze requirements and recommend a system topology
- Objective 1.3: Choose appropriate client-side technologies
- Objective 1.4: Choose appropriate server-side technologies
- Objective 1.5: Design state management

Real World

The application design process starts when management determines that a new application can fulfill a business requirement. As management describes what they need from the new application, your mind will race with all the reasons the application won't work the way they want. Pointing out every potential problem might feel like you're demonstrating your technical skill and preventing future frustrations, but in the real world, it hinders the design process, dampens creativity, and annoys management.

As developers, our minds have been tuned to spot and eliminate flaws. However, you need to be creative and positive during the application design process. Do your best to ignore the low-level challenges; troubleshooting is a job for coders. Designers must create.

Objective 1.1: Plan the Division of Application Logic

In the early days of the web, browsers did little more than render HTML and display images. Today, thanks to technologies such as JavaScript, Flash, and Silverlight, the browser can interact with the user, validate data, and communicate with servers without loading new webpages. Use these client-side capabilities properly, and you can make your web application feel faster, reduce bandwidth, and reduce user input errors.

Server-side processing still has its place, however. First, server-side code is much easier to develop, test, and maintain. Second, anything but the most trivial data validation must be performed on the server, because it is possible for malicious attackers to bypass client-side validation. Third, some clients do not support JavaScript, Flash, or Silverlight, requiring you to duplicate any mandatory client-side functionality on the server.

This objective covers how to:

- Choose whether to implement functionality on the client or server.
- Efficiently use client-side scripting languages.
- Explain the capabilities and drawbacks of rich, client-side plug-ins such as Flash and Silverlight.
- Partition applications according to the separation of concerns principle.
- Plan for long-running processes.

Choosing Between the Client Side and Server Side

Many tasks can be performed at either the client or the server. For example, if you ask the user to enter his address in a web form, you can provide a *DropDownList* named *Country DropDownList* that contains every country/region in the world. When the user selects a country, you can populate the *StateDropDownList* with a list of states or provinces in his country.

You can do this on either the server or the client:

- **Server**   In ASP.NET, set *CountryDropDownList.AutoPostBack* to *True*. In the *DropDownList.SelectedIndexChanged* event handler, populate *StateDropDownList*.

- **Client**   Create a JavaScript function that handles the *CountryDropDownList.OnChange* JavaScript event and populates the *StateDropDownList* on the client.

Neither approach is clearly superior, but they each have advantages. By populating the list on the server side, you keep more code in ASP.NET, which is generally easier to write, troubleshoot, and maintain than JavaScript. Additionally, server-side processing works when the client does not support JavaScript.

By populating the list on the client side, you improve performance for both the user and the server. Client-side processing avoids a browser postback to the server when the user selects her country. This eliminates a delay in data entry that could last several seconds. Additionally, by reducing the number of requests sent to the web server, it reduces the performance impact on the server, thus improving scalability.

EXAM TIP

The 70-519 exam does not require you to know JavaScript or Microsoft AJAX; those topics were covered by the 70-515 exam. In fact, the 70-519 exam does not require you to know how to write code at all. You do need to know the capabilities and limitations of JavaScript and AJAX, however, and have a higher-level understanding of the impact of writing different types of code.

Table 1-1 compares common tasks that can be performed at either the client or server, and how you write code to accomplish them. When validating user input, you typically validate it on the client (for immediate responsiveness) and again at the server (for security and for browsers that do not support JavaScript).

TABLE 1-1 Performing Different Tasks at the Client-side and Server-side

Task	Client-side feature	Server-side feature
Respond to a button click	JavaScript's *onClick* event	ASP.NET's *Button.Click* event
Access a SOAP web service	JavaScript SOAP clients or the *XMLHttpRequest* object	Import the definition, and access the methods directly
Update part of a page with data from the server	ASP.NET *UpdatePanel* control	Any server control

Task	Client-side feature	Server-side feature
Validate user input	*RequiredFieldValidator, RangeValidator, RegularExpressionValidator,* and *CustomValidator* (with the *ClientValidationFunction* property)	*RequiredFieldValidator, RangeValidator, RegularExpressionValidator,* and *CustomValidator* (with the *OnServerValidate* property)

Many tasks should always be done on the server, while other tasks should be performed on the client (when the client supports JavaScript). Table 1-2 lists tasks that can be done on the client, and situations that require you to perform the task on the server, instead.

TABLE 1-2 Client-side and Server-side Tasks

Client-side Tasks	Server-side Tasks
For convenience, notify users if they enter data in an invalid format. For example, if they enter too few numbers for a credit card.	For security and data integrity, verify that user data falls within specified bounds.
Dynamically add items to a menu, based on what the user does within a single webpage.	Add items to a menu for restricted pages that only authorized users can access.
Perform tasks that require access to the client computer, such as saving files using JavaScript or accessing the graphical processing unit (GPU) with Silverlight.	Perform tasks that require access to resources on the internal network that the server can access but are not exposed to the client.
Perform tasks that consume a great deal of bandwidth when communicating between the client and server.	Perform tasks that cannot be performed on the client, especially when the client lacks JavaScript, Flash, or Silverlight.
Process business logic that the end user is allowed to examine (because the user can access the source code).	Process business logic that should not be exposed to the end user.
Perform user-interface interactions, such as expanding menus and displaying slide shows.	Perform security-oriented tasks, such as processing credit cards and authenticating users.

If a task can be performed on either the client or the server, you should perform the task on the server because server-side programming is more efficient, the code is easier to debug, and the application is easier to maintain. Table 1-3 describes the key differences between client-side and server-side programming.

TABLE 1-3 Comparison of Client-side and Server-side Programming

Client-side Programming	Server-side Programming
Code is written in Microsoft Visual Studio 2010 with limited support for auto-complete.	Code is written in Visual Studio 2010 with full support for auto-complete, descriptions of all parameters, and integrated documentation.
Weak typing and run-time detection of errors.	Strong typing with compile-time detection of many errors

Client-side Programming	Server-side Programming
Must test in every supported operating system, browser, and browser version (which can be more than a dozen different environments).	Only need to test in a single-web-server environment.
Somewhat imprecise debugging provided by Microsoft Internet Explorer and Visual Studio 2010. Other browsers require browser-specific debugging tools.	Precise debugging provided by Microsoft Internet Information Services (IIS) and the Visual Studio 2010 ASP.NET runtime environment.
Code might never run if the client does not support JavaScript.	Code always runs regardless of client capabilities.
End users can view, manipulate, or bypass code.	Code is never exposed to the end user.

Partitioning According to Separation of Concerns

Separation of Concerns (SoC) is a software architecture concept for dividing code used for different purposes. For example, if you were designing a web application with SoC in mind, you might create different application layers for the user interface, the business logic, the data access, and the database itself.

Microsoft's early web development languages provided little opportunity for implementing SoC. However, the importance of SoC is reflected in each new web development model that Microsoft has released, as the following sections describe.

Classic ASP

In 1998, Microsoft released Active Server Pages (ASP), now known as Classic ASP. Classic ASP mixed the HTML user interface and all back-end code into a single file. To write output to part of a webpage, you had to write code at the appropriate spot in the HTML:

```
<p>First name:
<%
    Dim firstName
    firstName = "Kim" (Akers)
    Response.Write firstName
%>
</p>
<p>Last name:
<%
    Dim lastName
    lastName = "Akers"
    Response.Write lastName
%>
</p>
```

Because all the code was mixed together, a web designer who wanted to modify the user interface might accidentally change code that performed business logic or accessed the database. Similarly, if a database designer changed the layout of a table in the database, it might affect the user interface of the application. Performing quality assurance (QA) was difficult because you could not easily test individual components. Instead, developers had to simulate user input and then examine the resulting HTML output for an expected result. Different developers could not easily work on the same page at the same time.

ASP.NET

In 2002, Microsoft released ASP.NET, which allowed developers to use code-behind files to separate the HTML and the placement of server controls from the back-end code. This was a definite improvement for implementing SoC, but developers still created a single class for displaying output and responding to user input. This approach makes testing difficult because testing an individual page requires creating an instance of the page class, its child controls, and all dependent classes.

ASP.NET MVC

In 2009, Microsoft released ASP.NET MVC, which is named for the Model-View-Controller software architecture and provides three different layers of SoC:

- **Model**   The data and behavior of the application
- **View**   The user interface, which displays data provided by the model
- **Controller**   Accepts user input, and calls the model and view to generate a response

Figure 1-1 shows the MVC design pattern and the communications between the layers.

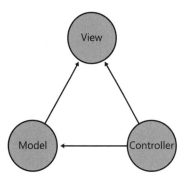

FIGURE 1-1 The MVC design pattern

By providing SoC, MVC provides several benefits. Support for test-driven development allows QA personnel to query the model directly to verify that it provides an expected output when given a specific input. Developers can modify views to update the user interface without any potential impact on the business logic or data access layers. Controllers completely abstract requests from the models and views responding to the request, allowing web architects to specify a structure for the user interface without defining the application architecture.

Implementing SoC can increase development time for smaller applications, albeit by a small margin. However, SoC can dramatically reduce debugging, QA, and maintenance time.

SoC also simplifies dividing development tasks between multiple developers. Therefore, the larger the development effort, the more important SoC becomes.

Planning for Long-Running Processes

Web users are impatient and will cancel a request or give up on a website entirely if pages do not load quickly. As a result, webpages typically need to be rendered in less than a second. That is enough time to query a database or a web service, but performing a longer-running task requires multiple requests.

Consider a travel agency web application that provides flight information from multiple airlines. If a user requests information about all flights between Boston and Chicago on a specific day, the web application might need to send web service requests to a dozen different airlines and wait for the responses before displaying the results to the user. One airline might respond in half a second, but another airline might take 10 seconds to respond.

If the web application queried each airline synchronously (in sequence, one after another), the response time would be delayed by the sum total of all the airline web services. It is more efficient to submit the web service queries asynchronously (in parallel, all at the same time). Then the response time is delayed only by the time required by the slowest web service.

When you create a method, such as a *Button.Click* event handler, the code in the method runs synchronously by default. In other words, the common language runtime (CLR) runs one line of code, waits for the results, and then moves on to the next line. This linear flow is easy for developers to understand, and it is efficient for short-running processes.

If you have long-running processes, such as waiting for a web service to respond, you can use asynchronous processing to allow the .NET Framework to perform other tasks instead of waiting for the response. When the asynchronous response is complete, you can retrieve the results and update the response to the user.

> **NOTE** **WRITING ASYNCHRONOUS CODE**
>
> Ideally, any task that is not dependent on the results of other tasks should be performed asynchronously. Using asynchronous programming techniques improves performance and scalability. In practice, however, you need to weigh the benefits against the complexity of writing and maintaining asynchronous tasks.

Designing a Webpage for a Long-Running Process

Figure 1-2 shows the typical flow of a synchronous webpage. With this model, however, the user gets no feedback until the server finishes rendering the response. If it takes the server more than a few seconds, the user is likely to cancel the request.

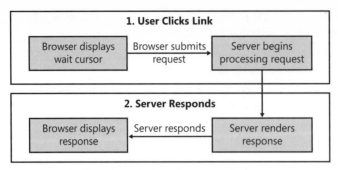

FIGURE 1-2 The flow of a typical synchronous webpage

Figure 1-3 shows the typical flow of an asynchronous webpage. With this model, the server informs the user that the response will take a few moments. A client-side script regularly checks the server to determine whether the results are ready. When the long-running, asynchronous process has completed, the final results are displayed to the user.

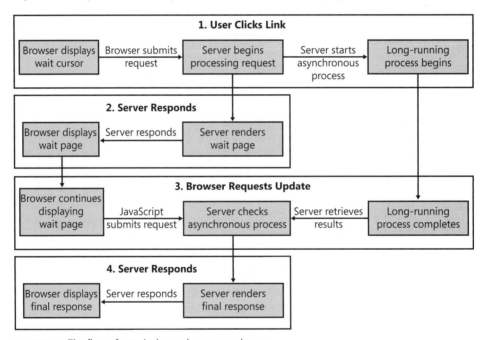

FIGURE 1-3 The flow of a typical asynchronous webpage

You can run a long-running process while remaining responsive to users. In the travel agency example, developers might take one of these two approaches:

- Display a loading page with a progress bar or other animation that shows the application is currently processing the request. This page uses JavaScript to communicate with the server. When the server reports that the results are ready, JavaScript loads the results page.

- Immediately display a formatted results page. Instead of showing the results, a progress bar indicates that the results are loading. In the background, the page runs JavaScript to connect to the server and wait for results. As the server returns results (either partially or all at once), JavaScript adds the results to the page.

For processes that might take more than a minute or two to complete, gather the user's email address and send her a notification with a link to retrieve the results.

Designing a Web Service for a Long-Running Process

Whereas web applications must render the HTML that the browser displays as the user interface, web services return raw data that the client application processes. Because the web service client creates the user interface, the web service developer does not need to decide how to communicate the delay to the user.

The web service developer does, however, need to design the web service to accommodate long-running asynchronous processes. If both the client and server are based on the .NET Framework, and the client is not protected by a firewall or Network Address Translation (NAT) device, you can use *WSDualHttpBinding*, *netTcpBinding*, *NetNamedPipeBinding*, *NetPeerTcpBinding*, or *NetTcpContextBinding* to create a callback contract on the client and then use that callback to notify the client that the process is complete.

> **NOTE** **DUPLEX HTTP FOR SILVERLIGHT AND .NET CLIENTS**
>
> Silverlight clients can use *PollingDuplexHttpBinding*, which supports duplex communications and allows the client to be located behind a firewall or NAT device. Unfortunately, .NET 4.0 does not include a polling duplex HTTP binding. However, you can download a sample custom channel that might suit your needs at *http://archive.msdn.microsoft.com/duplexhttp*.

If the binding type does not support duplex communications, or you must communicate through a firewall that prevents incoming connections to the client, you should handle long-running web service requests by immediately providing a token the client can use to later retrieve the results. To provide better feedback to the end user, you can also provide an estimated wait time that the client can use to display the progress to the user. Then have the client regularly poll the server to determine if the process is complete.

Use polling to retrieve the results of a long-running query that is using a web service by following this process:

1. The client sends the request to the web service. This might be, for example, "List all flights between Boston and Chicago on May 1."

2. The web service provides a unique token to the client and an approximate wait time. The token should be large and cryptographically random, such as a 20-byte value generated by *RngCryptoServiceProvider*. The wait time should be based on the actual wait time for similar requests.

3. The web service client displays a progress bar to the user to let him know the request is continuing and the application is responsive. The web service asynchronously calls a method to process the request and store the results in a database record associated with the token.

4. After an interval (for example, one-quarter of the estimated wait time), the web service client queries the web service for the results, providing the unique token. If the results are ready, the web service client formats and displays the data; otherwise, it repeats this step.

Objective Summary

- Use client-side scripting to provide users with a rich, responsive interface. However, you must write server-side code when security is important. Additionally, server-side code is more efficient to write, test, troubleshoot, and maintain.

- SoC simplifies development, testing, and updating of large-scale web applications. Strive to design applications with SoC dividing the functional layers of an application.

- To perform a long-running request while appearing responsive to the user, divide a request into multiple steps. In the first step, launch the long-running process asynchronously and display a wait page to the user. Embed JavaScript in the wait page that queries the server for the status of the long-running process and retrieves the final results page when processing is complete.

Objective Review

Answer the following questions to test your knowledge of the information in this objective. You can find the answers to these questions and explanations of why each answer choice is correct or incorrect in the "Answers" section at the end of this chapter.

1. You are designing an ASP.NET web application that allows members of the Administrators role to edit content by using a HyperLink control on each page named *EditHyperLink*. You do not want nonadministrators to discover the location of the administration pages. Which approach should you recommend?

   A. In the ASPX page, set the *EditHyperLink.Visible* property to *True*. In the JavaScript *window.onload* event handler, set the link's *style.display* property to none if the user is not a member of the Administrators role.

   B. In the ASPX page, set the *EditHyperLink.Visible* property to *False*. In the JavaScript *window.onload* event handler, set the link's *style.display* property to block if the user is a member of the Administrators role.

C. In the ASPX page, set the *EditHyperLink.Visible* property to *False*. In the *Page.Load* event handler, set the *HyperLink.Visible* property to *True* if the user is a member of the Administrators role.

D. In the ASPX page, set the *EditHyperLink.Visible* property to *False*. In the *EditHyper Link.Click* event handler, set the *HyperLink.Visible* property to *False* if the user is not a member of the Administrators role.

2. You are designing an ASP.NET web application that provisions virtual machines for a testing environment. Users can provision from 1 to 10 virtual machines at a time, and each virtual machine provision might take up to 60 seconds. For security reasons, the server hosting the virtual machines allows provisioning requests only from the web server. You need to design the application to keep users notified of the provisioning progress. Which approach should you recommend?

A. On the server, start asynchronous processes to provision each virtual machine. On the client, use JavaScript to query the server every five seconds for a status update.

B. On the server, synchronously provision each virtual machine. When complete, return a status update to the user.

C. On the server, calculate the approximate total provisioning time. On the client, use JavaScript to connect to the server hosting the virtual machines and initiate the provisioning.

D. On the client, use JavaScript to launch a separate asynchronous process for each virtual machine to be provisioned. Within each process, request a page from the web server that provisions a virtual machine.

3. You are creating a new website for an enterprise organization. The enterprise has a quality assurance team that requires developers to use test-driven development. Additionally, the application architecture must partition according to the principle of SoC. Which template should you use?

A. Use the ASP.NET 4.0 web application project template.

B. Use the ASP.NET MVC 2 web application project template.

C. Use the Silverlight application project template.

D. Create an ASP.NET 4.0 website.

In the following thought experiment, you apply what you've learned about the "Plan the Division of Application Logic" objective to predict how a theoretical website architecture will perform. You can find answers to these questions in the "Answers" section at the end of this chapter.

You are a developer for City Power & Light. You are working with management to assess the impact of moving an intranet application to the Internet. The application was created using ASP.NET 2.0. Only authorized and authenticated employees located on the high-speed intranet are allowed to use the application. Employees can enter a customer's identification number or street address, and then examine that customer's power usage over time by viewing a list of monthly statistics or a graphical chart. Typically, employees interpret the information over the phone when a customer calls and requests information about his bill.

Because many of the employee computers have low-powered processors and outdated browsers, the application was designed without any JavaScript or client-side logic. Employees complain that during peak hours, it can take five or ten seconds to load a page with a chart. Showing charts for different time periods requires waiting for a new page to load.

Management needs to give customers direct access to their usage information. Answer the following questions about the future performance of the application:

1. Which factors currently limit the responsiveness of the site: client processing, server processing, client bandwidth, or server bandwidth? How could you improve the performance?

2. How will the website perform if the company provides customers access to it across the Internet without modifying the application?

3. How would you create a reasonably accurate estimate of the server processing capabilities and the amount of bandwidth the site might need on the Internet?

4. How would you reduce the amount of server processing time required to generate the charts?

5. How could you avoid reloading the entire webpage when changing the time period of a chart?

6. How would generating charts on the client affect the site's performance? Which client-side technology would you use? How would you provide the raw data to the client?

7. How would using a content delivery network (CDN) reduce Internet bandwidth requirements? How might a CDN speed delivery of server-side or client-side charts?

Objective 1.2: Analyze Requirements and Recommend a System Topology

Large-scale Internet and intranet applications require you to create a logical design, map it to a physical server architecture, and choose how the different layers will interact. This objective includes an overview of common system topologies, describes how to select a binding for interapplication interactions, helps you choose a binding type, and provides best practices for cross-cutting concerns.

This objective covers how to:

- Design a system topology.
- Design interactions between applications.
- Map the logical design to the physical implementation.
- Validate nonfunctional requirements and cross-cutting concerns.
- Evaluate baseline needs.

Designing a System Topology

There are two system topologies with which you should be familiar: MVC (as described in Objective 1.1), and the three-tier architecture. The three-tier architecture consists of the following:

- **Presentation** The user interface. This tier is responsible for layout and formatting.
- **Application Logic** Also known as Business Logic, this tier is responsible for making decisions based on business rules. If this tier has multiple layers, you can refer to the architecture as an *n-tier* architecture.
- **Data** Typically implemented by a database, this tier is responsible for storing and retrieving information.

For a typical ASP.NET web application, the three-tier architecture might be implemented as follows:

- **Presentation** An IIS web server with an ASP.NET web application. The web application retrieves data from the logic tier by using Windows Communication Foundation (WCF), performs minor formatting and processing, adds it to a webpage, and returns it to the client's web browser.
- **Application Logic** A .NET Framework application exposing interfaces via WCF. The logic tier receives requests from the presentation tier, such as "How long will it take to ship this item?" or "Should I offer this customer a coupon?" The logic tier retrieves all data required to answer queries from the data tier.

- **Data**   A database server, such as Microsoft SQL Server. The data tier stores raw data, such as a table containing every item for sale and the number of items in inventory or a table with every customer and an index of their orders.

Whether you implement an MVC architecture, a three-tier architecture, or an n-tier architecture, you benefit from these advantages:

- **Easier to divide among different developers**   Let the database guys write the logic tier and the design guys write the presentation tier.

- **Easier to replace a single component**   For example, you could use existing Linux web servers for the initial deployment and later migrate to Windows. By separating the presentation layer, you would not have to rewrite the entire application—just the presentation.

- **Easier to scale**   You can add more web servers without making any changes to the presentation layer.

- **More flexibility**   Most web applications include logic and presentation in a single assembly. By separating the two, you simplify replacing the user interface. It also allows you to support multiple, different user interfaces, such as web, Microsoft Windows, and mobile interfaces.

- **Easier to test**   The only way to create a reliable application is to create a testable application. As described in Objective 1.1, providing SoC allows you to more easily test individual components.

If these three tiers aren't familiar to you as a web developer, it is because most web applications use a two-tier logical architecture that combines presentation and logic into a single set of classes. Unless you go out of your way, ASP.NET applications (other than MVC applications) use a two-tier architecture.

Designing Interactions Between Applications

Modern web applications are rarely isolated to themselves. They query databases, web services, and other applications to retrieve the data they need. They also provide updates by initiating order processing and signaling support.

Whether the communications are between different applications or different tiers within a single application, you should use WCF to implement it. WCF provides a powerful, flexible, and (optionally) standards-based way to communicate between processes, either on the same computer or across the network.

WCF supports many types of network protocols, implemented as bindings. If you need to be able to communicate across the Internet, choose one of the following HTTP bindings because HTTP communications are almost always allowed through firewalls:

- **wsHttpBinding**   A standards, SOAP-based web service, *wsHttpBinding* is perfect when you will be communicating with .NET Framework–based hosts or if you need to communicate across the Internet, where firewalls might block non-HTTP traffic. *wsHttpBinding* provides powerful security features, making it the binding type of choice for Internet communications. *wsHttpBinding* does not support streaming or duplex communications.

- **WSDualHttpBinding**   Like *wsHttpBinding*, except it provides duplex communications when the service needs to initiate communications to a client. As discussed in Objective 1.1, duplex communications will not work if the client is behind a firewall or Network Address Translation (NAT) device.

- **basicHttpBinding**   Like *wsHttpBinding*, *basicHttpBinding* is SOAP-based. However, it is based on earlier SOAP 1.1 standards and does not include the full set of *wsHttpBinding* features, such as encryption. *basicHttpBinding* is primarily useful for communicating with WS-Basic Profile conformant web services, such as ASMX-based web services.

- **webHttpBinding**   A REST-style binding that functions differently than SOAP. REST uses a wider variety of HTTP commands than SOAP, such as *GET*, *PUT*, and *DELETE*.

If you don't need to communicate across firewalls or the public Internet, and all hosts are .NET Framework–based, you can choose from these more powerful bindings:

- **netNamedPipeBinding**   The preferred binding type for communications between processes on a single computer.

- **netTcpBinding**   The most powerful binding type when all hosts are based on the .NET Framework.

- **NetMsmqBinding**   Useful when you need to queue messages for later processing. For example, the client might need to submit a task to a server that will not be able to process the message in a timely manner or is completely offline.

- **NetPeerTcpBinding**   Provides peer-to-peer communications when more than two hosts are involved.

Use the flowchart in Figure 1-4 to choose a binding type for your scenario. Although the flowchart does not include all binding types, it does cover the most common uses.

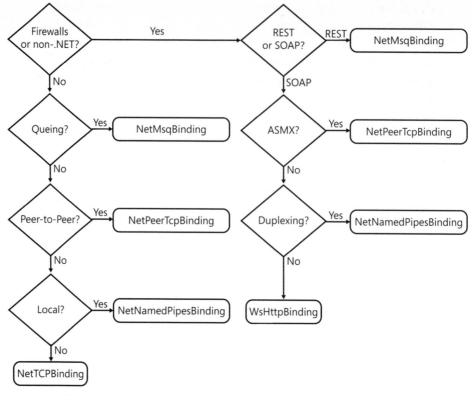

FIGURE 1-4 WCF binding decision flowchart

Any service you expose can use multiple bindings. Therefore, you can provide a binding based on *netTcpBinding* for .NET Framework–based hosts and a second *wsHttpBinding* for hosts that use open standards.

Although choosing the binding type is an important decision, it's relatively easy to change after the fact. Choose to define both the client and server bindings using configuration files, rather than hard-coding them into your application. Rely on discover protocols, such as Web Service Definition Language (WSDL), to save yourself from reconfiguring clients if the server settings change.

> **MORE INFO** **DESIGNING DATA ACCESS**
>
> For information about communicating with a database, refer to Chapter 3, "Designing Data Strategies and Structures."

When designing interactions between applications, consider whether your interactions will be chatty or chunky:

- Chatty application communications create many small requests. Chatty applications perform well when latency (the time it takes to send a message across the network) is low.
- Chunky application communications create fewer large requests. Chunky applications perform well when bandwidth (the total amount of data that can be sent across the network) is high.

Choose to bundle your communications together into chunks when the network infrastructure is high-latency and high-bandwidth, such as satellite or inter-continental communications. Use chatty communications by sending smaller messages immediately when the network infrastructure is low-latency and low-bandwidth, such as communications with mobile devices. The difference will be insignificant on most local area networks (LANs), which are low-latency and high-bandwidth.

Mapping the Logical Design to the Physical Implementation

After you have divided your application into layers to create your application's logical architecture, you need to design the physical architecture. The physical architecture defines the number of servers you will host the application on and how they are interconnected. At a high level, there are two different physical architecture philosophies:

- **Separate everything**   Place the web server, application server, and database servers on different computers. This approach provides greater scalability.
- **Combine everything**   Place all services on a single server. For the same cost, this approach provides better performance, reliability, and manageability.

Having a multitier logical architecture does not require you to deploy the same physical architecture. As Figure 1-5 illustrates, you can deploy all three logical layers to a single physical computer. Alternatively, you can deploy each layer to its own computer. You also have the option of deploying two layers to a single server, or of deploying ten web servers, three application servers, and a database cluster—the combinations are endless.

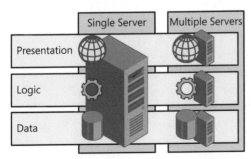

FIGURE 1-5 Single server vs. multiple servers for a three-tier web application

The physical architecture you choose depends on several factors. The single-server architecture has the following benefits:

- **Up-front costs**   Obviously, if you deploy an application to three servers, you have to buy more hardware. This factor can be eliminated by using virtualization software, such as Hyper-V, and creating virtual machines for each server instance. You also need more operating system licenses. However, you might be able to use a less-expensive operating system for the web server, such as Windows Server 2008 R2 Web Edition. Instead of dividing your hardware and software budget across multiple servers, you can put the same money into a single server and achieve much better performance.

- **Management costs**   The more computers you have, the more you need to manage. Over time, management costs typically exceed up-front costs.

- **Complexity**   Simple is always superior. The more servers you add, the more complex your configuration will be.

- **Reliability**   Each server you add to a web application is another component that can fail. If you deploy a three-tier application to three different servers, each server becomes a single point of failure; a failure of any one of the three servers would take the application offline. Similarly, scheduled downtime for any of the three servers requires scheduled downtime for the entire application. Additionally, communications between the servers becomes another single point of failure. If the network link between the servers fails, the entire application fails. You can use redundancy to overcome the decreased reliability of a multiple-server architecture, but your up-front and management costs will go up proportionately.

- **Efficient interprocess communications**   Communicating across a network, even a LAN, always introduces some latency. It will always be faster for the web, logic, and data tiers to communicate when they are located on the same server.

The multiple-server architecture provides these benefits:

- **Scalability**   With modern computing power, all but the busiest public web applications can be hosted on a single server. If your application requires more processing time or memory than a single computer can provide, dividing different tiers between physical computers can alleviate that concern.

- **Isolation**   Deploying a tier to a separate physical computers guarantees that the load on other tiers will not affect that tier's performance. For example, if you are concerned that a denial-of-service attack might cause IIS to consume 100 percent of the server's processing time, you can place the database on a separate physical computer to prevent the database from being affected. The hosted application is still inaccessible because of the load on the web server, but if other applications share the same database, those applications are not affected (unless, of course, the denial-of-service attack caused the website to submit costly database queries).

EXAM TIP

For the exam, know that you can move a service (such as a database server) to a different physical computer if you absolutely must ensure that load on the web server never affects the service.

Real World

I've had the opportunity to design the architecture for hundreds of websites, ranging from startups to Fortune 100 companies, and then monitor the performance of the websites over years. About 80 percent of the time, the clients think they need far more hardware then they ever end up using. Even during peak hours, most applications running on a single physical server are under 2 percent utilized.

There's the argument that websites must be designed to scale to sudden spikes in popularity, such as being featured in the news. That's a valid concern, but I typically recommend deploying a single-server architecture and then using load testing (for example, using the Microsoft Web Capacity Analysis Tool) to determine whether the architecture can scale. In most cases, the limiting factor to scalability is not insufficient processor or memory. Instead, applications tend to run into artificial connection limits, resource locking problems, and other software-related issues.

When those issues are resolved, further load testing tends to show developers that they need to make better use of .NET Framework caching, which can almost completely eliminate web and database server processing requirements. If the application is well designed and coded, your upstream bandwidth will limit your performance—a problem that can be resolved by caching content (especially multimedia content) by using a distributed content delivery network (CDN), such as Akamai or Amazon CloudFront.

Objective 6.3, "Plan for Scalability and Reliability," in Chapter 6, "Designing a Deployment Strategy," provides more detail about how to meet quality of service (QoS) requirements.

Validating Nonfunctional Requirements and Cross-Cutting Concerns

Cross-cutting concerns and nonfunctional requirements are noncore functions that affect many parts of an application. For example, management, monitoring, logging, and authentication affect all parts of the application, but they are not part of the core functionality.

As a developer, you should strive to create applications that systems administrators can configure and manage without needing development experience. You can do this by following these best practices:

- **Read all configuration settings from XML files, such as the Web.config file**   You can do this by using the *ConfigurationManager.AppSettings* property. Administrators should already be familiar with editing XML files, so storing commonly changed settings (such as the address of a server or number of seconds in a timeout) in the Web.config file allows administrators to change an application's behavior without contacting the developer.

- **Store application settings in an external .config file**   To allow an upgrade or re-installation to overwrite the Web.config file without affecting the application configuration, store application-specific settings in a separate XML file. You can reference this file by using the following syntax:

```
<configuration>
    <appSettings file="externalSettings.config"/>
</configuration>
```

- **Never store constants in a code file**   It might seem obvious not to store connection strings in a code file; however, you should also avoid storing the number of rows that appear on a page, the number of retries, or the path to a shared folder in a code file.

- **Use resource files**   It's often OK to store text, such as "OK" or "Cancel", in an .aspx file. However, you should never store text that appears in a user interface in a code file. Instead, reference a resource file that administrators can edit without recompiling the application.

- **Disable debugging by default, but allow it to be re-enabled**   Ideally, if a systems administrator cannot solve a problem, she describes it to the developer, who then re-creates the problem in a lab environment. In practice, however, some problems cannot easily be re-created, and you have no choice but to debug an application in the production environment. Plan for this by designing applications that allow debugging with proper authentication.

- **Allow back-ups**   Generally, web applications can be backed up as regular files. However, you must ensure that the data store you use can be backed up. If you use a SQL Server database, ensure that administrators know which tables to back up, and how frequently to back them up. Avoid keeping files locked, which might prevent them from being backed up.

- **Start correctly after a reboot**   Operations need to regularly restart servers. Although most web applications start automatically when the server comes back online, you should test your application to ensure that it functions properly after restarting either the web server, the database server, or both. In particular, avoid establishing database connections or reading important data in the *Application.Start* event, because the database server might be offline when the web server starts. A related trait to plan for is known as *graceful degradation* or *resiliency*, which allows the application to recover from a temporary network, database, or application server outage.

- **Plan for database changes**   Table structure can change over time. For example, a future version of an application might add a column to a table. To provide forward-compatibility and ensure that different versions of your application can interact with a single database, refer to table columns using names rather than column numbers. This is handled automatically if you use Entity Data Modeling.

- **Document thoroughly**   Naturally, you should comment both your code and configuration files. Additionally, you should write documentation for testing, deploying, configuring, monitoring, backing up, and restoring your application.

When you actually develop the application, avoid mixing functional and nonfunctional code. Instead, use the principals of aspect-oriented programming (AOP) and separate cross-cutting code into separate concerns.

> *MORE INFO*   **ASPECT-ORIENTED PROGRAMMING**
>
> For more information, read "Aspect-Oriented Programming" at *http://msdn.microsoft.com/library/aa288717.aspx*.

Evaluating Baseline Needs

During the design phase, you need to evaluate the baseline needs of your web application. Don't look too far into the future; instead, focus on what the application will need during the first six months. When the application is in production, you will be able to examine real-world performance factors and plan more accurately.

The following list describes the most important information you need to gather:

- **Uptime requirements**   These requirements are often expressed as 99% ("two nines"), 99.9% ("three nines"), or 99.99% ("four nines"). You need to determine whether a single server can meet the uptime requirements, factoring in planned downtime caused by updates.

- **Responsiveness**   How long users are willing to wait for a response from your server. With Internet applications, you must also factor in the network latency.

- **Peak number of simultaneous users**   The number of users who will be logged on simultaneously.
- **Peak number of requests per second**   The number of requests the web application will receive within a second. If this is less than one (as it is with most new web applications), you typically don't have to worry about processor capabilities, as even low-end shared web servers will be able to process most requests in less than a second.

MORE INFO   **RELIABILITY AND SCALABILITY**

For more information about planning for scalability and reliability, refer to Chapter 6.

Estimating these values allows you to create baseline infrastructure requirements, such as the following:

- **Disk capacity**   .NET Framework code typically takes very little disk space; however, databases can grow very large. Provide at least twice the estimated capacity of your data to allow for the inherent inefficiencies of database storage.
- **Number of processor cores**   Provide enough processing power to render pages faster than the peak number of requests per second. If the server cannot keep up with this number, the web server will queue requests. Short-term queuing might still occur when an abnormally high number of requests arrives within a few seconds, but the temporarily reduced responsiveness is typically acceptable.
- **Memory**   The amount of random access memory (RAM) your application will store. If you plan to store any large collections in memory rather than accessing them from a database, ensure the web server has at least twice that space available. The web server will use any excess memory for caching.
- **Bandwidth**   You can estimate the bandwidth requirements by multiplying the peak number of requests per second by the average page size (including images and video). Rendered webpages consume very little bandwidth. Instead, most web bandwidth is consumed by transmitting images and video.
- **Number of servers**   You might need multiple servers to provide redundancy to meet the uptime requirements. If you are planning for a high peak number of requests per second and a single server cannot provide the processing power, you might need multiple servers to meet your responsiveness requirement.
- **CDN needs**   For Internet applications, verify that your Internet connection has sufficient available bandwidth to meet peak requirements. If it is insufficient, use a web hosting provider with sufficient bandwidth or distribute the images and video by using a CDN.

Objective Summary

- The two most commonly used system architectures are MVC (discussed in Objective 1.1) and three-tier. The three-tier architecture creates an SoC between the presentation, application logic, and data tiers.

- Unless you are required to work with a system that does not support it, you should use MFC to communicate between applications. MFC provides a wide variety of protocols to meet interoperability, performance, and queuing requirements.

- When mapping logical design to physical implementation, use the minimum amount of servers required to meet your needs. Unless you need multiple servers for redundancy, scalability, or isolation, use a single server.

- Cross-cutting concerns such as monitoring, logging, operations, and security are not related to the application's core functionality. However, they contribute greatly to the manageability of the application. Whenever possible, use coding best practices that separate cross-cutting concerns into separate classes and store settings administrators might want to change separately from your code.

- Although baseline needs must be estimated, they are important because you can use them to specify hardware requirements. Typically, you should err on the side of using less expensive hardware, but provide a convenient path to upgrade in the event the application has higher requirements after it is in production.

Objective Review

Answer the following questions to test your knowledge of the information in this objective. You can find the answers to these questions and explanations of why each answer choice is correct or incorrect in the "Answers" section at the end of this chapter.

1. You need to design a physical architecture to meet these requirements:

   - The website will remain online if the web server is restarted.

   - The database server will not be affected by a denial-of-service attack against the web server.

   - You must minimize hardware costs.

   How many servers will you need?

   A. One

   B. Two

   C. Three

   D. Four

2. You need to design a physical architecture to meet these requirements:

- The website must be able to serve six requests per minute.
- The database server will store 2 TB of data.
- You must minimize hardware costs.

How many servers will you need?

A. One

B. Two

C. Three

D. Four

3. You are designing a three-tier web application. You need to choose the method of communication between the web and application layers to meet these requirements:

- The application server will use the .NET Framework 4.0.
- The application server must be physically isolated.
- The application server will be located on the same high-speed LAN as the web server and database servers.
- The web server will be located behind a firewall.
- The communications will be two-way.
- The communications must be as efficient as possible.

Which WCF binding type will you use?

A. *NetTcpBinding*

B. *NetNamedPipesBinding*

C. *WsHttpBinding*

D. *WSDualHttpBinding*

 THOUGHT EXPERIMENT
Planning for Scalability and Forward Compatibility

In the following thought experiment, you apply what you've learned about the "Analyze Requirements and Recommend a System Topology" objective to predict how a theoretical website architecture will perform. You can find answers to these questions in the "Answers" section at the end of this chapter.

You are a developer for Margie's Travel, an Internet-based business that provides travel reviews and recommendations. Margie's Travel has hired a developer to create an updated version of its website, and the company has asked you to review the design to verify that it meets its requirements for scalability and forward compatibility.

The new application is designed with a traditional three-tier architecture, as shown in Figure 1-6. Initially, all three layers will be implemented using a single server.

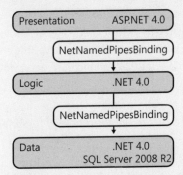

FIGURE 1-6 A three-tier application for Margie's Travel

Management wants to verify that the design meets its requirements. Answer the following question about the future performance of the application:

1. What changes will the company need to make to the application if it moves each tier to its own server?

2. What changes will the company need to make to the logic tier if it wants to create a Windows Presentation Foundation (WPF) application as a secondary presentation interface?

3. What changes will the company need to make if it replaces SQL Server 2008 R2 with a non-Microsoft database server?

4. What changes will the company need to make if it replaces the ASP.NET presentation interface with a Linux presentation interface? What impact will that have?

5. The company expects the website to get about 200 visitors per day. Will a single, dedicated server be fast enough?

Objective 1.3: Choose Appropriate Client-Side Technologies

Client-side technologies can make webpages feel responsive and interactive. However, because they run on the client, they can be challenging to plan. The richest client-side technologies require plug-ins, which some browser platforms do not support. Although JavaScript has become standard, many developers use client-side libraries that can increase bandwidth and page load times.

This section provides an overview of common client-side scripting languages and plug-ins, and it gives you the information you need to choose the right technology for different scenarios.

> **This objective covers how to:**
> - Use client-side scripting languages.
> - Use rich client-side plug-ins.

Using Client-Side Scripting Languages

In practice, there is only one client-side scripting language: JavaScript. The JavaScript syntax closely resembles C# syntax because it requires lines to end with a semicolon and uses brackets to group lines of code together (for example, to group the code that makes up a function or a for loop). However, the structure is looser than C#, and you don't always need to declare variables.

Here is a sample of JavaScript code to demonstrate the syntax. Because anyone with access to a page can examine the source code, JavaScript code rarely contains comments in the real world. To reduce bandwidth usage, JavaScript is almost always minified, which means unnecessary indenting and white space has been removed.

```
// Declare variables (without specifying a type)
numPics = 11;
secDelay = 7;

// Call the built-in functions Math.floor and Math.random
// Adding "var" identifies a local variable
var randomOffset = Math.floor(Math.random() * 11);

// A for loop
for (i = 1; i <= numPics; i++) {
    // Declare and define picNum
    picNum = i + randomOffset;

    // An if statement
    if (picNum > numPics) {
```

```
    picNum = picNum - numPics;
}

// Define a function call that will be passed to setTimeout using a string
// StartPic is a custom function not shown here
var sp = "StartPic(" + picNum + ", " + numPics + ", " + secDelay + ", '" +
    picUrl[picNum] + "')";

// setTimeout, a built-in function, runs the function declared by the first
// parameter after the delay, in milliseconds, specified by the second parameter
setTimeout(sp, secDelay * 1000 * (i - 1));
}
```

EXAM TIP

On the exam, you might see a reference to a second client-side scripting language: Microsoft VBScript. VBScript provides similar client-side capabilities as JavaScript; however, VBScript is supported only by the Microsoft Internet Explorer browser. Although most users currently use a version of Internet Explorer, most web developers prefer to write code that will work with as many browsers as possible, including Firefox, Opera, Chrome, and Safari. Only JavaScript works with each of those browsers. In the real world, almost all client-side code is written in JavaScript.

Microsoft is still maintaining VBScript; however, it is no longer releasing new versions of the scripting engine. For the exam, it is important to know that VBScript is a client-side scripting language with similar capabilities to JavaScript. However, VBScript is not an acceptable solution for scenarios that require compatibility with browsers other than Internet Explorer or operating systems other than Windows.

Client-Side Libraries

JavaScript itself is not as robust as the .NET Framework. For example, it could be time-consuming to write pure JavaScript code to retrieve data from a web service, sort it, and display it in a grid format, because JavaScript does not have built-in functions to do that. Even if you did write the large amount of code required to perform that task, you would then have to test and debug it using every different browser you planned to support.

To extend JavaScript's capabilities and provide better cross-platform support, the open-source community has created many JavaScript libraries. There are two you should be familiar with for the exam:

- **jQuery** jQuery is the most commonly used JavaScript library. It is only 29 KB in size when compressed (which the client must download before it can process any Java-Script), but it provides functions for easily selecting document elements, handling events, animating objects, and performing other AJAX actions.

- **Microsoft AJAX** A client-side JavaScript library created by Microsoft specifically to add client-side capabilities to ASP.NET.

Both jQuery and Microsoft AJAX are included with Visual Studio 2010. However, new versions of each are released regularly. Because they often contain important updates, you should always use the latest version available. Additionally, you should test and update references to new libraries for web applications you maintain.

> **MORE INFO** **JQUERY AND MICROSOFT AJAX**
>
> For more information about jQuery, visit *http://jquery.com*. For more information about Microsoft AJAX, visit *http://www.asp.net/ajax*.

Using a client-side library on your page requires the client to download the library from your server the first time a page requests it. For all subsequent requests, the client will normally have a copy cached. Unfortunately, the initial download of the library increases page load time and bandwidth usage. On a LAN, these differences might be negligible. On the public Internet, however, they can be significant.

For example, the jQuery library is only 29 KB in size when minified, which broadband users can download in a fraction of a second. However, the browser has to first download the page, parse the reference to the jQuery library, download jQuery from the server, and then process the library before it can begin executing any JavaScript. Depending on the client's bandwidth and latency (the delay it takes to send messages to and from your server), that can delay page-rendering time by up to a full second.

Because of the performance impact of loading client-side libraries and the importance of page load time to users and search engines, avoid using libraries for websites on the public Internet unless absolutely necessary. At times, however, using a library can save such a significant amount of development time that the performance impact becomes worthwhile.

Delivering Libraries with a CDN

To reduce the impact of downloading a library, you can use a CDN. A CDN stores copies of a library in many different locations on the Internet. Browsers download whichever copy of the library is closest to them, reducing latency and eliminating the extra bandwidth required of your web server. Additionally, if the browser has visited another webpage that uses the same version of the library from the same CDN, it can use the cached version, further improving page-load time.

Microsoft, Google, and Edgecast all provide CDN services for the jQuery library. Instead of referencing jQuery from your local server:

```
<script type="text/javascript" src="/Scripts/jquery/jquery-1.5.min.js" ></script>
```

you can reference it from Microsoft's CDN:

```
<script type="text/javascript" src="http://ajax.aspnetcdn.com/ajax/jquery/jquery-1.5.min.js" ></script>
```

you can reference it from Google's CDN:

```
<script type="text/javascript" src="http://ajax.googleapis.com/ajax/libs/jquery/1.5/
jquery.min.js"></script>
```

or you can reference it from Edgecast's CDN:

```
<script type="text/javascript" src="http://code.jquery.com/jquery-1.5.min.js"></script>
```

> **NOTE JQUERY VERSIONS**
>
> The .min in the file indicates that it is minified, which reduces file size. You need to reference the nonminified version only if you wanted to examine the jQuery library for debugging purposes. As developers release new versions of jQuery, you should test it and then update the version number in the script *src* property.

If a user has visited another page that used the same library from the same CDN, the browser will already have a cached copy of the CDN stored locally. Therefore, the more webpages that use a CDN, the more visitors will have already cached the library. As a result, you will get a greater performance benefit by using the most popular CDN.

To use the Microsoft CDN for Microsoft AJAX (your only option), simply set the *Script Manager.EnableCdn* property to *true*, as the following example shows:

```
<asp:ScriptManager
    ID="ScriptManager1"
    EnableCdn="true"
    Runat="Server" />
```

Using Rich Client-Side Plug-ins

JavaScript is capable of providing a moderately rich user interface that changes based on user actions. JavaScript can also display some video and animation. However, if you want to provide a rich user interface beyond JavaScript's capabilities, use high-performance or 3D graphics, or display some types of video, you need to use a plug-in. Two of the most common plug-ins are Adobe Flash and Microsoft Silverlight.

Flash and Silverlight are capable of complex, interactive animations, high-definition video, and games. They can also directly access some aspects of the computer that are not accessible to JavaScript, such as the video adapter's graphical processing unit (GPU), which is useful for accelerating graphics displays and performing some computations. However, Flash and Silverlight have several disadvantages:

- They require users to download and install a plug-in before they can be used.
- Users who already have the plug-in installed might have to update the plug-in before they can access content created for a newer version of the plug-in.
- Some browsers (such as the Safari browser built into the popular iPhone and iPad products) cannot support one or both of the plug-ins.

- The Flash and Silverlight objects must be stored in a separate file and embedded in a webpage. These objects tend to be large, increasing the size of the page and reducing page performance.

Because of these drawbacks, you should use plug-ins only when you can limit the impact of the drawbacks. For example, if you have a technology-savvy customer base that is willing to install and update the plug-in, or if you are deploying an intranet application and the Information Technology (IT) department will support the plug-in.

If you create web applications that use Flash or Silverlight and you must support a wide variety of browsers, create webpages that degrade gracefully. If a browser does not have the plug-in installed, provide a link so that users can install the plug-in. If a browser cannot support the plug-in, provide alternate content that duplicates as much of the functionality as possible using traditional HTML and JavaScript.

EXAM TIP

In the real world, Flash is much more widely supported than Silverlight because it has existed for many more years. The exam, however, prefers to reference Silverlight. Fortunately, you do not need to know how to create content for either plug-in. Instead, understand the capabilities and drawbacks of using rich client-side plug-ins.

Objective Summary

- JavaScript is the only widely accepted client-side scripting language, though Internet Explorer also supports VBScript. You can use client-side libraries to extend JavaScript's capabilities. Visual Studio 2010 has built-in support for two client-side libraries: jQuery and Microsoft AJAX.

- Rich client-side plug-ins, including Flash and Silverlight, provide a responsive and interactive experience rivaled only by desktop applications. However, they both require plug-ins to be installed in most browsers. Some browsers, especially those on mobile devices, do not support either plug-in. Therefore, when using a rich client-side plug-in, you need to plan to provide alternate code for clients that lack the plug-in.

Objective Review

Answer the following questions to test your knowledge of the information in this objective. You can find the answers to these questions and explanations of why each answer choice is correct or incorrect in the "Answers" section at the end of this chapter.

1. You are designing an ASP.NET web application that allows end users to chat live with customer support when they click a Button control. At times, it might take several minutes for customer support to respond to a user. You need to design the application to be responsive to users, even when customer support cannot immediately reply. You need to support a wide variety of browsers, including browsers built into mobile devices. Which approach should you recommend?

    A. In the *Button.Click* event handler, return a webpage that contains a real-time chat client implemented by using Flash. Configure the Silverlight client to communicate directly with customer support.

    B. In the *Button.Click* event handler, return a webpage that contains a real-time chat client implemented by using Silverlight. Configure the Silverlight client to communicate directly with customer support.

    C. In the *Button.Click* event handler, connect to the customer support chat client. Add the response to the webpage.

    D. In the *Button.Click* event handler, return a webpage that contains client-side Java-Script code that connects to a web service running on the server to send messages from the user and retrieve responses from customer support.

2. You are designing the client-side component of web application with the following requirements:

    - Retrieve data from a web service, and display it in a <div> element on the webpage.
    - Work with all common browsers.
    - Do not require client-side installation.

    Which two technologies should you recommend? (Choose all that apply. Each answer forms a complete solution.)

    A. Silverlight
    B. jQuery
    C. VBScript
    D. Microsoft AJAX

3. You are designing a 3D game that will run in client browsers. The platform you choose must be able to work in all common browsers and must support GPU acceleration. Which technology should you choose?

    A. Silverlight
    B. jQuery
    C. VBScript
    D. Microsoft AJAX

Evaluating the Impact of Rich Client Features

In the following thought experiment, you apply what you've learned about the "Choose Appropriate Client-Side Technologies" objective to predict how a theoretical website architecture will perform. You can find answers to these questions in the "Answers" section at the end of this chapter.

You are a development consultant. Coho Winery has asked you to review an MVC web application that its developer created to replace its public website at http://www.cohowinery.com. Their current public website is based on ASP.NET 2.0 and uses no JavaScript or other client-side technology. Management needs you to evaluate the application design to identify any problems that might occur prior to launch.

You interview the developer and determine that three components of the site use advanced client-side capabilities:

- The master page has a menu system that uses jQuery. jQuery is stored in the application's /Scripts/ folder.

- Product pages use AJAX to allow users to quickly browse different products without reloading the entire page.

- The home page displays a 500 KB Silverlight object that gives users a virtual tour of the winery.

Management needs to assess the future performance and compatibility of the site. In particular, they are concerned about bandwidth fees from their web hosting provider. Answer the following questions:

1. Will their bandwidth usage increase or decrease?

2. How can they change the design to reduce bandwidth usage?

3. Will any clients be unable to use parts of the site? How can they minimize the compatibility problems?

Objective 1.4: Choose Appropriate Server-Side Technologies

The .NET Framework is so robust that there are often many ways to accomplish a single task. This objective includes a high-level overview of the different server-side technologies and describes the scenarios in which you would use each of them.

> **This objective covers how to:**
> - Choose between different control types.
> - Use partial classes and methods.
> - Access server methods from client code.

> **MORE INFO**   HTML Helper Extensions
>
> For information about HTML helper extensions, refer to Objective 3.2.

Choosing Between Different Control Types

The .NET Framework provides many types of controls, including HTML, server, user, Web Parts, custom, and dynamic data. The sections that follow provide an overview of each type of control and describe the scenarios in which you would use each.

> **EXAM TIP**
>
> The 70-515 exam covers how to create and use controls. For the 70-519 exam, be sure you understand when you should choose each type of control.

HTML Controls

Use HTML controls when you need to create an HTML element without server-side logic. For example, you can create an input text box using either an HTML control or a server control. The Input (Text) HTML control simply creates the HTML <input> element, without directly providing server-side code access to anything the user types in the text box. If the user submits a form to the server, the contents of any HTML controls will be lost. You could still access the user input in an HTML control from client-side JavaScript, however.

Server Controls

ASP.NET renders server controls into HTML elements. For example, the *TextBox* server control is rendered into an HTML <input> element, similar to the Input (Text) HTML control. Server controls provide more robust features, however. With server controls, you can process user input from the code-behind file, and ASP.NET automatically maintains controls between page loads. Server controls require more processing time on the server, and their view state consumes additional bandwidth. As with HTML controls, you can access rendered server controls from client-side JavaScript.

Although the 70-519 exam does not test most of the details of implementing server controls, it does require you to know how to enable Cascading Style Sheet (CSS) styling for controls that have it disabled by default. These server controls were originally designed before CSS was commonly used, and as a result, they use tables for styling. All modern web applications should use CSS styling.

The .NET Framework provides different properties for different controls:

- **RenderOuterTable** Several server controls (including *FormView*, *Login*, and *Change Password*) have a property named *RenderOuterTable*. Set the *RenderOuterTable* property to *false* to control the appearance of the controls with CSS style sheets.

- **RepeatLayout** *RadioButtonList*, *CheckBoxList*, and *DataList* include the *RepeatLayout* property. Like *RenderOuterTable*, *RepeatLayout* uses a table for formatting. Set *Repeat Layout* to Flow (instead of the default Table) to control the appearance of the controls with CSS style sheets.

User Controls

User controls are custom server-side controls deployed using an .ascx file. Typically, user controls contain multiple server or HTML controls. You should create user controls under the following circumstances:

- You need to include a group of server controls in multiple ASPX pages.
- You need to deploy a custom control as a separate assembly.
- The layout is primarily static.

If you need to persist data between page loads, store the data in control state. Control state functions even when a developer has disabled view state.

Do not use user controls to display common user interface elements in the same position on every page within your site. Instead, use master pages. For example, if you want to display the weather in the upper-right corner of every page, you should add the weather element to your master page. However, if you want to display the weather in different locations on different pages, you should implement it as a user control.

Web Parts

Web Parts are controls that include built-in functionality to allow end users to customize their location, appearance, and functionality. You can use Web Part Connections to provide data to individual Web Parts. Choose Web Parts over other types of controls when user customization is important—for example, if you need the user to be able to move the control to a different spot on the webpage or change the colors of the control.

Custom Server Controls

Although user controls are typically composed of HTML and server controls, custom server controls provide you complete flexibility. You have complete control over how ASP.NET renders a custom server control into HTML, so you can accomplish almost anything. Custom server controls take more effort to create than user controls, however.

If your custom server control does not resemble any existing server controls, inherit from *System.Web.WebControls.WebControl*. Most of the time, however, you should inherit from an existing server control that provides similar functionality to your custom server control. For example, if you wanted to display a list of check boxes with associated images, you might inherit from the *CheckBoxList* class; add properties for the image URL, title, and alt tags; and then update the rendering to add the <img> information to the HTML output.

You can add custom controls to the Visual Studio toolbox, which you cannot do with user controls.

Dynamic Data Controls

Dynamic data controls are among the most complex controls in the .NET Framework. Dynamic data controls connect to a LINQ-to-SQL object model or LINQ-to-Entities object model and display data in a tabular format, allowing for sorting, filtering, and paging. Users can use links to edit and delete records directly from a dynamic data control.

Choose dynamic data controls when you want to view or edit data in a database with minimal development time and a standard tabular display will suffice.

Using Partial Classes and Methods

When you create a new website or web application, Visual Studio automatically generates a large amount of code. This auto-generated code includes many of the most important classes in your application, including your *Page* class and your data classes. By automatically generating code based on the template you chose, Visual Studio saves you from writing hundreds of lines of code just to provide basic website functionality.

You can use partial classes and methods to add your own custom code to the auto-generated code. A partial class allows you to add entirely new properties, methods, and events to a class, without editing the auto-generated code or rewriting the class from scratch. Similarly, a partial method allows you to add code to an auto-generated method.

Use partial classes and methods when Visual Studio auto-generates a class or method but you need to extend its functionality.

Accessing Server Methods from Client Code

The most common way to call a server-side method from the client is to configure a server control, such as a *Button* control, to run the method for its *Click* event handler. However, this technique requires a postback.

If you prefer not to reload the page, you can use one of these techniques to allow client-side code to call server-side methods and process the results:

- **UpdatePanel**   You can place server controls within an *UpdatePanel* container, and trigger the *UpdatePanel* to refresh itself when a trigger occurs. Often, triggers are clicking a button or changing a drop-down list selection. Using an *UpdatePanel* does not require manually writing JavaScript code.

- **UpdateProgress**   *UpdateProgress* is visible only when an associated *UpdatePanel* control is updating. *UpdateProgress* is designed to give users feedback about the *UpdatePanel* asynchronous request.

- **Page methods**   Mark the static method you want to expose with the *WebMethod* attribute, add a *ScriptManager* server control, and set *ScriptManager.EnablePageMethods* to *true*. Then you can use the *PageMethods* object within JavaScript to call server-side methods and process the results.

- **Web services**   Microsoft AJAX and jQuery are both capable of easily consuming web services. Therefore, you can write client-side code to consume any static method that you expose by using *WebMethod*. To access the method using the JSON format, also add the *ScriptService* attribute.

Using an *UpdatePanel* requires less code than using a page method, but it transfers view state as well, so the request and response are larger than page method calls. With a page method control, you can't access the contents of server controls, such as what a user typed into a *TextBox*, directly from a page method called by the client. Instead, you need to pass values to the page method as parameters.

Objective Summary

- HTML controls provide high performance with minimal overhead, but server controls provide much easier access to their properties and values. User controls allow you to easily combine multiple server controls into a single object. Web Parts provide robust capabilities and allow end users to personalize their appearance and move them to different locations. For the ultimate in flexibility, create custom server controls. Dynamic data controls automatically adjust their appearance to the underlying data source, allowing you to quickly display and manage data.

- Partial classes and methods allow you to extend classes that Visual Studio automatically generates.

- HtmlHelpers provide an easy way to add HTML controls to MVC views. You can create custom HtmlHelper extensions for HTML elements that are not provided with the built-in HtmlHelpers.

- You can access server methods directly from client JavaScript code, saving a full page load. The easiest way to do this is to use a page method with Microsoft AJAX.

Objective Review

Answer the following questions to test your knowledge of the information in this objective. You can find the answers to these questions and explanations of why each answer choice is correct or incorrect in the "Answers" section at the end of this chapter.

1. You are creating a new web application. You must meet these requirements:

   - Use the *Login* control to allow users to authenticate.

   - Allow a web designer to configure the appearance of all controls using classes in CSS style sheets.

   How should you configure the *Login* control? (Choose two. Each answer forms part of the complete solution.)

   A. Define the CssClass property.

   B. Set the *RenderOuterTable* property to *true*.

   C. Set the *RenderOuterTable* property to *false*.

   D. Define the *LoginButtonType* property.

2. You are planning to write client-side JavaScript that must retrieve and display a string value returned by a server-side method. You want the messages sent between the client and server to be as small as possible. Which approach should you choose?

   A. Create a partial class.

   B. Use an *UpdateProgress* control.

   C. Use an *UpdatePanel* control.

   D. Use a Microsoft AJAX page method.

3. You are creating a view for an MVC application. You need to create a non-standard HTML control that should be rendered on the server. You must minimize the amount of client and server resources used as well as your development time. Which approach should you choose?

   A. Use the jQuery library to dynamically add the HTML control to the document object model.

   B. Create an HtmlHelper extension.

   C. Create a custom server control.

   D. Create a custom Web Part.

THOUGHT EXPERIMENT
Evaluating a Real-Time Web Application Design

In the following thought experiment, you apply what you've learned about the Choose Appropriate Server-Side Technologies objective to predict how a theoretical website architecture will perform. You can find answers to these questions in the "Answers" section at the end of this chapter.

You are a developer for Contoso Pharmaceuticals. Recently, Contoso acquired a smaller pharmaceutical company, Trey Research. The developers at Trey are in the process of planning a new web application. Your manager has asked you to review the Trey developer's plans.

The application is designed to provide management with real-time information about the progress of drug development, whether the manager is in the office, at home, or on a mobile device. To support mobile clients, one of the design requirements is to minimize bandwidth. Managers want to be able to open a webpage and leave it open, and have it automatically update with current project status.

Trey developers designed an application with the following features:

- A user control that displays all the information about a project
- An *UpdatePanel* control that contains one user control for every project that a manager wants to monitor
- A *Timer* control that triggers the *UpdatePanel* control to refresh every 30 seconds

Answer the following questions about the future performance of the application:

1. Is a user control the right choice for displaying information about a project? Which other technologies might be more efficient?

2. Is the combination of an *UpdatePanel* and *Timer* trigger the right choice to allow the page to be dynamically updated? Which other technologies might be more efficient?

Objective 1.5: Design State Management

As a user visits a website, he might interact with multiple controls on a page, submit a single page multiple times, and view multiple, different pages in a single site. Often, the user will return later to the same site.

Throughout these interactions, your application needs to keep track of state. You need to know any values the user types or selects in a form. Often, you need to track information about a user as he visits multiple pages or makes multiple visits to your site at different times.

Keeping track of this information in a web application is a challenge, however, because HTTP communications are inherently stateless, a web application might run on multiple web servers, and a single user might switch between different networks or clients. Fortunately, ASP.NET provides several state management techniques that can meet almost any need.

This objective includes an overview of those different state management techniques, along with a description of the advantages of each. Most of this objective reviews topics covered by the 70-515 exam. However, the 70-515 exam focused on the details of implementing state management technologies, while the 70-519 exam focuses on choosing the appropriate state management technology for a given scenario. Therefore, the content in this objective is very high level.

> **This objective covers how to:**
> - Use application state.
> - Use the Cache object.
> - Evaluate user state technologies
> - Use session state.
> - Create custom page state persisters.

Using Application State

ASP.NET provides the *Application* object, which you can use to store information that can be accessed by any page or user session. The *Application* object is a dictionary that is useful for storing small amounts of frequently accessed data that is the same for all users.

However, the *Application* object was primarily intended for backward compatibility with ASP applications. A better alternative is to store application state in global static objects. Global static objects perform better than the *Application* object and provide strong typing.

Because application state is stored in memory, accessing it is much faster than querying a database. Consider these factors when using application state:

- Application state is lost when a server is restarted. Therefore, you must initialize data in the *Application_Start* method in the Global.asax file.
- Application state is not shared between servers in a web farm. If you need to share data between servers, use session state, or store it in a shared database.

- Application state is stored in memory. If you store large amounts of data in application state, it reduces the amount of memory available for other applications and caching. Use the *Cache* object to allow the .NET Framework to automatically remove objects you no longer need from memory.

- Application state is free-threaded. Because multiple threads can access application state at the same time, you must write thread-safe code that locks and unlocks data so that it is written to by only one thread at a time. Writing thread-safe code increases development time.

Using the *Cache* Object

Just like the *Application* object, the *Cache* object is a dictionary that is available to all pages and sessions in your application. However, while *Application* stores objects until the application restarts, *Cache* stores them only until they expire or ASP.NET determines that it needs to free up memory.

When you add an object to the Cache, you have the option of providing an expiration policy. For example, the following code configures ASP.NET to remove the object after one minute:

Sample of Visual Basic.NET Code

```
Cache.Insert("MyItem", "MyValue", Nothing, DateTime.Now.AddMinutes(1.0), TimeSpan.Zero)
```

Sample of C# Code

```
Cache.Insert("MyItem", "MyValue", null, DateTime.Now.AddMinutes(1d),
    System.Web.Caching.Cache.NoSlidingExpiration);
```

Alternatively, you can create sliding expiration policies and policies that cause a cached object to expire when a file or directory is updated.

You should use the *Cache* object any time you might need to access the same data again and that data is relatively difficult to retrieve or create. When choosing between storing data in the *Cache* and *Application* objects, choose the *Cache* object in the following circumstances:

- The original data source might change.

- You might run low on memory.

- You will not need the value for the entire lifespan of the application.

Evaluating User State Technologies

User state is any information the server maintains between multiple user requests. ASP.NET provides several ways to store user state:

- **Cookies** Short strings provided by the server that the client includes with each subsequent request. You can store any string on the client and instruct the client to store it for a few seconds or many years, providing a simple and persistent storage technique. Because cookies do not store data on the server, they do not affect server scalability. However, cookies provide no inherent security; they can be easily intercepted or modified. Additionally, because the client must send cookies with every request, large cookies can increase bandwidth usage and slow page response times.

- **Query strings** You can add query strings to hyperlinks on your pages to pass data to other pages. For example, if you link to a page that lists a store's inventory, you might specify the link like this to show only audiobooks under $10: http://www.contoso. com/products.aspx?category=audiobook&maxprice=10. Within the Products.aspx code-behind file, you could check for the values *Request.QueryString["category"]* and *Request.QueryString["maxprice"]*. Unlike other forms of application state, query strings are typically maintained if a user shares a link. Relying heavily on query strings can make it more difficult for search engines to index your site.

- **Hidden fields** You can store information within a form by using HTML hidden fields. If the user submits the form, the browser will submit the contents of the hidden field along with any other fields in the form. However, the hidden field won't be visible to the user. To add a hidden field, simply add an <input> element to the form and set the type to hidden, as this example shows:

```
<input type="hidden" name="code" value="93">
```

- **Session state** Clients identify themselves with a unique session ID, usually using a cookie. The server then retrieves a collection of session data using the user's unique session ID. Sessions expire after 20 minutes by default and will not be available if the user changes devices. Therefore, session state is useful only for short-term storage.

- **View state** ASP.NET stores view state in encrypted hidden fields in a web form. View state allows ASP.NET to track control values across multiple requests even if session state is disabled. View state can significantly increase page size in a way that cannot be compressed as efficiently as standard HTML. Therefore, you should disable view state when you do not need it.

- **Control state** Control state functions exactly like view state, except it is defined as part of a user control. If a developer disables view state for a page but a user control uses control state, that control state will remain intact.

- **Authentication** If you authenticate users, you can store any information about the user in a database and associate it with their user ID. This allows state to be persistent between visits, even if the user switches devices. However, users must log on to retrieve the state.

You should use cookies to store information about user preferences. Use view state and control state to store data between requests to the same web form on an intranet. Any data requiring security, such as a user's address, should be stored on a database and accessed only on the server after the user authenticates.

Table 1-4 compares the features of the different application-state storage techniques.

TABLE 1-4 Application-State Storage Techniques

Cookies	Query strings	Hidden fields	Session state	View state/Control state	Authentication
Uses server resources					
			X	X	X
Can be shared in a link					
	X				
Can increase bandwidth significantly					
X		X		X	
Provides some security					
			X	X	X
Works across multiple views of the same page					
X	X	X	X	X	X
Works across different pages in a single visit					
X	X	X	X		X
Works across multiple visits from the same device					
X					X
Works across multiple visits from different devices					
					X

Using Session State

Session state involves both a client and server component:

- The client must identify itself to the server by using a unique session ID.
- The server must use the session ID to look up that client's unique Session collection.

The sections that follow discuss the decisions you can make about both the client side and the server side of session state.

Tracking Session on the Client

You have different options for both the client and server components. For the client, you can choose between using cookies or cookieless session state. Using cookies is the default setting, and it is the right choice for the vast majority of websites. Although every modern browser supports cookies, you might be faced with a scenario that requires you to support sessions without cookies.

Cookieless session state appends the unique session ID to the webpage URL. For example, if a client's session ID is ow2j32ieo233kj4i2ogfj9320, the URL might be http://www.contoso.com/(S(ow2j32ieo233kj4i2ogfj9320))/default.aspx. The altered URL creates several problems:

- Search engines might receive a different session ID on different visits, causing the search engine to identify different paths to seemingly duplicate content.

- If a user bookmarks a page and visits it after the session has expired (20 minutes by default), the session ID will no longer be valid.

- The URL is much longer than normal, making it more difficult for users to share (especially using short message formats such as Twitter).

- If a user shares a URL with a session ID embedded, the other user can access information stored within her session. This creates a potential security risk.

Because of these concerns, you should choose cookie-based sessions (the default) unless clients cannot use cookies and you must rely on session state.

Storing Session on the Server

Your web server can store session state in one of three ways:

- **InProc**   The default, this setting stores session state in the server's memory. Session state is not shared between different web servers, and it is lost if the web server is restarted.

- **State Server**   This setting stores session state on a separate server. Multiple web servers can share state server session state, allowing clients to transparently switch between different web servers in a server farm. Session state is lost if the state server is restarted.

- **SQL Server**   This setting stores session state on a computer running SQL Server. Like a state server, multiple web servers can share state server session state. Additionally, session state is maintained if the state server is restarted. If session state must be maintained during a server outage, you can store state in a SQL Server cluster.

InProc session state is sufficient for most applications that use a single web server. If you use multiple web servers (for example, as part of a network load-balancing cluster) and requests from a single client might be sent to a different server, you need to store state on a state server or SQL Server. In this scenario, you must define the same <machineKey> setting (located within <configuration><system.web> in the Web.config file) on every web server.

Because a machine key is automatically generated by default, you need to manually generate a machine key and set the value on every web server. You can use this online tool to quickly generate a <machineKey> value: *http://aspnetresources.com/tools/machineKey*. The setting in the Web.config will resemble the following:

```
<configuration>
    <system.web>
        <machineKey
validationKey="8E8992656E0CD2811EA23ADA31DD7F75F199EE9476947E0860FFC9C767992AEDE0B5CFDAB
A73D059E67AB166491E1342E4101B814135CFE40BC51D55E4F6B4DE"
decryptionKey="8D02DDC2E9CE3647E5F2649DF5BA0F7A30CFAE2D5AE436AE809CA11D3A3F2121"
validation="SHA1" decryption="AES" />
    </system.web>
</configuration>
```

Creating Custom Page State Persisters

View state has a significant disadvantage: it can dramatically increase page size. This page size increase is especially dramatic when you are using complex controls such as *DataGrid*. At times, view state size can approach 1 MB, which takes about 15 seconds to transfer across a 512 Kbps link. You can offset this page size increase by disabling view state for controls that don't need to be persisted between requests, but often that is not sufficient.

View state is the default mechanism for persisting page state, and usually it is the best choice. However, it is not the only choice. View state uses the class *System.Web.UI.HiddenField PageStatePersister*, which derives from the *PageStatePersister* class. If view state does not meet your needs, you can use the other built-in page state mechanism, *SessionPageStatePersister*, or derive your own custom class from *PageStatePersister*.

SessionPageStatePersister stores view state data along with session state data. This eliminates the extra bandwidth consumed by sending view state data back and forth between the client and the server. However, it consumes more server resources by increasing session state size. Additionally, it can fail if you make use of iframes, pop-ups, or AJAX, or if users have multiple pages open simultaneously.

To use a different page state persister, register a custom *PageAdapter* class. Within the class, override the *GetStatePersister* method and return an instance of your *PageStatePersister*. Then use the custom *PageAdapter* class instead of the default page adapter. This example demonstrates how to use *SessionPageStatePersister*:

Sample of Visual Basic.NET Code

```
Public Class SessionPageAdapter
    Inherits System.Web.UI.Adapters.PageAdapter

    Public Overrides Function GetStatePersister() As PageStatePersister
        Return New SessionPageStatePersister(Page)
    End Function 'GetStatePersister

End Class 'SessionPageAdapter
```

Sample of C# Code

```csharp
public class SessionPageAdapter : System.Web.UI.Adapters.PageAdapter {
    public override PageStatePersister GetStatePersister() {
        return new SessionPageStatePersister(Page);
    }
}
```

> **MORE INFO** **PAGE STATE PERSISTERS**
>
> For more information about storing page state in sessions, read "SessionPageStatePersister Class" at *http://msdn.microsoft.com/en-us/library/system.web.ui.sessionpagestatepersister. aspx*. For detailed information about creating a custom page state persister, read "PageStatePersister Class" at *http://msdn.microsoft.com/en-us/library/system.web. ui.pagestatepersister.aspx*.

Objective Summary

- The *Application* object provides a dictionary that can be accessed by any page and session. Use it sparingly because any object you add remains in memory until the application restarts.

- The *Cache* object provides a dictionary that can be accessed by any page and session, just like the *Application* object. However, the *Cache* object allows you to link an item to a dependency so that the item will be automatically removed from the cache.

- The .NET Framework provides many ways to track user state, including cookies, sessions, and view state. Cookies tend to be reliable, but the browser has to send any information you store in a cookie with every request. Sessions are less reliable and can be used only for temporary information. ASP.NET uses view state to track server control properties between page requests.

- By default, ASP.NET stores session state information in memory. If you deploy your application to multiple web servers, you should store session state information in a state server or a SQL Server database. By default, ASP.NET uses cookies to identify clients with a specific session. If clients do not support cookies, you can choose cookieless sessions instead. However, cookieless sessions add the session ID to the page URL, which can cause a variety of issues.

- View state can significantly increase page size. You can reduce view state page size requirements by using a custom page state persister. ASP.NET provides a built-in page state persister that uses session state; however, it only works reliably if users access only one page at a time.

Objective Review

Answer the following questions to test your knowledge of the information in this objective. You can find the answers to these questions and explanations of why each answer choice is correct or incorrect in the "Answers" section at the end of this chapter.

1. You are designing a web application that will be deployed across ten servers in a web farm. The servers will be load-balanced using NLBS. Sessions must be maintained if a user is directed to a different server mid-session. Which session type should you use? (Choose all that apply. Each answer forms a complete solution.)

   A. InProc session state

   B. State server session state

   C. SQL Server session state

   D. Cookieless session state

2. You recently deployed an ASP.NET web application. Although the application performs well on the intranet, mobile users complain that pages take too long to load. You investigate the problem and determine that the size of the view state is very large, increasing page size. How can you solve the problem? (Choose all that apply. Each answer forms part of the complete solution.)

   A. Create a custom *PageAdapter* class that uses *SessionStatePersister*.

   B. Create a custom *PageAdapter* class that uses control state.

   C. Disable view state.

   D. Use dynamic data controls.

3. Recently, systems administrators scaled a web application you designed from one web server to three web servers. Requests are distributed between the servers using round-robin DNS. Since the upgrade, the administrators have noticed that sessions are reset when a user request is sent to a different server. How can you solve the problem? (Choose all that apply. Each answer forms part of the complete solution.)

   A. Use the *StateServer* session state mode.

   B. Use cookieless session state.

   C. Create a custom *PageStatePersister*.

   D. Configure all web servers with the same machine key.

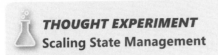

THOUGHT EXPERIMENT
Scaling State Management

In the following thought experiment, you apply what you've learned about the "Design State Management" objective to predict how a theoretical website architecture will perform. You can find answers to these questions in the "Answers" section at the end of this chapter.

You are a developer for Northwind Traders. You are working with management to assess how an Internet application's current state management techniques will scale as they grow from one web server to four.

The application was created by using ASP.NET 4.0. The following aspects of the application rely on state management:

- **Shopping carts**   User shopping carts are stored in InProc session state. Administrators increased the session timeout to one hour.

- **User information**   User names and addresses are stored in a SQL Server 2008 R2 database. Users are allowed to shop without logging on, but they must log on before checking out.

- **Inventory**   Inventory is stored in the database. When a user browses a list of inventory, the web application stores the collection of inventory in the *Cache* object.

- **Support chat status**   When support staff are available, the web application provides a link users can click to chat in real time with a support technician. The web application allows support staff to specify whether they are available by adjusting the *Boolean Application["OnlineSupport"]* object.

Northwind Traders has systems administrators on staff. However, the company outsources its web development. As a result, the company would like to minimize the amount of development time needed. Answer the following questions about the change in physical implementation:

1. Which features will require developer time to work properly in the web farm, and why? About how many hours of development effort will be required?

2. What changes will the administrators have to make so that the other features work in a web farm environment?

Chapter Summary

- Client-side scripting provides users with a rich interface, but it lacks the robustness and security of server-side code. SoC simplifies development, testing, and the updating of large-scale web applications by dividing the functional layers of an application. To perform a long-running request while appearing responsive to the user, divide a request into multiple asynchronous steps.

- The two most commonly used system architectures are MVC and three-tier. MFC allows different applications to communicate with a variety of bindings that provide different levels of features, performance, and compatibility. Unless you need multiple servers for redundancy, scalability, or isolation, use a single server. Whenever possible, use coding best practices that separate cross-cutting concerns into separate classes and store settings administrators might want to change separately from your code.

- JavaScript is the only widely accepted client-side scripting language, and it can be extended with the jQuery and Microsoft AJAX libraries. When you need more capabilities than JavaScript can provide, use a plug-in such as Flash or Silverlight. However, you will need to write extra code to provide down-level functionality for browsers that do not support the plug-in.

- HTML controls provide high performance with minimal overhead, but server controls provide much easier access to their properties and values. Custom server controls require extra development effort but provide the most flexibility. Use HtmlHelper extensions to add custom HTML elements to MVC views. To improve page responsiveness, update individual elements within a page using Microsoft AJAX page methods.

- The *Application* and *Cache* objects provide dictionaries that can be accessed by any page and session. You can use cookies and sessions to track information about individual users. ASP.NET stores view state in hidden fields within a page, allowing it to recall server control properties when a page is posted back.

Answers

Objective 1.1: Review

1. **Correct Answer:** C

    A. Incorrect: This approach would display the link only to administrators. However, because the processing is performed on the client, users could view the page source, see that the link existed (even though the browser would not render it), and identify the page it linked to.

    B. Incorrect: Setting the *Visible* property to *False* on the ASPX page would prevent ASP.NET from rendering the control at all. Therefore, JavaScript would not be able to display the control.

    C. Correct: This approach displays the link only to users who are members of the Administrators group, even if the user views the page source. Because it performs the processing on the server, security is maintained.

    D. Incorrect: This approach would never display the link to a user, even if the user was a member of the Administrators group. Additionally, the *HyperLink* control does not have a *Click* event. To initiate a postback when a user clicks a link, you would need to use the *LinkButton* control.

2. **Correct Answer:** A

    A. Correct: This approach blends server-side and client-side programming to provide a responsive user interface. The web server communicates directly with the server hosting the virtual machines because the client would not have authorization.

    B. Incorrect: Although this approach would work, the server would not return a response to the user until after all virtual machines had been provisioned. The lack of responsiveness would be unacceptable to most users.

    C. Incorrect: This approach would work only if the server hosting the virtual machines allowed provisioning requests from the client. However, the server hosting the virtual machines allows provisioning requests only from the web server.

    D. Incorrect: This approach would work if you use JavaScript to initiate web service requests rather than page requests. However, you should not use JavaScript to request webpages unless you intend to display them.

3. **Correct Answer:** B

   A. **Incorrect:** ASP.NET 4.0 web application projects do not allow individual classes to be easily testable. Additionally, ASP.NET 4.0 web applications provide no inherent SoC.

   B. **Correct:** The MVC architecture provides SoC, which also allows individual classes to be testable.

   C. **Incorrect:** Silverlight is not designed to create websites.

   D. **Incorrect:** Like ASP.NET 4.0 web applications, ASP.NET 4.0 websites do not allow individual classes to be easily testable and provide no inherent SoC.

Objective 1.1: Thought Experiment

1. Bandwidth is not a concern because the site is located on a high-speed intranet, and no client-side processing is performed. Therefore, server processing must be limiting the performance of the site. To improve the performance, increase the server's processing capabilities by upgrading the server hardware or adding more servers.

2. With page load times of more than five seconds, the site is already performing unacceptably slowly during peak hours. Adding traffic would cause it to be even slower.

3. You could use Performance Monitor to record the processing time and bandwidth under the current load, and then multiply that by the expected load to estimate the total requirements. To be even more accurate, you could take the site offline and use load-testing software to generate artificial load on the server, and record the performance information by using Performance Monitor.

4. You could generate the charts on the client rather than on the server.

5. You could either generate the charts on the client or use AJAX to replace the chart without reloading the webpage.

6. Generating charts on the client would reduce the processing requirements of the server. You could use JavaScript, Silverlight, or Flash to render the charts on the client. You could provide the raw data to the client by embedding it as an array in the page itself, or you could create a separate web service and have the client chart component retrieve the data from the web service.

7. Because the website provides per-customer information, caching the webpages and charts would have no impact on bandwidth and would actually increase page load times. However, you could reduce bandwidth usage and improve page load times by caching static embedded objects, such as the website logo, JavaScript, Flash, and Silverlight objects.

Objective 1.2: Review

1. **Correct Answer:** C

   A. **Incorrect:** Refer to answer C.

   B. **Incorrect:** Refer to answer C.

   C. **Correct:** To allow the website to remain online if a web server is restarted, you need to configure two web servers. To isolate the database from a denial-of-service attack, you must place it on a separate, third server.

   D. **Incorrect:** Refer to answer C.

2. **Correct Answer:** A

   A. **Correct:** The website needs to serve six requests per minute, which is an average of one request every ten seconds. Although the amount of processing time per request varies based on the application, very few applications have requests that take more than ten seconds to process, even on very low-end hardware. The database storage requirement can be met by a single hard disk in a single server. There is no compelling reason to physically separate the web and database servers, so a single server for both roles is the best use of the hardware budget.

   B. **Incorrect:** Refer to answer A.

   C. **Correct:** Refer to answer A.

   D. **Incorrect:** Refer to answer A.

3. **Correct Answer:** A

   A. **Correct:** Although you could use *WSDualHttpBinding*, *NetTcpBinding* is more efficient.

   B. **Incorrect:** *NetNamedPipesBinding* is intended for communications between processes on the same computer.

   C. **Incorrect:** *WsHttpBinding* does not support two-way (duplex) communications.

   D. **Incorrect:** *WSDualHttpBinding* meets all the requirements; however, *NetTcp Binding* is more efficient.

Objective 1.2: Thought Experiment

1. The company will need to change from *NetNamedPipesBinding* (which only works between processes on a single server) to *NetTcpBinding*. If the developer stored the binding configuration in the .config files, this might only require updating the configuration files. If the developer hard-coded the bindings, that code will need to be edited, but it should be a simple change.

2. The company will need to add a secondary binding type to the logic tier, such as *Net TcpBinding*.

3. The company will need to change only the connection string for the data assembly.

4. The company will need to change the logic tier's binding type to an open-standards based binding type, such as *WsHttpBinding*. It will have a minor, but perhaps not noticeable, negative impact on performance.

5. It's impossible to say without testing the application to determine how many resources each request requires, how many requests each visitor makes, and how quickly visitors send requests at peak hours. However, most low-end servers can handle tens of thousands of visitors per day.

Objective 1.3: Review

1. **Correct Answer:** C

   A. **Incorrect:** Although a Flash chat client could provide a very rich and responsive user interface, it would be incompatible with some browsers.

   B. **Incorrect:** As with answer A, Silverlight is incompatible with some browsers.

   C. **Correct:** Responsiveness is key here, and this approach relies on client-side Java-Script and a separate server process to manage the communications. Because the chat client is running entirely in JavaScript, the server could return a page immediately without waiting for customer service.

   D. **Incorrect:** Although this approach would work, the server would not return a webpage until after customer service typed a response. Most users are not willing to wait several minutes while a page loads.

2. **Correct Answers:** B and D

   A. **Incorrect:** Silverlight requires client-side installation.

   B. **Correct:** jQuery, a JavaScript plug-in, meets all these requirements.

   C. **Incorrect:** VBScript does not work with all common browsers. It natively works only with Internet Explorer, limiting its usefulness in Internet applications.

   D. **Correct:** Microsoft AJAX, a JavaScript plug-in, meets all these requirements.

3. **Correct Answer:** A

   A. **Correct:** Of these choices, only Silverlight provides GPU acceleration. Flash also provides GPU acceleration.

   B. **Incorrect:** jQuery works with all common browsers and can be used for simple animations. However, at the time of this writing, it does not support GPU acceleration.

   C. **Incorrect:** VBScript lacks GPU acceleration and natively works only with Internet Explorer.

   D. **Incorrect:** Microsoft AJAX works with all common browsers and can be used for simple animations. However, at the time of this writing, it does not support GPU acceleration.

Objective 1.3: Thought Experiment

1. Their bandwidth usage will increase for two reasons. First, every client who visits the site will need to download jQuery from the server. Second, clients who visit the home page will need to download the relatively large 500 KB Silverlight object.

2. The easiest way to reduce bandwidth usage is to reference the jQuery library from a CDN, such as that provided by Microsoft. This will also improve page load times for many users. The Silverlight object is very large relative to the size of a typical page; if they reduce the size of that object or remove it entirely, bandwidth usage will be much lower.

3. JavaScript and jQuery are widely accepted, so they should not pose a problem. However, any browser that does not have Silverlight installed (including mobile devices that cannot currently support it) will be unable to view the virtual tool. This is an easy problem to work around; simply determine whether the browser supports Silverlight, and provide alternate content to browsers without the necessary plug-in.

Objective 1.4: Review

1. **Correct Answers:** A and C

    A. **Correct:** Set the *CssClass* property (and, optionally, the *LoginButtonStyle.CssClass*, *TextBoxStyle.CssClass*, *LabelStyle.CssClass*, *TitleTextStyle.CssClass*, and *ValidatorText Style.CssClass* properties) to specify the class assigned to the rendered control in HTML. A web designer can use this class name to associate a set of styles with the control in a CSS style sheet.

    B. **Incorrect:** When *RenderOuterTable* is set to *true*, ASP.NET uses an HTML table to format the control, rather than allowing the control to be formatted by using CSS style sheets.

    C. **Correct:** Set *RenderOuterTable* to *false* to allow a control to be styled by using CSS style sheets.

    D. **Incorrect:** The *LoginButtonType* property controls whether the button is styled as a button, an image, or a link. Setting this value does not help you meet the requirements.

2. **Correct Answer:** D

    A. **Incorrect:** Partial classes allow you to add functionality to an auto-generated class. They do not provide any client-server communication capabilities.

    B. **Incorrect:** An *UpdateProgress* control displays the progress of updates to an *UpdatePanel* control. It does not allow you to retrieve string values from a server method.

C. **Incorrect:** You could display an updated string value by using an *UpdatePanel* control. However, the messages would be much larger than if you used a Microsoft AJAX page method.

D. **Correct:** A Microsoft AJAX page method allows you to call server methods without transmitting view state. This minimizes the size of the messages sent between the client and the server.

3. **Correct Answer:** B

A. **Incorrect:** Although you could use jQuery to insert custom HTML into a page after it is rendered, the requirements specify that the control should be rendered on the server.

B. **Correct:** HtmlHelper extensions allow you to create custom Html methods that render HTML code as strings. They are rendered on the server but do not require view state, so they are relatively efficient.

C. **Incorrect:** Custom server controls provide a great deal of flexibility; however, you can meet the requirements by using an HtmlHelper extension, and an HtmlHelper extension requires less development time.

D. **Incorrect:** Custom Web Parts require extra development and consume more client and server resources than an HtmlHelper extension.

Objective 1.4: Thought Experiment

1. Although there are many ways to display the information, a user control is a good choice if it provides enough flexibility to meet the company's requirements. User controls are easy to develop, and it would be simple to add multiple instances of a user control to the *UpdatePanel* container, based on which projects a manager wants to monitor.

2. An *UpdatePanel* and *Timer* will work well to automatically refresh a portion of the page on a regular interval. However, it probably won't be the most efficient way. A more bandwidth-efficient technique would be to create client-side JavaScript that made web services requests (such as page methods) to a server method to retrieve the raw data about a project, and then render it on the client. This technique reduces bandwidth usage and server load, but increases development time. Additionally, although this technique requires only a few lines of server-side code, it would require dozens of lines of client-side JavaScript, which tends to be more difficult to troubleshoot and maintain. Therefore, the trade-off is not entirely clear, and management would need to weigh the benefits of reduced bandwidth against the additional development costs.

Objective 1.5: Review

1. **Correct Answers:** B and C

   A. **Incorrect:** InProc session state stores session information in the web server's memory. If a user is sent to a different web server, the web server will create a new session for the user.

   B. **Correct:** When you use state server-based session state, the web servers store and retrieve session state on a central server. All web servers have access to the same session state information, allowing users to move between servers mid-session.

   C. **Correct:** When you use SQL Server–based session state, the web servers store and retrieve session state on a database server. All web servers have access to the same session state information, allowing users to move between servers mid-session.

   D. **Incorrect:** Cookieless session state allows browsers that do not support cookies to participate in a session. It does not provide for centralized session state management, however.

2. **Correct Answers:** A and C

   A. **Correct:** *SessionStatePagePersister* stores view state data within the session on the server instead of using hidden fields that must be sent back and forth between the client and server. *SessionStatePagePersister* can be problematic in some applications, but if users open only one page at a time, it can work properly.

   B. **Incorrect:** Control state stores data in hidden fields, just like view state. Therefore, using control state would not change the size of the pages.

   C. **Correct:** Disabling view state would completely remove the hidden fields that increase page size. However, it might prevent the application from working properly. Additionally, disabling view state does not disable control state.

   D. **Incorrect:** Dynamic data controls use view state by default.

3. **Correct Answers:** A and D

   A. **Correct:** By default, ASP.NET uses the InProc session state mode, which stores session state information in memory. Although this is very efficient, it does not allow multiple web servers to share session state. You should use StateServer or SqlServer session states any time you use multiple web servers and store information in session state.

   B. **Incorrect:** Cookieless session state changes how clients identify the session that they are currently using. However, it does not change how the server stores that session data.

C. Incorrect: A custom *PageStatePersister* could change the default view state storage mechanism. However, the default view state mechanism of storing data in hidden fields would work properly with multiple web servers and does not need to be changed.

D. Correct: Whether you use StateServer or SqlServer session state, you need to synchronize the machine key on all web servers.

Objective 1.5: Thought Experiment

1. The only feature that will require developer time is the support chat status. Because each web server has an isolated instance of the Application object, changing the status would require either updating the *Application["OnlineSupport"]* object on all four servers or writing code to store the support chat status in the database server. Either approach should take only an hour or two of development time (not including testing).

2. Administrators will not need to make any changes to the user information or inventory features; they should work fine in a web farm environment. Naturally, thorough testing will be required to be confident, however. Each web server will maintain a separate cache, but developing a distributed cache might not be worthwhile. They will need to change the session state configuration to use either a state server or the SQL Server, and then update the machine key on all servers.

CHAPTER 2

Designing the User Experience

After designing your application architecture, you are ready to design the user experi-ence. The first component of the user experience is the site structure, which determines the external URLs of your application, how you segment the application, and how you centralize formatting.

The second component of the user experience requires you to consider the different platforms with which users might access your site. For example, you might need to disable some page components for mobile users. Depending on your site, you might need to create an entirely separate user interface.

The third component of the user experience is globalization. For applications used only by a single community, globalization might not be a concern. However, the Internet enables users worldwide to access websites. To reach the largest audience, plan for globalization by translating the user interface and customizing the display for different cultures.

Objectives in this chapter:

- Objective 2.1: Design the site structure
- Objective 2.2: Plan for cross-browser and/or form factors
- Objective 2.3: Plan for globalization

Objective 2.1: Design the Site Structure

This objective provides an overview of how to use the Microsoft .NET Framework features and web standards to design both the external and internal structures of your site. This objective first describes the .NET Framework features that support application segmenta-tion. Next, this objective covers two techniques for centralizing formatting settings: Cascad-ing Style Sheets (CSS) and themes. Finally, this objective discusses how to configure the Model-View-Controller (MVC) routing engine.

Much of this objective will be a high-level review of topics covered by the 70-515 exam, with a focus on designing applications using technologies with which you might already be familiar.

This objective covers how to:

- Design application segmentation.
- Use style sheets.
- Use themes.
- Render element modes.
- Configure the routing engine.

Designing Application Segmentation

If an application grows beyond 10 or 20 pages, you need to segment the application to prevent its structure from becoming confusing. The most common techniques are these:

- **Master pages**   Most websites have common elements that appear on every page on the site, such as a header, footer, and navigation menu. Use master pages to define these common elements. If multiple content pages will access the same instances of objects, create the object in the master page, and access it from content pages using Master.<*Object*>.

- **Nested master pages**   You can nest master pages within each other to create a hierarchy for both layout and objects. For example, you might create a top-level master page for every content page on your site. Different segments within your site could have segment-specific master pages nested within the top-level master page.

- **Shared views**   MVC applications use views to render information into HTML pages. Typically, each controller has its own action which, in turn, has its own view. Create shared views to associate a single view with multiple controller actions by adding the shared view to the \Views\Shared folder using the same name as the actions you want to match.

- **Areas**   MVC applications are inherently segmented into model, view, and controller. However, large MVC applications can still become cluttered with large numbers of files. Use areas to further segment your MVC application. Each area has its own subfolders for models, views, and controllers.

> **NOTE SEGMENTING NON-MVC APPLICATIONS**
>
> If you need to segment a standard ASP.NET application, simply create subfolders.

Master pages and shared views do not change the URL that users will see as they browse the pages on your site; they exist primarily to improve site manageability. Areas and subfolders do visibly change URLs, however. Because URLs are visible in the browser address bar and in search results, you should choose area and subfolder names that will be meaningful to users and search engines.

You can use breadcrumbs to show users and search engines your site structure. Breadcrumbs reveal the path from the root of your site to the current page, much like a folder name reveals the path from the root of your drive to the current file. However, breadcrumbs consist of human-friendly names. A webpage about the Microsoft 70-519 certification exam might have the URL http://contoso.com/exam.aspx?pageid=132. The breadcrumb path could be the much more readable "Contoso Home > Certifications > Microsoft > Developer > 70-519".

If you want search engines to be able to display the breadcrumbs to your site, read "Breadcrumbs" on Google Webmaster Central at *http://www.google.com/support/webmasters/bin/answer.py?answer=185417*. As shown in Figure 2-1, some search engines display the breadcrumb path to a specific page, allowing users to jump directly to higher-level pages on your site from the search results.

Exam 70-519 - Microsoft
Jul 2, 2010 **...** This **exam** is designed to test the candidate's knowledge on designing and developing Web applications using Microsoft .NET 4 and Visual **...**
www.microsoft.com › ... › Training Catalog › Exam - Cached - Similar

Exam 70-515 OR **70-519** ?
7 posts - 5 authors - Last post: Sep 21, 2010
For MCPD Web Developer, the required **exam** is **70-519**. What if I took 70-515 ? Will it count as a creadit to the Certification ? **...**
social.microsoft.com › ... › Learning Forums › Training and Certification - Cached

70-519 exam prerequisites for ASP.NET 3.5 MCPD
2 posts - 1 author - Last post: Jul 30, 2010
NET 3.5, is **exam 70-519** what is equivalent for .NET 4.0 ? also what are the prerequisites for my case to be able to take **exam 70-519** ? **...**
social.microsoft.com › ... › Learning Forums › Training and Certification - Cached

FIGURE 2-1 A search engine displaying the breadcrumb path to search results

Another way to segment your site and optimize it for search engines is to make the URL reflect the site structure, make it human readable, and provide default pages for each virtual folder. Continuing the previous example URL http://contoso.com/exam.aspx?pageid=132, you might make the URL http://contoso.com/certifications/microsoft/developer/70-519.aspx and use routing to display the correct page. Each folder in the URL relates to an application segment. A default page for the root of each folder should display a list of pages within that segment.

Using Style Sheets

You can centrally manage the colors, fonts, and layout of your site by using style sheets. Style sheets contain a list of element types, classes, and IDs, as well as default attributes for matching elements. Visual Studio includes a default style sheet, \Styles\Site.css, that defines default appearance settings for new websites.

For example, the default style sheet includes these settings for text within the <body> HTML element:

```
body
{
    background: #b6b7bc;
    font-size: .80em;
    font-family: "Helvetica Neue", "Lucida Grande", "Segoe UI", Arial, Helvetica,
                 Verdana, sans-serif;
```

```
margin: 0px;
padding: 0px;
color: #696969;
}
```

Pages must reference any style sheet that should be applied. Typically, you add a reference to the style sheet to your master page. By default, Microsoft Visual Studio adds the following reference to the <head> element of the master page:

```
<link href="~/Styles/Site.css" rel="stylesheet" type="text/css" />
```

Pages can reference multiple style sheets. For example, if you add an open source JavaScript slideshow to a webpage, it might reference its own style sheet. Browsers have to submit a separate request for each style sheet, so combine all style settings into a single style sheet whenever possible.

You can define style settings by using element types (such as the default style definition for the <body> element shown previously), class names, and IDs. For example, if you plan to have several *TextBox* controls containing password information, you can format them the same by setting their CssClass property to *"passwordTextBox"*. This causes ASP.NET to add the class attribute to the HTML element, as the following example shows:

```
<input type="text" class="passwordTextBox"/>
```

Within the style sheet, you can configure the appearance for any element with the same CSS class by prefixing the class name with a period:

```
.passwordTextBox
{
    font-size: 1.1em;
    color: White;
}
```

Classes are useful for associating multiple HTML elements with a single set of attributes. If you need to associate formatting with a single HTML element, you can specify the element ID.

Within your style sheet, specify a style for an ID by prefixing the ID name with a pound sign (#), as this example shows:

```
#submitButton
{
    text-align: right;
    padding-right: 10px;
}
```

When using ASP.NET server controls, ASP.NET automatically assigns a dynamic ID that can vary each time the webpage is displayed. Although this ensures the ID is unique, this behavior makes it impossible to reference HTML elements by ID. You can control how ASP.NET generates the client ID by setting the *ClientIDMode* property. In addition to *inherit*, this property has three possible values:

- **AutoID**   ASP.NET generates a dynamic ID when rendering the control. It's impossible to reliably reference automatically generated IDs.

- **Predictable**   ASP.NET generates the same ID every time it renders the control. Render the webpage once, examine the page source, and use the assigned ID when referencing the HTML element.

- **Static**   ASP.NET assigns the ID you specify using the ID property. This is the easiest way to reference rendered HTML controls.

Using Themes

Like style sheets, themes centralize formatting settings. However, although style sheets rely on the client browser to download and apply the settings, ASP.NET processes themes on the server by setting control properties to specified defaults prior to rendering.

Themes are stored in the App_Themes\<theme_name>\ folder and consist of one or more skin files. Each skin file contains a list of controls with default property settings. Skin file definitions closely resemble controls in an ASPX file. However, skin files never specify an ID property.

Skin files contain two types of definitions: default skins and named control skins. Default skins, such as the following for a *Button* control, provide the defaults for any controls of the same type:

```
<asp:Button runat="server" Text="OK" Font-Bold="True" ForeColor="#00CC00" />
```

Named control skins specify the *SkinID* property. To apply the named control skin settings to a control, set the same value for the controls' *SkinID* property. For example, suppose that you created the following named control skin:

```
<asp:GridView runat="server" SkinId="gridviewSkin" BackColor="White" >
    <AlternatingRowStyle BackColor="Blue" />
</asp:GridView>
```

You can apply the named control skin's settings to a control in an .aspx file by using this control definition and setting the *Page.Theme* property to the theme name:

```
<asp:GridView
    ID="GridView1" runat="server" SkinID="gridviewSkin">
</asp:GridView>
```

Both themes and style sheets are useful for quickly changing the appearance of an entire site. For example, if you need to change the color of <h1> headings on any page from black to green, you can do so by changing a single value in either the style sheet or the theme. If you need to automatically select a different theme at runtime (for example, based on client browser capabilities), derive the pages on your site from a custom *Page* subclass that overrides the *Page_PreInit* method and sets the *Page.Theme* property to the correct value.

To simplify troubleshooting, use style sheets to specify the appearance of HTML elements and use themes to specify server-side values.

Configuring the Routing Engine

The ASP.NET MVC Framework includes a URL routing engine that you can use with both MVC and standard ASP.NET applications. The URL routing engine reads each URL requested by a web browser and chooses a webpage (for ASP.NET web applications) or controller (for MVC applications) to process the request.

The routing engine allows you to build an internal structure for the site completely separate from the public URL structure. If you later decide to change the internal structure of the site, you can modify the routing engine to maintain the existing public URLs to allow links and bookmarks to continue to function.

You configure the routing engine by using the *RegisterRoutes* method in the Global.asax file. The *Application_Start* method calls *RegisterRoutes* to configure the routing engine before the application processes any user requests. This structure is built into the ASP.NET MVC 2 Web Application template, though you can add it to any ASP.NET application.

The routing engine is flexible enough to allow you to pass any incoming request to any page or controller. Additionally, the routing engine can automatically convert parts of the requested URL into parameters. For example, consider the following default route:

Sample of Visual Basic.NET Code

```
' MapRoute takes the following parameters, in order:
' (1) Route name
' (2) URL with parameters
' (3) Parameter defaults
routes.MapRoute( _
    "Default", _
    "{controller}/{action}/{id}", _
    New With {.controller = "Home", .action = "Index", .id = UrlParameter.Optional} _
)
```

Sample of C# Code

```
routes.MapRoute(
    "Default", // Route name
    "{controller}/{action}/{id}", // URL with parameters
    new { controller = "Home", action = "Index", id = UrlParameter.Optional }
        // Parameter defaults
);
```

If a user requests the root page of a website, the routing engine passes the request to the Index action of the Home controller. If a user requests /Home/Index/25, the routing engine also passes 25 as a URL parameter. If a user requests /Store/Catalog/36, the routing engine passes the request to the *Catalog* action of the *Store* controller with an ID URL parameter of 36.

Routes work similarly for non-MVC sites. For an ASP.NET site, use the *MapPageRoute* method instead. The following code sample directs requests to either ShowCategory.aspx or ShowPicture.aspx, depending on whether the file name is index.htm or anything else:

Sample of Visual Basic.NET Code

```
routes.MapPageRoute("CategoriesWithIndexHtm", _
    "photos/{folder}/index.htm", "~/ShowCategory.aspx")

routes.MapPageRoute("Pictures", _
    "photos/{folder}/{pictureName}.htm", "~/ShowPicture.aspx")
```

Sample of C# Code

```
routes.MapPageRoute(
    "CategoriesWithIndexHtm",            // Route name
    "photos/{folder}/index.htm",     // URL with parameters
    "~/ShowCategory.aspx"    // Web forms page to handle it
);

routes.MapPageRoute(
    "Pictures",             // Route name
    "photos/{folder}/{pictureName}.htm",      // URL with parameters
    "~/ShowPicture.aspx"    // Web forms page to handle it
);
```

EXAM TIP

For the exam, remember that routing allows you to abstract the URLs end users see from the internal site structure. MVC applications use the *MapRoute* method, while non-MVC applications can use the *MapPageRoute* method.

Objective Summary

- ASP.NET provides several technologies that you can use to segment your application, including putting common content into master pages and nesting master pages within each other. MVC applications benefit from inherent segmentation as well as the ability to store common display logon in shared views, and to divide the application into areas.

- CSS style sheets store formatting information common to an entire application. For example, you can use style sheets to define the font used for headings and body text throughout an application. Later, if you change one of those fonts, you only need to update the style sheet.

- Like style sheets, themes centralize formatting settings. However, unlike style sheets, themes are processed on the server. Additionally, themes can define values for any server control property, even those not related to formatting.

- The .NET Framework routing engine is an integral part of all MVC applications, allowing you to separate the external and internal structures of an application by directing any request to any controller and action. You can also use the routing engine from ASP.NET applications, providing a way to design your site URLs separately from your ASP.NET page file names.

Objective Review

Answer the following questions to test your knowledge of the information in this objective. You can find the answers to these questions and explanations of why each answer choice is correct or incorrect in the "Answers" section at the end of this chapter.

1. You are creating an intranet web application that dozens of different organizations will deploy. You need to provide a way for web designers to specify custom logos, fonts, and colors for all pages in the application. You do not want the web designers to need any knowledge of ASP.NET. What should you do?

   A. Specify all styles in the App_Themes\Default\Skinfile.skin file. Set the master page's *Theme* property to *Default*.

   B. Specify all styles in the App_Themes\Default\Skinfile.skin file. Set each page's *Theme* property to *Default*.

   C. Specify all styles in the Styles\Site.css file. Link to the file in your master page.

   D. Define settings in the Web.config file. In the *Page_Load* method, read and apply the settings.

2. You are creating a web application that allows users to select one of four different themes. You have defined each of the themes in the App_Themes folder. How can you apply the correct theme to a page?

   A. Switch to the appropriate theme in the master page's *Load* method.

   B. Switch to the appropriate theme in each content page's *PreRender* method.

   C. In the master page, override the *Page_Load* method and change the style sheet reference in the <head> element to the appropriate theme.

   D. In each content page, override the *Page_Load* method and change the style sheet reference in the <head> element to the appropriate theme.

3. You are designing a large MVC application. The application will be divided into five areas: home, products, services, support, and investor relations. Every page on the site must have a logo at the top of the page and copyright information at the bottom of the page. Within each section, developers must define navigation links that will be used on every page in that section. How should you define the application structure to maximize consistency and minimize development time?

   A. Define the logo and copyright footer in a master page. Define the navigation links in nested master pages within each area.

   B. Create custom user controls for the logo and copyright footer. Create master pages within each area that contain the custom user controls and define the navigation links.

   C. Define the logo and copyright footer in a master page. Derive master pages containing the navigation links for each area from the root master page.

D. Define the logo and copyright footer in a master page. Apply area-specific themes to define the navigation links.

THOUGHT EXPERIMENT
Designing a Site for Maintainability

In the following thought experiment, you apply what you've learned about the "Design the Site Structure" objective to predict how a theoretical website architecture will perform. You can find answers to these questions in the "Answers" section at the end of this chapter.

You are a developer for Adventure Works. You are working with management to assess the impact of migrating the company's current static HTML site to a database-driving MVC application.

Currently, the Adventure Works site consists of static HTML created with an early version of Microsoft FrontPage. The site consists of a home page, a contact page, and a list of 30 adventure trips visitors can purchase.

Although the site remains functional, management is frustrated with the time required to update content. For example, when the company changed its logo recently, it had to manually update more than 30 pages.

The new MVC version of the site uses a master page to define the header and footer. Additionally, all styles are defined by using a CSS style sheet. Information about each of the 30 trips is stored within a database.

Answer the following questions about the future manageability of the application:

1. How many different files will the company need to update if it changes the logo again?

2. How would the company change the font used for all body text on the site?

3. How will the web designers use the standard fonts and colors when they add new pages?

4. How will the company be able to create a single layout for each of its 30 trip pages?

5. The new MVC site uses different file names than the existing site. However, Adventure Works has many existing direct backlinks to product pages, and it wants to continue to use the existing URLs. How can the company do that?

Objective 2.2: Plan for Cross-Browser and/or Form Factors

This objective provides an overview of how to identify different browser types and modify your content to suit each platform's capabilities. First, this section describes the considerations for different platforms, including bandwidth, processing capabilities, and support for rich-media plug-ins. Next, this section discusses browser files and user agents, which you will use to identify each visitor's browser type. Finally, this section provides an overview of different techniques for rendering multiple levels of content, based on the browser capabilities.

This objective covers how to:

- Evaluate the impact of features.
- Decide when to apply the browser's file.
- Examine the user agent and browser capabilities.
- Identify structural approaches.

Evaluating the Impact of Features

Client browsers differ in several ways that can affect how your site functions:

- **Screen resolution**   Computer screen resolution varies widely, and although you can read the screen resolution with JavaScript, browsers do not report their resolution with each request. Therefore, most web designers create applications about 960–980 pixels wide. That width is perfect for displays that are 1024 pixels wide. Although computer monitor resolutions vary, all mobile clients of a specific type have the same resolution. Therefore, you can detect specific mobile browser and serve pages formatted for their screens.

- **Bandwidth**   You can't reliably determine a user's bandwidth. Therefore, you need to optimize your site for the lowest-bandwidth clients. Alternatively, you can detect mobile clients (which often have low bandwidth) and serve bandwidth-optimized pages.

- **Processor speed**   Although mobile and desktop computers typically have sufficient processing capability for any JavaScript you might create, including client-side behaviors built into complex server controls such as the *DataGrid*, mobile devices might run complex JavaScript very slowly. Test your application on different devices, and if JavaScript performance is unacceptable, use a postback so that the server handles tasks such as sorting.

- **Support for plug-ins**   Although almost every browser supports JavaScript, many browsers are incapable of supporting Adobe Flash or Microsoft Silverlight. You can detect these browsers and provide an HTML page that does not rely on those plug-ins.

- **User input method** Users tend to interact with mobile devices and tablets using a touch-screen interface, rather than a keyboard and mouse. You can create HTML that takes advantage of these features. For example, you can allow users to swipe their finger across the screen to select the next item in an e-commerce store's inventory.

> *NOTE* **USING EMULATORS TO TEST DEVICE-SPECIFIC PAGES**
>
> You need to test every change to your site with every device and browser you support. As with a virtual machine, you can use emulators to simulate using a mobile device on your computer. The best emulators are those developers use to write mobile applications and are available directly from the device manufacturer. You can also find online emulators that run within a browser. Many emulators are unreliable, however, and might not submit the correct user agent or render pages exactly like the mobile device. Additionally, emulators cannot accurately simulate the experience of using a touch-screen interface. It is always better to test sites using physical mobile devices, but emulators are useful when that is not possible.

Deciding When to Apply the Browsers File

To determine the capabilities of a client browser, ASP.NET compares identifying information provided by the browser to a series of .browser files. At runtime, you can examine the browser capabilities to customize the page for that specific browser type.

For example, you might identify mobile browsers and provide a lower-bandwidth version of the site. Alternatively, if a specific browser interprets HTML formatting differently, you might work around this by providing different HTML to different browsers. In fact, the .NET Framework uses this technique to modify built-in server controls to different browser types.

ASP.NET includes standard browser definitions at %windir%\Microsoft.NET\ Framework\<*ver*>\CONFIG\Browsers. Each .browser file contained within that folder is an XML file that includes information allowing the definition to match a specific browser and attributes of that browser type. For example, the following excerpt from iemobile.browser includes a user agent that requests must match and defines *IsMobileBrowser* as *true*.

```
<browsers>
    <!-- Mozilla/4.0 (compatible; MSIE 6.0; Windows CE; IEMobile 8.12; MSIE Mobile 6.0)
-->
    <browser id="IEMobile" parentID="Mozilla">
        <identification>
            <userAgent match="IEMobile.(?'version'(?'major'\d+)(\.(?'minor'\d+)?)\w*)">
        </identification>

        <capture>
          <userAgent match="MSIE (?'msieMajorVersion'\d+)" />
        </capture>

        <capabilities>
            <capability name="layoutEngine"    value="Trident" />
```

```
<capability name="browser"        value="IEMobile" />
<capability name="majorversion"   value="${major}" />
<capability name="minorversion"   value="${minor}" />
<capability name="type"           value="IEMobile${msieMajorVersion}" />
<capability name="isMobileDevice" value="true" />
```

Typically, you will not need to create custom browser definitions; the definitions provided by ASP.NET meet most requirements. If you discover that you need to customize your site for a specific browser and ASP.NET is unable to detect it (for example, if a new browser is released), you can add a custom browser definition by creating the App_Browsers application subfolder and then adding a custom .browser file.

If you want all applications on a given computer to access a .browser file, add it to the %windir%\Microsoft.NET\Framework\<ver>\CONFIG\Browsers folder and then run %windir%\ Microsoft.NET\Framework\<ver>\aspnet_regbrowsers.exe to recompile them.

When creating a custom .browser file, you should determine two properties:

- **The user agent** Every browser identifies itself with a user-agent string included with the HTTP request. The user-agent string is visible in the Trace.axd file, or you can examine it at runtime by using the *Requst.UserAgent* string.

- **The parent browser** To simplify configuring your browser definition file, use the *parentID* attribute of the <browser> element to specify that the definition inherits from an existing browser file. You should inherit from whichever built-in browser most closely matches the browser you are defining.

After you define these two properties, you can specify any properties that differ from the parent browser.

> *MORE INFO* **CREATING CUSTOM .BROWSER FILES**
>
> For detailed information about creating custom .browser files, read "Browser Definition File Schema" at *http://msdn.microsoft.com/library/ms228122.aspx*.

Examining User Agents and Browser Capabilities

When a browser requests a page from a website, it provides a user agent to define the browser type. For example, Microsoft Internet Explorer 9.0 running on Windows 7 provides the following user agent:

Mozilla/5.0 (compatible; MSIE 9.0; Windows NT 6.1; WOW64; Trident/5.0)

However, Safari running on an iPhone 4 provides the following user agent:

Mozilla/5.0 (iPhone; U; CPU iPhone OS 4_3_2 like Mac OS X; en-us) AppleWebKit/533.17.9 (KHTML, like Gecko) Version/5.0.2 Mobile/8h7 Safari/6533.18.5

User agents are formally defined by RFC (Request for Comments) 1945 (available at *http:// www.ietf.org/rfc/rfc1945.txt*), but the unofficial structure is more important to understand:

- **Mozilla/<version>** The first part of the user agent is used only if the web server cannot more precisely identify the browser. Most modern browsers identify themselves as "Mozilla/5.0". Mozilla was the codename of Netscape Navigator, the first free, widespread browser, and modern browsers continue to identify their basic functionality with the Mozilla name. The Opera browser identifies itself as "Opera", and search engine bots use unique identifiers.

- **(<System information>)** A precise description of the browser and operating system.

- **<Platform> (<Platform details>)** The browser's low-level platform. Internet Explorer does not provide this or any further fields by default.

- **<Browser enhancements>** Some plug-ins, such as Microsoft Live Meeting, add information about themselves to the user agent.

If you provide alternate pages for specific devices (an approach that is often required for mobile devices because of the varying form factors), examine the user-agent string directly by using *Request.UserAgent*. The following example shows how to examine the user agent to detect requests from iPhones, and then transfer processing to a device-specific page:

Sample of Visual Basic.NET Code

```
If Request.UserAgent.ToLower().Contains("iphone") Then
    ' If this is an iPhone user, send them to the iPhone page
    Server.Transfer("~/IphonePage.aspx")
End If
```

Sample of C# Code

```
if ( Request.UserAgent.ToLower().Contains("iphone") )
{
    // If this is an iPhone user, send them to the iPhone page
    Server.Transfer("~/IphonePage.aspx");
}
```

If you plan to create more generalized pages, such as pages for all mobile devices, you do not have to interpret browser strings directly. Instead, use the *Request.Browser* object, which ASP.NET creates by comparing the user agent to the browser's files.

Because different clients have different capabilities, your website content should degrade gracefully when a client does not support every feature of your site. At runtime, examine *Request.Browser* (an instance of *HttpBrowserCapabilties*) to determine the features the browser supports, and modify the output page accordingly. The most important *Request.Browser* properties are the following:

- **Type** The name and major version of the browser, such as "IE9" or "Chrome12".

- **Browser** The name of the browser.

- **Version** The version of the browser.

- **Crawler** Indicates whether the browser is a bot. This is typically used by search engines to index content.

- **IsMobileDevice** One of the most useful properties, this indicates whether the browser is a mobile device.

- **InputType** Indicates whether user input is provided by one of these values: *virtualKeyboard*, *telephoneKeypad*, or *keyboard*.

- **Frames** Indicates whether the browser supports HTML frames.

- **Cookies** Indicates whether the browser supports cookies.

- **VBScript** Indicates whether the browser supports VBScript. Only Internet Explorer supports VBScript.

- **JavaApplets and JavaScript** Indicates whether the browser supports JavaScript.

- **ActiveXControls** Indicates whether the browser supports ActiveX controls. Note that the browser might support ActiveX controls, and thus return True, but your website or the user might not have privileges to install and run ActiveX controls. Only Internet Explorer supports ActiveX controls.

Some properties, such as *ScreenPixelsHeight* and *ScreenPixelsWidth*, might seem useful but do not always provide accurate values. For a complete list of properties, read "Http-BrowserCapabilities Class" at *http://msdn.microsoft.com/library/system.web.httpbrowsercapabilities.aspx*.

> **NOTE DETERMINING THE SCREEN SPACE**
>
> To retrieve the usable window resolution, examine the client-side JavaScript objects *window.screen.availHeight* and *window.screen.availWidth*.

Identifying Structural Approaches

There are four main approaches you can use to provide different layouts based on client browser capabilities:

- **Conditionally alter control properties at runtime** You can use a simple *If* statement to evaluate the client browser capabilities and then selectively change the properties of server controls to customize the content of a page. For example, you might set the *Visible* property for a control containing a reference to a Silverlight object to *False* for mobile browsers. This technique allows you to create and maintain only a single copy of each page.

- **Use Server.Transfer to render a different page** *Server.Transfer* causes ASP.NET to render a different page without redirecting the browser or changing the page address. Therefore, you can examine the user agent in the code-behind file and transfer processing to a page optimized for mobile users. This technique allows greater flexibility (especially if you need to render several versions of a page); however, it requires you to create and maintain multiple pages.

- **Use Response.Redirect to direct clients to a different page**   If you determine that a client requires a different version of a page, you can use *Response.Redirect* to cause the client browser to request an alternate URL. Many websites use different domain names for desktop and mobile versions of a site, such as www.<*domain*>.com and m.<*domain*>.com or <*domain*>.mobi. If a mobile client visits the desktop version of the site, you can detect it at runtime and automatically redirect the client to the mobile version. This technique allows search engines to separately index the content and displays the version of the site being used in the address bar.

- **Use JavaScript**   You can examine the user agent by using JavaScript and redirect the client to a different page or hide specific elements. Using JavaScript has an important advantage: the logic will work with content delivery networks (CDNs) that cache recently retrieved copies of your pages. If you use any server-side solution, a CDN caches the version of the page last requested and serves it to any client, regardless of their user agent. Therefore, if you use ASP.NET to alter pages or redirect users, and you use a CDN to cache your web pages, mobile users might receive the desktop version of the page.

> *NOTE* **PREVENTING INDEXING OF DUPLICATE CONTENT**
>
> If you provide different versions of the same content with different URLs (for example, by using a different domain name for mobile-optimized pages), edit your robots.txt file to instruct search engines to disregard the duplicate content. Indexing duplicate content can diminish your search ranking and cause search engines to direct users to the incorrect version of a page.

Objective Summary

- When considering supporting different form factors, evaluate the screen resolution required by your site, the bandwidth used, the processing requirements of any JavaScript, and whether the form factors support any plug-ins you might require.

- ASP.NET uses .browser files to determine browser capabilities based on the client's user agent. You can create custom .browser files for new devices that ASP.NET does not automatically detect.

- User agents provide detailed information about the client's browser and platform. It also provides fallback compatibility information in case the server is not aware of the browser and platform type.

- There are several structures you can consider using to provide content for multiple form factors. You can use a single page or view, but selectively enable and disable components based on client capabilities. Alternatively, you can create completely separate pages and use *Server.Transfer* to process a different page. If you want the client to open a different URL, such as the URL of a mobile-specific version of your site, use *Response.Redirect*.

Objective Review

Answer the following questions to test your knowledge of the information in this objective. You can find the answers to these questions and explanations of why each answer choice is correct or incorrect in the "Answers" section at the end of this chapter.

1. You are designing a web application that includes two different interfaces: desktop and mobile. Which object would you examine to change the layout at runtime for mobile clients?

    A. *Request.Browser*

    B. *Request.HttpMethod*

    C. *Response.IsClientConnected*

    D. *Response.Status*

2. Recently, your IT department began issuing users a new type of mobile device. An existing web application does not detect the device as a mobile device. How can you allow the device to be properly detected without changing application code?

    A. Alter the *Request.Browser* object.

    B. Add a .browser file.

    C. Add a new user agent to the Web.config file.

    D. Restart the web server.

3. You are designing a web application that provides separate interfaces for desktop and mobile clients using different .ASPX files. By default, default.aspx receives requests for both desktop and mobile clients. How can your application process default-mobile. aspx instead without changing the path in the browser's address bar?

    A. *Server.Execute*

    B. *Response.Clear*

    C. *Server.Transfer*

    D. *Response.Redirect*

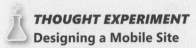

In the following thought experiment, you apply what you've learned about the "Plan for Cross-Browser and/or Form Factors" objective to predict how a theoretical website architecture will perform. You can find answers to these questions in the "Answers" section at the end of this chapter.

You are a consultant for Wide World Importers. Management has contracted you to review an updated design for the company's website that better supports mobile devices.

World Wide Importers' current website, *http://www.wideworldimporters.com*, allows customers and suppliers to view the status of shipments as they are shipped, travel in transit, and received. The user interface was designed for desktop users with a mouse, and it has proved difficult for mobile users to access. Additionally, the home page includes a Silverlight animation describing the company, and most mobile users cannot see the animation. Finally, the website currently shows large images of each product, which causes the website to load slowly on mobile devices.

World Wide Importers' internal developers have designed a new website that they feel addresses the needs of mobile users. The website will be located at *http://mobile.wideworldimporters.com*. The mobile site's user interface is optimized for smaller displays, lower bandwidth, and touch interfaces. If a mobile user attempts to access the desktop version of the site, which remains at *http://www.wideworldimporters.com*, a JavaScript pop-up will appear and prompt them to be redirected to *http://mobile.wideworldimporters.com*.

Though developers have assured management that this is the best possible design, management has some concerns and wants your opinion. Answer the following questions about the future performance of the application:

1. Management does not expect users to remember to visit the mobile version of the site. If mobile users visit the standard version of the site, how much of a delay will there be before they are redirected?

2. Is there a way mobile users could be automatically redirected to the mobile site? How would that work?

3. What drawbacks might there be to maintaining a separate mobile site?

4. Is there a way to display a mobile version of the site by using the existing URLs? How would that work?

5. If a new mobile device comes out, will it be automatically detected? If not, how could management properly address the new device?

Objective 2.3: Plan for Globalization

This objective provides an overview of designing web applications for an international audience. Reaching users beyond a single language and country/region requires two primary considerations:

- Displaying text in the user's preferred language
- Displaying information such as dates and currencies using the standards of the user's country

ASP.NET includes features to handle both scenarios. In fact, after you set the user's culture, ASP.NET handles many aspects of globalization automatically. In some cases, however, you will need to develop a custom solution to provide flexibility and performance.

> **This objective covers how to:**
> - Handle language and culture preferences.
> - Design to support culture preferences.
> - Choose between *CurrentCulture* and *CurrentUICulture*.
> - Display controls for different cultures.
> - Translate web applications.
> - Handle Unicode data.

Handling Language and Culture Preferences

Most browsers read the user's language preference from the operating system settings. In Internet Explorer, users can also set their language and culture preferences using the Languages button on the General tab of the Internet Options dialog box.

Browsers send a user's language preferences using the *HTTP_ACCEPT_LANGUAGE* header. For example, if you are from Mexico and prefer Spanish (es-MX) but are also comfortable with US standards and the English language (en-US), Internet Explorer sends the following header with each web request:

HTTP_ACCEPT_LANGUAGE: es-MX, en-US

You can access the browser's list of languages by using the *Request.Browser.UserLanguages* string array. *Request.Browser.UserLanguages[0]* contains the user's preferred language and culture, though not all browsers provide it in the same format. At runtime, you can verify that the user's language is in an acceptable format and then set *Thread.CurrentThread.CurrentUI Culture* and *Thread.CurrentThread.CurrentCulture*.

Real World

There are several ways to provide globalized content to users. Recently, I redesigned an English-only website to support eight different languages and cultures. The website stored text content for thousands of pages in a database, and it routed all requests to three ASPX pages, which retrieved the content for the request page based on the requested URL.

First, I needed to modify the database layout to support multiple languages. So, I moved text content into tables separate from other data, and then added an indexed column for the language code. When a translator translated a page into a different language, the management tools added a new row to the database and specified the language code.

Next, I needed to update the routing mechanism to support displaying content in different languages. I chose to use www as the hostname for English-language content to maintain the existing URLs, and replace www with the two-letter language code for other URLs.

In addition to the primary content stored in the database, the website had static English-language content stored in labels. I updated these to retrieve values from resource files instead, and had that text translated. For labels that were populated in the code-behind file, I had to update the code to access the resource file, instead.

Finally, I needed to allow users to select content in other languages. Most users find the site organically through search engines, so searching in their native language should bring them directly to their preferred language. Additionally, I added links on every page to allow users to manually select a different language. In the master page, I added code to examine the hostname being requested and set the *Current Culture* and *CurrentUICulture* appropriately. I updated the data access layer to retrieve the appropriate row for the requested language.

ASP.NET can automatically adjust to a user's language and culture preferences. To have ASP.NET set the *CurrentCulture* and *CurrentUICulture* to the first language supported by the client's browser settings, set both properties to auto in either the Web.config or the @ *Page* directive. To specify a default language, use *auto:<default_language>*, as the following two examples show:

Example of Web.config

```
<globalization uiCulture="auto:en-US " culture="auto:en-US" />
```

Example of @ Page directive

```
<%@ Page uiculture="auto:en-US" culture="auto:en-US" %>
```

Visual Studio automatically sets both *Culture* and *UICulture* to auto in the @ *Page* directive of new pages. To declaratively configure a particular page or application to use a specific culture, simply remove auto and specify the appropriate language and culture.

Designing to Support Cultural Preferences

Objective 2.2 discussed how to format a site differently for different browser types. Objective 2.3 covers how to manage multiple versions of a site for different languages and cultures. These require different design approaches because search engines should index only a single version of desktop-formatted and mobile-formatted pages as well as pages formatted for different cultures. Typically, however, you want search engines to separately index pages translated into multiple languages because the primary content, the text, would be unique. Therefore, you might not want to automatically select a translation based on the browser's preferred language, because search engines do not attempt to retrieve individual pages in different languages.

To make a translated site easy to index, design the site so that each version of a page has a unique URL. Although there are other ways to do this (including using query parameters), the three most common approaches are these:

- **Changing the page path**   Add a language identifier to the page path. For example, the language identifier for English is en and for Spanish it is es. Therefore, you might identify different language versions of a page as http://contoso.com/en/page.aspx and http://contoso.com/es/page.aspx.

> **NOTE   CHANGING THE PAGE PATH**
>
> MSDN inserts the language culture name at the beginning of each page path. Visit any MSDN page using a browser set for the English language, and you will see "en-us" embedded in the URL, such as *http://msdn.microsoft.com/en-us/library/ms123401.aspx*. You can translate the page into Chinese by changing "en-us" to "zh-cn", or into French by changing "en-us" to "fr-fr".

- **Changing the top-level domain**   Register multiple versions of your domain name with country-specific registrars. For example, you might use .com for the English-language version of the site and .es for the Spanish-language version of the site.
- **Changing the hostname**   Change the hostname—but not the domain name—for different versions of your site. For example, you might use www.contoso.com or en.contoso.com for the English-language version of your site, and use en.contoso.com for the Spanish-language version of your site.

Choosing Between *CurrentCulture* and *CurrentUICulture*

The .NET Framework provides two related classes for setting a page's culture. Both classes are members of *Thread.CurrentThread* and require the *System.Threading* namespace:

- **CurrentCulture**   Defines how ASP.NET renders server controls. For example, English speakers in the United States abbreviate dates using the format mm/dd/yyyy, while English speakers in the United Kingdom prefer the format dd/mm/yyyy. If the date is January 31, 2012, setting *CurrentCulture* to *en-US* (United States English) will cause *DateTime.Now.ToShortDateString* to render as "01/31/2012". Setting *CurrentCulture* to en-GB (Great Britain English) causes the same method to render as "12/01/2031".

- **CurrentUICulture**   Defines which language-specific resources ASP.NET chooses when server controls are linked to a resource file. Set *CurrentUICulture* when a single page has been translated into multiple languages.

EXAM TIP

The naming difference between *CurrentCulture* and *CurrentUICulture* makes them easy to confuse. After all, they can both cause changes to the user interface. Remember to use *CurrentUICulture* when you have translated text in resource files, and *CurrentCulture* when you want to take advantage of the .NET Framework's built-in globalization capabilities.

Displaying Text for Differing Cultures

After setting *CurrentCulture*, use *String.Format()* to help ensure data is properly formatted. For example, the following code sample shows how to display a value as currency in both English (as "$1,999.99") and French (as "1 999,99 €"). It requires the *System.Threading* and *System.Globalization* namespaces.

Sample of Visual Basic.NET Code

```
Dim money As Double = 1999.99

' Set the UI culture to English
Thread.CurrentThread.CurrentCulture = New CultureInfo("en")

' Format a double as currency using the current culture
USLabel.Text = [String].Format("{0:C}", money)

' Set the UI culture to French
Thread.CurrentThread.CurrentCulture = New CultureInfo("fr")

' Format a double as currency using the current culture
FRLabel.Text = [String].Format("{0:C}", money)
```

Sample of C# Code

```
double money = 1999.99;

// Set the UI culture to English
Thread.CurrentThread.CurrentCulture = new CultureInfo("en");

// Format a double as currency using the current UI culture
USLabel.Text = String.Format("{0:C}", money);
```

```
// Set the UI culture to French
Thread.CurrentThread.CurrentCulture = new CultureInfo("fr");

// Format a double as currency using the current UI culture
FRLabel.Text = String.Format("{0:C}", money);
```

> **MORE INFO** **FORMATTING STRINGS**
>
> For detailed information about formatting strings, read "Formatting Types" at *http://msdn. microsoft.com/library/26etazsy.aspx.*

If you configure ASP.NET to automatically set the culture based on the supported languages provided by the browser, all you need to do is format data with *String.Format* when populating the *Text* properties of *Label* and *Literal* controls.

Plan ahead to allow controls to be formatted to different cultures. Specifically, test any controls that display text with both left-to-right and right-to-left languages. Verify that calendar controls have sufficient room when different cultures are selected.

Translating Web Applications

ASP.NET provides support for using resource files to automatically render server controls in the proper language. After creating an ASPX page in Visual Studio, click the Tools menu and then click Generate Local Resources. Visual Studio creates a .resx file using the name of the ASPX page and adds *meta:resourcekey* properties to every server control so that values are populated from the new resource file. The new resource file includes values for every *Text*, *ToolTip*, *Title*, *Caption*, and other visible text properties on the page.

Next, copy the resource file for every language you plan to translate the site into. Add the language code to the file name before the .resx extension. For example, if the default English resource file is named Default.aspx.resx, you can create Spanish and French resource files named Default.aspx.es.resx and Default.aspx.fr.resx. Then have translators add appropriate text to the resource files.

ASP.NET automatically uses the text from the resource file that matches the *CurrentUICulture* value. Some controls include built-in translations. For example, ASP.NET always renders the *Calendar* control by using month names in the language defined by *CurrentUICulture*.

At runtime, use the *Resources* object to access translated resource files. For example, the following code sets the current page's title based on the *PageTitle* value in the Translations resource file:

Sample of Visual Basic.NET Code

```
Page.Title = Resources.Translations.PageTitle
```

Sample of C# Code

```
Page.Title = Resources.Translations.PageTitle;
```

If you currently retrieve text from a database, you need to develop a custom solution to retrieve the proper language from the database. For best results, add the translation functions in the data access layer so that the proper language text is automatically retrieved from the database, based on the *CurrentUICulture* setting.

Handling Unicode Data

The .NET Framework uses Unicode (specifically, UTF-16) to store most text data, including strings. However, HTTP communications are converted to UTF-8 by default. Most browsers support UTF-8, so this default behavior is typically acceptable.

If you have clients that do not support Unicode, you can specify a different encoding type by setting the *requestEncoding* and *responseEncoding* attributes in either the Web.config file or the @ *Page* directive. Additionally, if the ASPX page is encoded in something other than Unicode, you can specify the correct encoding by using the *fileEncoding* attribute in the Web.config file. The following examples demonstrate how to use the Japanese Shift-JIS encoding:

Example of Web.config

```
<configuration>
  <system.web>
    <globalization
       requestEncoding="shift-jis"
       responseEncoding="shift-jis"
       fileEncoding="shift-jis"
   />
  </system.web>
</configuration>
```

Example of @ Page directive

```
<%@ Page requestEncoding="shift-jis" responseEncoding="shift-jis" %>
```

Objective Summary

- Users set their language preference in their operating system. Browsers send this preference along with every request. By default, ASP.NET will set both the *Culture* and *UICulture* properties according to the preference sent by the browser. However, you can override this by setting the *Culture* and *UICulture* properties of the @ *Page* directive, or at runtime by setting *Thread.CurrentThread.CurrentUICulture* and *Thread. CurrentThread.CurrentCulture*.

- If you need to have different URLs for different languages, you can add a language code to the path, change the hostname, or use country-specific top-level domains.

- Use *CurrentCulture* for regional formatting, such as changing the layout of dates and currency. Use *CurrentUICulture* to translate text using resource files.

- Server controls automatically format their output based on the *CurrentCulture*. However, if you add *String* output to a *Label* or other control, you must use *String.Format* to use culture-specific formatting rules.

- Visual Studio can automatically generate resource files containing all the visible text in server controls on an ASPX page. You can then create language-specific resource files by adding the language code immediately before the .resx file extension. ASP.NET automatically chooses the resource file that most closely matches the *CurrentUICulture* value.

- ASP.NET outputs Unicode text by default. Although Unicode is universally accepted by modern browsers, you can define different encoding by setting the *requestEncoding* and *responseEncoding* attributes of the <configuration><system.web><globalization> configuration element. You can also use the @ *Page* directive to set *requestEncoding* and *responseEncoding* on a per-page basis.

Objective Review

Answer the following questions to test your knowledge of the information in this objective. You can find the answers to these questions and explanations of why each answer choice is correct or incorrect in the "Answers" section at the end of this chapter.

1. You are developing multilingual blog software. Writers will create a new blog entry in their native language by typing it into a web form, which the application stores in a database. Translators will then translate the blog entry into other languages, and editors will review the translation before approving it. Additionally, static text information (such as the copyright details) is stored in language-specific resource files. You must choose how to display the version of a blog entry in the reader's preferred language. What should you do? (Choose two. Each answer forms part of the complete solution.)

   A. Set *Thread.CurrentThread.CurrentUICulture*.

   B. Set *Thread.CurrentThread.CurrentCulture*.

   C. Store translated blog entries in the database, and then read the correct entry based on the user's language preference.

   D. Store translated blog entries in resource files.

2. You are designing an English language website for users in several countries. The countries each have their own standards for displaying dates and currencies. How can you customize the display of information according to the standards of each user's country? (Choose two. Each answer forms part of the complete solution.)

   A. Set *Thread.CurrentThread.CurrentUICulture*.

   B. Set *Thread.CurrentThread.CurrentCulture*.

   C. Using *String.Format* to display dates and currency.

   D. Use *Object.ToString* to display dates and currency.

3. You have created resource files that include translations for the text properties of all server controls in a new web application. You need to test the website to verify that it displays the French language translations correctly. Which of the following could you do? (Choose two. Each answer forms a complete solution.)

A. In *Page.Load*, set *Thread.CurrentThread.CurrentUICulture* to a new instance of *CultureInfo* created with the string "fr".

B. In *Page.Load*, set *Thread.CurrentThread.CurrentCulture* to a new instance of *CultureInfo* created with the string "fr".

C. Add uiculture="fr" to the @ *Page* directive.

D. Add culture="fr" to the @ *Page* directive.

THOUGHT EXPERIMENT
Designing a Multilingual Website

In the following thought experiment, you apply what you've learned about the "Plan for Globalization" objective to predict how a theoretical website architecture will perform. You can find answers to these questions in the "Answers" section at the end of this chapter.

You are a developer for Contoso Pharmaceuticals. You are working with management to assess the current plans for translating a website into multiple languages, and then maintaining the multilingual site.

The public website displays information about the business' thousands of drugs, including their usage and side effects. Because the information provides medical safety data, the legal and medical departments must review all translated information before it is published. The developers created a database design to store the content for each page in multiple languages. It also supports review status for translated pages.

Information not related to products, such as menu items, will be stored in resource files and manually translated when required.

In addition to the translated drug information, the website must display currency and dates using local formats. Developers plan to set the *CurrentCulture* and *CurrentUICulture* values according to the user's region.

Management needs to give customers direct access to their usage information. Answer the following questions about the future performance of the application:

1. Is it the best choice to store the product information in the database? Why?

2. When displaying product information, how will the webpages determine which language to retrieve from the database?

3. Is it the best choice to store menu information in resource files? Why?

4. When displaying menu information, how will the master page determine which language to display?

Chapter Summary

- ASP.NET provides several technologies to allow you to segment your application, including master pages and MVC. You can use HTML to centralize formatting information in CSS style sheets, and ASP.NET provides similar capabilities using server-side themes. If you do not want your site structure to be visible to users, use routing.

- Different clients have different processing capabilities, bandwidth, and support for JavaScript and plug-ins. ASP.NET compares the user agent provided by clients to built-in and custom .browser files to determine client capabilities. Using the *Request. Browser* object, you can inspect these capabilities and disable specific controls, transfer processing to another page with *Server.Transfer*, or redirect the client using *Response. Redirect*.

- ASP.NET sets *Culture* and *UICulture* according to user preferences, but you can override them declaratively and at runtime. Use *CurrentCulture* for regional formatting, such as changing the layout of dates and currency, and use *CurrentUICulture* to translate text using resource files. If you add String output to a *Label* or other control, you must use *String.Format* to use culture-specific formatting rules. You can change the encoding standard from Unicode by defining the *requestEncoding* and *response Encoding* attributes of the <configuration><system.web><globalization> configuration element or the @ *Page* directive.

Answers

Objective 2.1: Review

1. **Correct Answer:** C

    A. **Incorrect:** You cannot set the *Theme* property for master pages; instead, you should set the *Theme* property for content pages.

    B. **Incorrect:** Although this approach would centralize the appearance of all controls, web designers would need to understand the structure of an ASP.NET application to modify the settings.

    C. **Correct:** Style sheets provide a way to centralize an application's appearance by using open standards that any web designer will be able to modify.

    D. **Incorrect:** Although this approach would centralize the appearance of all controls, web designers would need to understand your application-specific settings to modify the application's appearance.

2. **Correct Answer:** B

   A. **Incorrect:** You cannot set the *Theme* property for master pages; instead, you should set the *Theme* property for content pages.

   B. **Correct:** You can change themes in the *Page.PreRender* method. To simplify coding, create a custom *Page* class that changes the theme, and derive all pages from the custom class.

   C. **Incorrect:** This approach modifies the CSS style sheet, which is separate from the ASP.NET theme.

   D. **Incorrect:** Refer to the explanation for answer C.

3. **Correct Answer:** A

   A. **Correct:** Nested master pages provide a straightforward and flexible way to define a hierarchy of common elements for multiple pages on a site.

   B. **Incorrect:** Custom user controls can simplify repeating the same element on multiple pages. However, each area developer would have to add the controls to every page, increasing development time. Additionally, developers might not place the controls in the same location, reducing consistency.

   C. **Incorrect:** Although you can create custom page classes, you cannot derive a master page from another ASPX page.

   D. **Incorrect:** Themes would allow each area developer to specify custom properties for controls defined in the master page. However, themes would not provide area developers with the flexibility they need to specify their own navigation links.

Objective 2.1: Thought Experiment

1. The company will need to update only the master page.

2. The company would need to update only the CSS style sheet.

3. The web designers will need to add the class attribute to HTML elements, and reference a class defined in the CSS style sheet.

4. The company will be able to create a controller, action, and a view for the trip pages, and it can populate information about the specific trip based on the URL requested.

5. Routing allows any incoming URL to be processed by a specified controller and action.

Objective 2.2: Review

1. **Correct Answer:** A

   A. **Correct:** The *Request.Browser.IsMobileDevice* property is the best way to determine if the current client is mobile.

   B. **Incorrect:** The *Request.HttpMethod* indicates whether the request was made by using an HTTP *Get*, *Put*, or other method. It does not give any indication of whether the client is mobile.

   C. **Incorrect:** The *Response* object allows you to configure different aspects of the web server's HTTP response. It contains no useful information about the client. *Response.IsClientConnected* indicates whether the client has reset the connection to the server.

   D. **Incorrect:** *Reponse.Status* is the HTTP status returned by the server.

2. **Correct Answer:** B

   A. **Incorrect:** You cannot alter the *Request.Browser* object because it is created by ASP.NET at runtime.

   B. **Correct:** You can create a new .browser file that matches the user agent provided by the mobile device and sets *IsMobileDevice* to *true*.

   C. **Incorrect:** You should not add user agents to the Web.config file. Instead, create new .browser files.

   D. **Incorrect:** Restarting the web server would have no effect.

3. **Correct Answer:** C

   A. **Incorrect:** *Server.Execute* runs an .asp file and should be used only when working with ASP applications.

   B. **Incorrect:** *Response.Clear* erases the current response from memory.

   C. **Correct:** *Server.Transfer* begins processing the specified page without communicating that change to the client.

   D. **Incorrect:** *Response.Redirect* sends a message back to the client requesting that the client submit a second request with a different URL.

Objective 2.2: Thought Experiment

1. Users will need to confirm that they want to be redirected, and then their mobile device will need to load the mobile version of the page. This could take several seconds.

2. Yes. The JavaScript could simply load the new page automatically without prompting the user. Alternatively, you could check *Request.Browser.IsMobileDevice* at runtime and issue a *Server.Redirect* to the mobile site.

3. One drawback to this approach is that mobile users must make an extra request to visit the mobile site, reducing page load time. Another drawback is that your site displays two copies of the same content. If you do not rely on search engines indexing the content, this might not be a problem. If search engines are important, you would need to block the mobile site from being indexed.

4. Yes. You could check *Request.Browser.IsMobileDevice* at runtime and issue a *Server.Transfer* to the mobile version of the page.

5. Maybe, but maybe not. A new iPhone, for example, would probably still identify itself as an iPhone, and ASP.NET would apply an appropriate .browser file that still identified the device as mobile. An entirely new mobile device, however, might not be detected. In that case, you could create a new .browser file with the device's user string that sets *IsMobileDevice* to *true*.

Objective 2.3: Review

1. **Correct Answers:** A and C

    A. **Correct:** Setting *CurrentUICulture* causes ASP.NET to read the correct language from the language-specific resource files.

    B. **Incorrect:** Setting *CurrentCulture* causes ASP.NET to format information, including dates and currency, using the current culture's standards. However, the scenario does not mention that type of information.

    C. **Correct:** Database entries provide the flexibility and performance required for a blog system.

    D. **Incorrect:** Resource files should not be used for dynamic information such as blog entries. Additionally, resource files do not provide an editorial review process.

2. **Correct Answers:** B and C

   A. **Incorrect:** Set *CurrentUICulture* to configure which language-specific resources ASP.NET reads from the resource file.

   B. **Correct:** Set *CurrentCulture* to configure how information such as dates and currencies is displayed.

   C. **Correct:** ASP.NET uses the *CurrentCulture* setting to determine how to format information rendered using *String.Format*.

   D. **Incorrect:** You cannot format numeric values as currency using *Object.ToString*. Instead, use *String.Format*.

3. **Correct Answers:** B and C

   A. **Correct:** You can set the *UICulture* at runtime by creating a new instance of *CultureInfo* and using it to define *CurrentUICulture*.

   B. **Incorrect:** CurrentCulture defines layout and formatting, but not resource translation.

   C. **Correct:** By default, ASP.NET sets the *Culture* and *UICulture* properties automatically based on the language preferences defined by the browser. You can override this by setting *Culture* and *UICulture* in the @ *Page* directive. To use translation resources, define *UICulture*.

   D. **Incorrect:** Culture defines layout and formatting, but not resource translation.

Objective 2.3: Thought Experiment

1. Yes, a database is the correct choice. If the company needed to store only a few pieces of information, it could use resource files. However, using a database allows the developers to implement content control mechanisms to ensure translations are reviewed before being published.

2. For consistency, webpages should use the *CurrentUICulture* setting when accessing the database.

3. Yes, resource files are the best choice for displaying static strings in multiple languages because resource files allow efficient development and ASP.NET provides the correct translation automatically.

4. The master page automatically displays the correct language, because developers plan to set the *CurrentUICulture* setting.

CHAPTER 3

Designing Data Strategies and Structures

All web applications provide data to users, and most collect input from users, too. Although accessing data is a common task, designing data access, presentation, and validation is a complex topic. If you make poor choices during the design phase, the application can still work, but development or maintenance might be more costly, input errors might cause data integrity problems, or malicious attackers might compromise the security.

This objective domain provides an overview of data access, presentation, and validation technologies, and describes the scenarios for which each technology is best suited. Like the 70-515 exam, "Web Applications Development with Microsoft .NET Framework 4," most of the content is focused on MVC applications, which access data very differently than traditional ASP.NET applications.

Like all objectives for the 70-519 exam, this objective domain is design-oriented. Therefore, the content focuses on making high-level decisions, rather than writing code. Before you attempt to understand the design-level concepts, you should already understand how to implement the technologies and you should have passed the 70-516 exam, "Accessing Data with Microsoft .NET Framework 4."

Objectives in this chapter:

- Objective 3.1: Design data access
- Objective 3.2: Design data presentation and interaction
- Objective 3.3: Plan for data validation

Objective 3.1: Design Data Access

Any time you are accessing a database directly from a .NET application, you should use the Entity Framework as your data access layer. If clients need to access a database across the Internet, use WCF data services (formerly known as ADO.NET data services) to implement an open, standards-based Open Data Protocol (OData) and a Representational State Transfer (REST) service.

As discussed in Objective 1.2, the Windows Communication Foundation (WCF) is the preferred way to create web services, which allow you to expose both data and application logic to local or remote applications. Additionally, the Microsoft .NET Framework still supports creating ASP.NET web services, which build upon Internet Information Services (IIS) to expose methods to web clients.

This objective provides an overview of the available data access technologies and describes the scenarios in which you should choose each.

> **This objective covers how to:**
>
> - Describe when to use ADO.NET, the Entity Framework, and WCF data services to implement the Data layer.
> - Describe when to use WCF web services and ASP.NET web services to implement the Application Logic layer.

Using ADO.NET

ADO.NET provided early versions of the .NET Framework with basic, but direct, access to databases. First, you use a connection string to create a connection object. Using the connection object, you can run stored procedures, read data by using *DataSet* and *DataTable* objects, and submit updates to the database.

Although you can still use ADO.NET, recent versions of the .NET Framework support the Entity Framework (sometimes called the ADO.NET Entity Framework). The Entity Framework provides an additional layer of abstraction between the application and the database, making data easier to work with, especially for developers who do not have a database development background. For the 70-515 exam, you should be familiar with ADO.NET technologies and aware that ADO.NET is never the best choice for data access in a new application.

Using the Entity Framework

Databases are relational, which means tables with rows and columns relate to each other through keys and indexes. Relational databases support queries and stored procedures, which act on tables as separate entities.

The .NET Framework, however, is object-oriented. Objects can relate to each other by using references, which closely resemble the structure of a relational database. Object-oriented application design provides many powerful features that cannot be directly supported by relational databases. For example, objects can have parent-child relationships, which allow developers to easily access child and parent objects. Objects can also support methods to provide built-in behavior and logic.

The Entity Framework creates a mapping from object-oriented programming to relational databases. In a few seconds, Microsoft Visual Studio can use the Entity Framework to examine an existing database and create a complex object-oriented class structure with built-in relationships and methods, allowing you to access data by using classes. With the Model First capabilities of Model-View-Controller (MVC), Visual Studio can even create a new database based on an MVC model. Translating between a relational database and an object-oriented application does not require you to give up the power of queries, however—Language-Integrated Query (LINQ) provides SQL-like querying for collections, including those implemented using the Entity Framework.

Developers often add an Entity Framework model directly to their project to act as the data access layer. If you need to use a single Entity Model as the data access layer for multiple applications, create a separate Visual Studio project containing only the Entity Model. After you add the project to your solution, create a reference to the Entity Model project and to *System.Data.Entity*. Then add the connection string to your new project's configuration file.

> **MORE INFO**   **CREATING A SEPARATE DATA ACCESS PROJECT**
>
> For more information, watch "Consuming an Entity Data Model from a Separate .NET Project" at *http://msdn.microsoft.com/data/ff628208*.

Using WCF Web Services

The .NET Framework version 3.0 created the WCF to combine and update several communication technologies: enterprise services, Active Server Methods (ASMX) web services, Web Service Extensions (WSE), Microsoft Message Queuing (MSMQ), and .NET Remoting. WCF web services is the most powerful, flexible, and secure way to provide Application Logic layer services to a Presentation layer, whether the Presentation layer is part of the same application or a different one.

> **MORE INFO**   **WCF**
>
> For more information about WCF, refer to Objective 1.2.

Using WCF Data Services

Formerly known as ADO.NET data services, WCF data services allows you to quickly build an OData or REST service. OData and REST are HTTP-based open standards for exposing data across the web, where they can be consumed by clients built on a wide variety of platforms, including .NET, Microsoft Silverlight, jQuery, PHP, and JavaScript.

WCF web services and WCF data services have similar names, but they should be used in very different ways. WCF data services implement the Data layer (as described in Objective 1.1); use them when you need to provide low-level access to database tables, queries, and stored procedures. WCF web services are better suited to implementing the Application Logic layer; use them when your code needs to make decisions about the underlying data.

To create a WCF data service, follow these steps:

1. Add a data model to your project.

2. Add a WCF data service project to your solution.

3. Specify your data source class name as the type for the new generic *DataService* class.

4. Set the rules used to indicate which entity sets and service operations are available and what privileges users have. For example, you can use *SetEntitySetAccessRule* to allow users to read or write a table. Visual Studio provides example methods that are commented out by default.

Now the application exposes your data by using OData and REST. You can view the WCF data service in a browser by right-clicking the service in Solution Explorer and then clicking View In Browser. Accessing the data using OData requires providing specially formed URLs with your query information. For example, the following request provides the entire Widget table (which has an entity framework collection name of Widgets) in XML format:

/WcfDataService1.svc/Widgets

To view the row with the primary key of three, use the following path:

/WcfDataService1.svc/Widgets(3)

You can create LINQ queries by adding query parameters. For example, the following path sorts the Widgets collection by title, and then shows you the second set of 10 results:

/WcfDataService1.svc/Widgets?$orderby=title&$skip=10&$top=10

You can also filter results, draw data from related tables, and do almost anything else you can do with LINQ. Naturally, you do not typically consume a WCF data service using your browser directly. Instead, you create a client that consumes the data. If you create a JavaScript client, the data service automatically provides data in the JSON format.

MORE INFO **WCF DATA SERVICES**

For more information about implementing WCF data services, watch "Getting Started with OData Part 1: Building an OData Service" at *http://msdn.microsoft.com/en-us/data/gg601462*, and then watch the other videos in the same series.

Using ASP.NET Web Services

Although WCF web services (discussed in Objective 1.2) are the best choice for most new web services, ASP.NET web services can be easier to implement as part of an existing web application. You can create an ASP.NET web service by adding an .asmx file to an application and marking methods that you want to be accessible with the *WebMethod* attribute.

To a client, a WCF web service and an ASP.NET web service can be indistinguishable. Most of the code you write for either service is the same, too. Following is a list of the key difference between the technologies:

- WCF web services provide many types of bindings.
- WCF web services are written to implement contracts defined by interfaces.
- For ASP.NET web services, you add attributes to the methods. For WCF web services, you add attributes to the interfaces.
- ASP.NET web services must be hosted in IIS, but WCF web services can be either self-hosted or hosted in IIS.
- WCF provides more features, including support for transactions, binary serialization, message queuing, and guaranteed message delivery.

Choosing a Data Access Technology

This objective requires you to understand the different data access technologies and when you use each. In the real world, you can use any of the technologies for many scenarios, but you should choose the Entity Framework when you have direct access to the database server; choose WCF data services when you will access the database server across HTTP (such as when you access it from JavaScript); and choose WCF web services when you must provide access to both data and application logic. The guidelines that follow will help you select the correct data access technology.

Choose the Entity Framework when you

- Are implementing the Data layer.
- Connect to the database server without network protocol restrictions.
- Require rapid application development.
- Require strongly typed objects.

Choose WCF data services when you:

- Are implementing the Data layer.
- Connect to the database server by using HTTP.
- Require access from JavaScript.
- Require application-level control over access to the data.

Choose WCF web services when you:

- Are implementing the Application Logic layer.
- Require specific network protocols, such as WS-Security, SOAP, or REST.
- Require multiple binding types for supporting different types of clients.
- Require access from JavaScript.

Choose ASP.NET web services when you:

- Are implementing either the Application Logic layer or the Data layer for a remote application.
- Need to add web services to an existing ASP.NET application.
- Will host the application only in IIS.
- Require only basic HTTP communications.

Objective Summary

- ADO.NET provided earlier versions of the .NET Framework direct access to databases. Although ADO.NET is still supported, it should not be used for new applications.
- The Entity Framework is the preferred technology for accessing databases from .NET Framework applications.
- WCF web services is the preferred technology for providing remote applications access to the Application Logic layer. When WCF data services are insufficient, you can also use WCF web services to provide access to the underlying data.
- WCF data services is the preferred technology for providing remote applications access to the Data layer.
- ASP.NET web services provide a simple way to expose ASP.NET methods as web services. Although ASP.NET web services is still supported, WCF web services is now the preferred technology.

Objective Review

Answer the following questions to test your knowledge of the information in this objective. You can find the answers to these questions and explanations of why each answer choice is correct or incorrect in the "Answers" section at the end of this chapter

1. You are designing a data access service that will allow several types of clients to access a back-end database server running Microsoft SQL Server Express Edition. Non-.NET client developers plan to access the data access service across the Internet by using secure open standard protocols. Developers creating .NET clients plan to access the service by using faster, .NET-only protocols that use TCP. Which approach should you use?

   A. Create an ASMX page.

   B. Create a WCF web service.

   C. Configure the firewall to forward Internet traffic to the database server.

   D. Generate an ADO.NET Entity Data Model.

2. You are designing a data access layer for a WCF application that will connect to an existing database running on the local network. You want to develop the layer as efficiently as possible, use strongly typed data objects, and use an object-oriented development model. Which data access technology should you use?

   A. ADO.NET

   B. WCF data services

   C. ASP.NET web services

   D. WCF Entity Framework

3. You are designing a data access layer that will be accessed by remote clients on the Internet. Clients might be running JavaScript or the .NET Framework. You would like to create the data access layer with the least amount of development effort. Which data access technology should you use?

   A. ADO.NET

   B. WCF data services

   C. ASP.NET web services

   D. WCF Entity Framework

THOUGHT EXPERIMENT
Exposing the Application Logic and Data Layers

I n the following thought experiment, you will apply what you have learned about the "Designing Data Access" objective to predict how a theoretical website architecture will perform. You can find answers to these questions in the "Answers" section at the end of this chapter.

You are a consultant for City Power & Light. As part of an effort to more transparently expose information about its operations to the public, City Power & Light has decided to allow third-party developers to connect directly to both the Application Logic and Data layers of its existing ASP.NET web application. The company's goal is to allow developers to either create new user interfaces that connect directly to its Application Logic layer or create entire applications that access its database directly.

The developers have designed a solution with these features:

- Decorate the methods that the Application Logic layer consists of with the *WebMethod* attribute.

- Enable port forwarding for TCP port 1433 on its firewall to allow Internet connections directly to the SQL Server.

Management wants your opinion on the application design. Answer the following questions about the future performance of the application:

1. Will third-party developers be able to create a new Presentation layer that connects to the Application Logic layer?

2. What would be the benefits of using WCF instead of ASP.NET web services?

3. Would it require more development time if the company used WCF instead of ASP.NET web services? Why?

4. Will third-party developers be able to create a new application that connects to the database?

5. What are some of the challenges third-party developers will have connecting to the database?

6. Do you think the City Power & Light database administrators will have concerns about this architecture?

7. What benefits would WCF data services offer?

Objective 3.2: Design Data Presentation and Interaction

All applications show data to users, and most applications also allow users to update some of the data. The .NET Framework provides many ways to display and edit your data, and each technique requires a different amount of development, testing, and maintenance time. Additionally, some techniques provide better responsiveness and security. This objective provides an overview of the various techniques and helps you decide which technique to choose in different scenarios.

> **This objective covers how to:**
>
> - Bind server controls to data sources.
> - Bind MVC views to data sources.
> - Bind client controls to data sources.

Binding Server Controls to Data Sources

The simplest way to display data is to bind a server control to a data source. Data sources can be collections, queries, database tables, XML files, and more. When you bind a server control to a data source, the server control intelligently displays the contents of the data source.

For example, if you created a data entry form that requires the user to select a country/region, you would have three options for populating the list:

- Type every country name into the drop-down list.
- Query the database, and then use a For Each loop to add each result to the drop-down list.
- Bind a database query directly to the drop-down list.

Whichever method you used would be transparent to the end user, but binding to the data source requires less code and is much easier to maintain.

The sections that follow describe how to bind data to server controls at design time and at runtime.

Binding at Design Time

Using Visual Studio 2010, you can bind data server controls to data sources at design time without writing any code. For example, if you create a project with an Entity Model, you can view the contents of a table by following these steps:

1. Add a *GridView* control to a page.

2. Select the *GridView*. In the Properties pane, click the *DataSourceID* list, and then select New Data Source.

3. Follow the prompts that appear to configure the data source.

Now you can run the project and view the contents of the data source you selected. If you set *AutoGenerateDeleteButton*, *AutoGenerateEditButton*, and *AutoGenerateSelectButton* to *true*, the *GridView* control provides a user interface that allows you to make changes to the underlying data source. If you set *AllowPaging* and *AllowSorting* to *true*, you have a simple create, read, update, and delete (CRUD) web application with absolutely no code.

Binding at Runtime

Many server controls can be bound directly to collections, such as the *EntityCollection* result of a LINQ-to-Entities query. For example, the following code sample stores the results of a sorted query in the *categories* object. The query is used to populate the *CategoriesDropDown List* by specifying *categories* as the data source and then specifying the fields to use for the text and values.

Sample of Visual Basic.NET Code

```
Using context = New ratingsEntities
    ' Query the database
    Dim categories = From c In context.categories _
                        Where c.title.StartsWith("A") _
                        Order By c.title _
                        Select c.id, c.title

    ' Associate the drop-down list with the results of the query
    CategoriesDropDownList.DataValueField = "id"
    CategoriesDropDownList.DataTextField = "title"
    CategoriesDropDownList.DataSource = categories

    ' Bind the data
    DataBind()
End Using
```

Sample of C# Code

```
using (var context = new ratingsEntities())
{
    // Query the database
    var categories = from c in context.categories
                        where c.title.StartsWith("A")
                        orderby c.title
                        select new { c.id, c.title };

    // Associate the drop-down list with the results of the query
    CategoriesDropDownList.DataValueField = "id";
    CategoriesDropDownList.DataTextField = "title";
    CategoriesDropDownList.DataSource = categories;

    // Bind the data
    DataBind();
}
```

The *GridView* control displays a data source in a table, automatically adding rows and columns as needed. In the previous example, you can display the results of the query in a *GridView* by adding these two lines of code:

Sample of Visual Basic.NET Code

```
ProductsGridView.DataSource = categories
ProductsGridView.DataBind()
```

Sample of C# Code

```
ProductsGridView.DataSource = categories;
ProductsGridView.DataBind();
```

As you do when binding at design time, set *AutoGenerateDeleteButton*, *AutoGenerate EditButton*, and *AutoGenerateSelectButton* to *true* to allows users to change the data.

Binding MVC Views to Data Sources

Unlike traditional ASP.NET applications, MVC views are linked directly to model data. Visual Studio automatically generates basic views that allow viewing lists of data as well as viewing, editing, and deleting individual records. This makes displaying the data remarkably easy. In fact, views almost never require a code-behind file, even when displaying complex data.

The sections that follow describe how to display data in MVC views, how to allow data to be edited, how model binders process form input, and how to create custom HTML helper extensions.

Displaying Data in Views

In MVC, views are ASPX pages that display data provided by the model. Displaying data is exceptionally easy in MVC, and it can typically be done without creating a code-behind page for the view.

To display data in a view, pass an instance of the object containing the data using *ActionResult*, and then embed the strongly typed model properties directly within the HTML.

First, in your controller, provide a method that returns an *ActionResult*. *ActionResults* provide an instance of a model object to the view associated with the method. For example, Visual Studio automatically generates the following *Edit* method as part of a new controller to allow users to edit an instance of the custom *Person* object model class with a specified ID. The method finds the *Person* object with the associated ID and passes it to the view using the *ActionResult*.

Sample of Visual Basic.NET Code

```
' GET: /Person/Edit/5
Public Function Edit(id As Integer) As ActionResult
    Dim person As Person = db.People.Find(id)
    Return View(person)
End Function
```

Sample of C# Code

```csharp
// GET: /Person/Edit/5
public ActionResult Edit(int id)
{
    Person person = db.People.Find(id);
    return View(person);
}
```

Visual Studio generates generic views based on your model, making it easy to display data using strong types. The page header shows that this page is inherited from the *Person* model, which means code running in the context of the page has access to any instance of *Person* that the action method returned as part of the *ActionResult*.

```
<%@ Inherits="System.web.Mvc.ViewPage<MVCApp.Models.Person>" %>
```

You can display data in a form by using *Model.<Property>*. Though using strong types is always preferred, you can also call *Html.DisplayText* and specify the name of the property. The following ASPX code segment uses both techniques to display information from a model that includes address details:

```
Street: <%: Html.DisplayText("Street") %><br />
City, State, and Zip: <%: Model.City %>, <%: Model.State %> <%: Model.Zipcode %>
```

Though this book focuses on ASPX syntax, the Razor view engine provides more efficiency and readability. The same code written in Razor looks like this:

```
Street: @Html.DisplayText("Street")<br />
City, State, and Zip: @Model.City, @Model.State @Model.Zipcode
```

> **MORE INFO   RAZOR**
>
> For more information about Razor, read "Introducing "Razor" – a new view engine for ASP.
> NET" at *http://weblogs.asp.net/scottgu/archive/2010/07/02/introducing-razor.aspx*.

In the previous examples, the model was a single object. If your view's model is a list (as it is for the default Index view), you can iterate through the list with a For Each loop, as the following example demonstrates:

```
<% foreach (var item in Model) { %>
    Street: <%: Html.DisplayFor(modelItem => item.Street) %><br />
    City, State, and Zip: <%: Html.DisplayFor(modelItem => item.City) %>,
        <%: Html.DisplayFor(modelItem => item.State) %>
        <%: Html.DisplayFor(modelItem => item.Zipcode) %>
<% } %>
```

Allowing Data to be Edited

MVC makes it simple to allow model data to be edited. In Visual Studio, right-click the Edit method in your controller, and then click Add View. The default settings, as shown in Figure 3-1, create a strongly typed view.

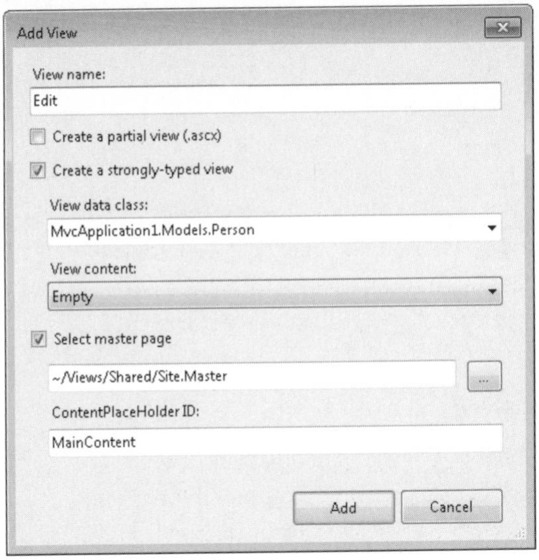

FIGURE 3-1 Creating an Edit view

Using *HtmlHelpers*, the automatically generated view includes labels and text boxes for every property in the model. For example, the following ASPX code generates an HTML label, text box, and validation message for the *Street* property of the model:

```
<% using (Html.BeginForm()) {%>
    <%: Html.LabelFor(model => model.Street) %>:
    <%: Html.EditorFor(model => model.Street) %>
    <%: Html.ValidationMessageFor(model => model.Street) %>
<% } %>
```

Any input fields that MVC generates use ID names that match the model's property names, as the following code demonstrates. This code displays an HTML validation message only if a user attempts to input data and validation fails. When a user submits the form, model binders examine the IDs and can automatically generate a model object.

```
<label for="Street">Street</label>: <input id="Street" name="Street"
 type="text" value="" />
```

> **MORE INFO** **VALIDATION**
>
> **For more information about validation, refer to Objective 3.3.**

The *Html.EditorFor* method automatically chooses an HTML input type, based on the property type. You can override the default behavior for both editing and displaying data by decorating a property with the *DataType* attribute (part of the *System.ComponentModel. DataAnnotations* namespace). The examples that follow demonstrates a data model with three common *DataType* values.

Sample of Visual Basic.NET Code

```
<DataType(DataType.EmailAddress)> _
Public Property email() As String
End Property

<DataType(DataType.Password)> _
Public Property password() As String
End Property

<DataType(DataType.MultilineText)> _
Public Property biography() As String
End Property
```

Sample of C# Code

```
[DataType(DataType.EmailAddress)]
public string email { get; set; }

[DataType(DataType.Password)]
public string password { get; set; }

[DataType(DataType.MultilineText)]
public string biography { get; set; }
```

> **MORE INFO   DATA TYPES**
>
> For a complete list of data types, read "DataType Enumeration" at *http://msdn.microsoft. com/library/system.componentmodel.dataannotations.datatype.aspx.*

Note that setting the *DataType* attribute configures only how HTML Helpers will display controls based on the property; they do not provide validation. For example, defining the *DataType* to *DataType.EmailAddress* will not prevent users from entering an invalid email address. However, the *DataAnnotationsExtensions.EmailAttribute* does. For more information about validation, refer to Objective 3.3.

Using Default Model Binders

When users submit data in a form, your application needs to read that data from the POST form values or the URL and store it in strongly typed objects that your action can process. In a traditional ASP.NET application, you might access the *Request.Params* or *Request.Form* collections and convert the string into the object you need. In MVC, model binders make the process much more elegant by automatically binding form data to your model's complex types.

You can manually call a model binder in an action method by calling the *UpdateModel* or *TryUpdateModel* method and passing an instance of an object. For example, the following code sample shows an action method that accepts a standard *FormCollection*. It calls the *UpdateModel* method to create an instance of the model object (an instance of the *Person* class) without accessing the individual form elements.

Sample of Visual Basic.NET Code

```
public ActionResult Update(FormCollection collection)
{
    Person person = new Person();
    UpdateModel(person);
    return View(person);
}
```

Sample of C# Code

```
public ActionResult Update (FormCollection collection)
{
    Person person = new Person();
    UpdateModel(person);
    return View(person);
}
```

For more security, provide a list of the parameters that you want *UpdateModel* to process, as this example demonstrates:

Sample of Visual Basic.NET Code

```
Public Function Create(collection As FormCollection) As ActionResult
    Dim person As New Person()
    UpdateModel(person, New () {"Id", "Name", "State", "Zipcode"})
    Return View(person)
End Function
```

Sample of C# Code

```
public ActionResult Create(FormCollection collection)
{
    Person person = new Person();
    UpdateModel(person, new [] {"Id", "Name", "State", "Zipcode"});
    return View(person);
}
```

You can also provide a list of strongly typed parameters, and MVC will automatically parse the form data, match it to method parameters based on names, and convert it automatically. The following code sample performs the same function as the previous code sample, but it manually populates several properties of the instance of *Person*. Because it processes only specific properties, it is more secure than creating the entire instance by using default model binding.

Sample of Visual Basic.NET Code

```
Public Function Update(Id As Integer, Name As String, Street As String, Zipcode As
Integer) As ActionResult
    Dim person As New Person()
    person.Id = Id
    person.Name = Name
    person.Street = Street
    person.Zipcode = Zipcode

    Return View(person)
End Function
```

```
public ActionResult Update(int Id, string Name, string Street, int Zipcode)
{
    Person person = new Person();
    person.Id = Id;
    person.Name = Name;
    person.Street = Street;
    person.Zipcode = Zipcode;

    return View(person);
}
```

A more efficient approach is to use the *Bind* attribute and specify parameters to include or exclude. The following example is functionally equivalent to the previous example:

Sample of Visual Basic.NET Code

```
Public Function Details(Bind(Include := "Id, Name, Street, Zipcode")> person As Person)
As ActionResult
    Return View(person)
End Function
```

Sample of C# Code

```
public ActionResult Details( [Bind(Include="Id, Name, Street, Zipcode")] Person person)
{
    return View(person);
}
```

Though doing so is less secure, you can replace the *Include* with *Exclude* in the previous example to list specific properties that you do not want the model binder to process.

At their simplest, model binders work completely automatically. When your model's properties match the form element names, MVC's default model binder intelligently extracts the data from the HTTP request, populates the object properties, and passes it to your action method as a parameter. Therefore, instead of accessing the default *FormCollection* in your action method, you can directly access the model. The following example shows how to use automatic model binding to create an instance of the *Person* custom class:

Sample of Visual Basic.NET Code

```
Function Details(ByVal person As Person) As ActionResult
    Return View(person)
End Function
```

Sample of C# Code

```
public ActionResult Details(Person person)
{
    return View(person);
}
```

Creating Custom Model Binders

Though the default model binder works for most scenarios, you can create a custom model binder by implementing the *IModelBinder* interface and then associating it with a type or specific methods. To create a custom model binder, implement the *IModelBinder.BindModel* method, extract the information from the *ControllerContext*, and return an instance of the object. If you encounter an error, call the *ModelBindingContext.ModelState.AddModelError* method. The following example demonstrates this by concatenating input from two form fields (FirstName and LastName) to generate the *Person.FullName* property:

Sample of Visual Basic.NET Code

```vb
Public Class PersonBinder
    Implements IModelBinder
    Public Function BindModel(controllerContext As ControllerContext, _
            bindingContext As ModelBindingContext) As Object
        Dim person As New Person()
        Dim personId As Integer
        If Integer.TryParse(controllerContext.HttpContext.Request("Id"), personId) Then
            person.Id = personId
        Else
            ' Add a binding error if the ID could not be parsed
            bindingContext.ModelState.AddModelError("Id", "The ID must be an integer.")
        End If

        ' Concatenate the FirstName and LastName fields
        person.FullName = [String].Format("{0} {1}", _
                    controllerContext.HttpContext.Request("FirstName"), _
                    controllerContext.HttpContext.Request("LastName"))

        Return person
    End Function
End Class
```

Sample of C# Code

```csharp
public class PersonBinder : IModelBinder
{
    public object BindModel(ControllerContext controllerContext, ModelBindingContext
                            bindingContext)
    {
        Person person = new Person();
        int personId;
        if (int.TryParse(controllerContext.HttpContext.Request["Id"], out personId))
        {
            person.Id = personId;
        }
        else
        {
            // Add a binding error if the ID could not be parsed
            bindingContext.ModelState.AddModelError("Id", "The ID must be an integer.");
        }

        // Concatenate the FirstName and LastName fields
        person.FullName = String.Format("{0} {1}",
            controllerContext.HttpContext.Request["FirstName"],
            controllerContext.HttpContext.Request["LastName"]);

        return person;
    }
}
```

To associate a model binder with a specific type for your entire application, add code such as the following to *Application_Start* in your global.asax file:

Sample of Visual Basic.NET Code

```
ModelBinders.Binders.Add(GetType(Person), New PersonBinder())
```

Sample of C# Code

```csharp
ModelBinders.Binders.Add(typeof(Person), new PersonBinder());
```

To associate a model binder individually for different methods, add the *ModelBinder* attribute to the action method parameters, as the following example shows:

Sample of Visual Basic.NET Code

```
<AcceptVerbs(HttpVerbs.Post)> _
Function Edit(<ModelBinder(TypeOf PersonBinder)> ByVal person As Person) As ActionResult
```

Sample of C# Code

```csharp
[AcceptVerbs(HttpVerbs.Post)]
public ActionResult Edit([ModelBinder(typeof(PersonBinder))] Person person)
```

You can replace the default binder that is used for all types by setting *ModelBinders. Binders.DefaultBinder* to an instance of your custom binder in *Application_Start*, as the following example shows:

Sample of Visual Basic.NET Code

```
ModelBinders.Binders.DefaultBinder = New PersonBinder()
```

Sample of C# Code

```
ModelBinders.Binders.DefaultBinder = new PersonBinder();
```

> **MORE INFO**   **MODEL BINDERS**
>
> For more information about model binders, read "How to use the ASP.NET MVC Model-Binder" at *http://weblogs.asp.net/melvynharbour/archive/2008/08/29/how-to-use-the-asp-net-mvc-modelbinder.aspx* and "Dive Deep Into MVC — IModelBinder Part 1" at *http://mgolchin.net/posts/20/dive-deep-into-mvc-imodelbinder-part-1*.

Creating Custom *HtmlHelper* Extensions

You can use the *HtmlHelper* class in MVC applications to render HTML controls. Each HTML helper simply returns text, usually as a string. Some of the most commonly used HTML helpers include the following:

- **Html.Action()** and **Html.RenderAction()**   Outputs the results of an action. *Html. RenderAction* outputs the results directly to the *Response*, which is more efficient.

- **Html.Partial()** *and* **Html.RenderPartial()**   Outputs a partial view directly to either a string or the *Response*.

- **Html.ActionLink()**   Generates a clickable hyperlink to an action.

- **Html.BeginForm()** and **Html.EndForm()**   Generates the beginning and closing tags of an HTML <form>.

- **Html.CheckBox()**, **Html.DropDownList()**, **Html.ListBox()**, **Html.RadioButton()**, **Html.TextBox()**   Generates various HTML controls.

Typically, you use HTML helpers directly within a view's ASPX page, as this example shows:

```
<% using (Html.BeginForm())
{ %>
    <label for="name">Name: </label>
    <%= Html.TextBox("name")%>
    <input type="submit" value="Register" />
<% } %>
```

You can create custom HTML helpers simply by writing a method that returns a string. For example, this method creates a <div> element and specifies the class:

Sample of Visual Basic.NET Code

```
Public Shared Function Div(cssclass As String, contents As String) As String
    Return [String].Format("<div class='{0}'>{1}</div>", cssclass, contents)
End Function
```

Sample of C# Code

```
public static string Div(string cssclass, string contents)
{
    return String.Format("<div class='{0}'>{1}</div>", cssclass, contents);
}
```

You can also create HTML helper extension methods to add new methods to the standard classes. When you create an extension method, you can access it as a member of the *Html* class, just like the other HTML helpers.

To create an HTML helper extension in C#, define the method as static, specify the first parameter as an instance of *HtmlHelper*, and precede it with the keyword *this*. To create an HTML helper extension in Microsoft Visual Basic.NET, add the *System.Runtime.Compiler Services.Extension* attribute to the method, define the method as *Shared*, and specify the first parameter as an instance of *HtmlHelper*. The following examples demonstrate both techniques.

Sample of Visual Basic.NET Code

```
<System.Runtime.CompilerServices.Extension> _
Public Shared Function Div(helper As HtmlHelper, cssclass As String, contents As String) As String
    Return [String].Format("<div class='{0}'>{1}</div>", cssclass, contents)
End Function
```

Sample of C# Code

```
public static string Div(this HtmlHelper helper, string cssclass, string contents)
{
    return String.Format("<div class='{0}'>{1}</div>", cssclass, contents);
}
```

> **MORE INFO   HTML HELPER EXTENSIONS**
>
> For a detailed discussion of how to create HTML helper extensions that display model data, read "TextBoxFor(u => u.Name) – Unleash the power" at *http://codebetter.com/karlseguin/ 2008/11/13/textboxfor-u-gt-u-name-unleash-the-power/*.

Binding Client Controls to Data Sources

You can also bind data to JavaScript running on the client. This is not efficient if a user is viewing only a single page of data. However, as discussed in Objective 1.1, if the user might need to browse through several pages of data or submit updates, using client controls can improve responsiveness by eliminating extra postbacks.

As discussed in Objective 1.3, the most popular client technologies are JavaScript add-ons: jQuery and Microsoft AJAX. Either can connect to a wide variety of web services, including WCF data services (discussed in Objective 3.1). After you retrieve the data, you can display it in a list or grid by using templating.

Binding Using Inline Expressions

To bind a collection to an AJAX client control, follow these high-level steps:

1. Create a class that the web service will return to the AJAX client control. Decorate the class with the *DataContract* attribute. Decorate each public attribute that you want the web service to send to the AJAX client with the *DataMember* attribute.

    Sample of Visual Basic.NET Code

    ```vbnet
    <DataContract> _
    Public Class Person
        <DataMember> _
        Public Property Id() As Integer
        End Property

        <DataMember> _
        Public Property Name() As String
        End Property

        <DataMember> _
        Public Property Age() As Integer
        End Property

        Public Sub New(_id As Integer, _name As String, _age As Integer)
            Me.Id = _id
            Me.Name = _name
            Me.Age = _age
        End Sub
    End Class
    ```

    Sample of C# Code

    ```csharp
    [DataContract]
    public class Person
    {
        [DataMember]
        public int Id { get; set; }

        [DataMember]
        public string Name { get; set; }

        [DataMember]
        public int Age { get; set; }

        public Person(int _id, string _name, int _age)
        {
            this.Id = _id;
            this.Name = _name;
            this.Age = _age;
        }
    }
    ```

2. Add an AJAX-enabled WCF web service to your project. This creates a class with the *ServiceContract* attribute, creates an .svc file that references the class, and adds the necessary service configuration information to the Web.config file.

Sample of Visual Basic.NET Code

```
<ServiceContract([Namespace] := "")> _
<AspNetCompatibilityRequirements(RequirementsMode :=
AspNetCompatibilityRequirementsMode.Allowed)> _
Public Class PersonService
End Class
```

Sample of C# Code

```
[ServiceContract(Namespace = "")]
[AspNetCompatibilityRequirements(RequirementsMode =
AspNetCompatibilityRequirementsMode.Allowed)]
public class PersonService
{
}
```

3. Within your *ServiceContract* class, create a member method that exposes the data that the client control needs, and add the *OperationContract* attribute to the method. The AJAX client will query this method.

Sample of Visual Basic.NET Code

```
<OperationContract> _
Public Function GetPeople() As Person()
    Dim people As Person() = New Person(3) {}

    ' Populate the people array with fake data
    ' This would be replaced with a database query

    people(0) = New Person(1, "Tony", 37)
    people(1) = New Person(2, "Chelsea", 26)
    people(2) = New Person(3, "Madelyn", 7)
    people(3) = New Person(4, "Sandi", 7)

    Return people
End Function
```

Sample of C# Code

```
[OperationContract]
public Person[] GetPeople()
{
    Person[] people = new Person[4];

    // Populate the people array with fake data
    // This would be replaced with a database query
```

```
    people[0] = new Person(1, "Tony", 37);
    people[1] = new Person(2, "Chelsea", 26);
    people[2] = new Person(3, "Madelyn", 7);
    people[3] = new Person(4, "Sandi", 7);

    return people;
}
```

4. Create the ASPX page and client controls that will query the web service.

5. If you are creating an ASP.NET web page, add a *ScriptManager* with a *ScriptReference* to MicrosoftAjaxTemplates.js.

```
<asp:ScriptManager ID="ScriptManager1" runat="server">
    <Scripts>
        <asp:ScriptReference Name="MicrosoftAjaxTemplates.js" />
    </Scripts>
</asp:ScriptManager>
```

If you are creating an HTML page or an MVC view, reference the static JavaScript files directly:

```
<script type="text/javascript" src="MicrosoftAjax.js"></script>
<script type="text/javascript" src="MicrosoftAjaxTemplates.js"></script>
```

6. To the <body> of the ASPX page, add a JavaScript template to format the data. This template simply adds the *Id*, *Name*, and *Age* properties to a bulleted list.

```
<ul id="peopleListView" class="sys-template">
    <li>{{ Id }}: {{ Name }}, age {{ Age }}</li>
</ul>
```

7. To the head of the page or to your CSS style sheet, add a style that hides the template so that it is not directly visible to the user. If you add it to the head of the page, it should resemble the following:

```
<style type="text/css">
    .sys-template { display:none; }
</style>
```

8. Finally, add JavaScript code to the *<head>* of the ASPX page that runs during the JavaScript *pageLoad()* event and uses the AJAX *Sys.UI.DataView* class to retrieve the data and format it using your template.

```
<script type="text/javascript">
    function pageLoad() {
        $create(
```

```
                Sys.UI.DataView,
                {
                    autoFetch: "true",
                    dataProvider: "PersonService.svc",
                    fetchOperation: "GetPeople"
                },
                {},
                {},
                $get("peopleListView")
            );
        }
    </script>
```

You can add any JavaScript expression that evaluates as a string to an inline expression. For example, you can replace the HTML template with the following to cause JavaScript to divide each record's *Age* property by two:

```
<ul id="peopleListView" class="sys-template">
    <li>{{ Id }}: {{ Name }}, age {{ Age / 2 }}</li>
</ul>
```

Live Binding

You can use live binding to automatically update a web page when the client data source is updated. The client data source is a copy of the server data source, so changes to the data source on the server are not automatically reflected on the webpage.

To use live binding, simply replace the {{ <*Property*> }} syntax with {binding <*Property*> }. For example, you can change the template in the previous example to the following:

```
<ul id="peopleListView" class="sys-template">
    <li><span>{binding Id}</span>: <span>{binding Name}</span>,
        Age: <span>{binding Age}</span></li>
</ul>
```

Live binding does not cause the server to notify the client of any changes that occur on the server. Therefore, by default, live binding shows only changes that might be made to the data source on the client. To update client data with any changes that have been made on the server, call the *DataView.fetchData* function from the client JavaScript. For example, you can add an HTML refresh button control that calls *DataView.fetchData*.

Two-Way Data Binding

Two-way data binding provides live binding's ability to automatically update client controls when the client data source is updated, and it also updates the client data source when the contents of a bound client control are changed. For example, if you performed two-way data binding from a client data source to a text input control, user changes to the text box are automatically reflected in the client data source.

To take advantage of two-way data binding, add the *mode=twoWay* attribute to the bound client control. For example:

```
<input type="text" value="{binding Name, mode=twoWay}" />
```

MORE INFO   **BINDING MODES**

For a complete list of binding modes, refer to "Sys.BindingMode Enumeration" at *http://msdn.microsoft.com/library/dd393733.aspx*.

You can use live binding with formatted data by specifying JavaScript functions for the *convert* and *convertback* properties. For example, if you want to allow users to edit the age in years, but the underlying data source stores the age in days, you can create JavaScript functions that convert between days and years. Then you can specify the functions by using the following syntax:

```
<input type="text" value="{binding Age, convert=toYears, convertBack=fromYears}"/>
```

MORE INFO   **DATA BINDING AND TEMPLATES**

This objective is focused on providing a design-level understanding of the technologies rather than implementation-level knowledge. For more detailed information, read "ASP. NET AJAX Templates" at *http://msdn.microsoft.com/library/dd448879.aspx*, "Live Data Binding in ASP.NET AJAX 4.0" at *http://msdn.microsoft.com/magazine/ee819084.aspx*, and "How to: Create an Editable View with Two-Way Data Binding" at *http://msdn.microsoft.com/library/dd448863.aspx*.

Updating Server Data from Client Controls

If you need to allow users to update the data using client controls, use one of the following three classes with an instance of *DataView*:

- *DataContext*
- *AdoNetServiceProxy*
- *AdoNetDataContext*

The sections that follow describe these classes in more detail.

DATACONTEXT

The ASP.NET AJAX *Sys.Data.DataContext* class connects to a WCF data service or WCF AJAX-enabled web service and reads, updates, and inserts data from a JavaScript client. With *DataContext*, you can develop a CRUD application using nothing but client-side JavaScript code, providing responsiveness similar to a Microsoft Windows application within the browser environment.

Typically, you use a *DataView* client control to present the *DataContext* to the user. Set the *DataView:DataProvider* to the instance of *DataContext,* and use live-binding markup in the template to allow users to edit the data. When the user has indicated that she is done making changes (such as by clicking a Submit button), call the *DataContext.saveChanges* JavaScript function.

This example demonstrates using *DataContext* and *DataView* together to connect to an ASP.NET web service:

```
<script type="text/javascript">
    var dataContext = new Sys.Data.DataContext();
    dataContext.set_serviceUri("../Services/peopleService.svc");
    dataContext.set_saveOperation("SavePerson");
    dataContext.initialize();
</script>

<button onclick="dataContext.saveChanges()">Submit Changes</button>

<ul sys:attach="dataview" class="sys-template"
    dataview:autofetch="true"
    dataview:dataprovider="{{ dataContext }}"
    dataview:fetchoperation="GetPerson"
    dataview:fetchparameters="{{ {orderBy: 'Name'} }}"
>
  <li>
    <input type="text" value="{binding Name}"/><br/>
    <input type="text" value="{binding Address}"/>
  </li>
</ul>
```

ADONETSERVICEPROXY

You can use the ASP.NET AJAX *Sys.Data.AdoNetServiceProxy* class to read, update, add, and delete records exposed by a WCF data service using REST. After you create an instance of *AdoNetServiceProxy* by specifying the location of the WCF data service, you can call the query and update, insert, remove, and invoke JavaScript functions to perform individual operations, or you can call the *createActionSequence* JavaScript function to run several operations together.

> **NOTE   AdoNetServiceProxy**
>
> The name AdoNetServiceProxy makes sense if you remember that WCF data services had previously been called ADO.NET data services.

This example demonstrates using *AdoNetServiceProxy* and *DataView* together to connect to a WCF web service:

```html
<head>
  <script type="text/javascript" src="../MicrosoftAjax/MicrosoftAjax.js"></script>
  <script type="text/javascript" src="../MicrosoftAjax/MicrosoftAjaxTemplates.js">
    </script>
  <script type="text/javascript" src="../MicrosoftAjax/MicrosoftAjaxAdoNet.js"></script>
  <script type="text/javascript">
      var peopleService = new Sys.Data.AdoNetServiceProxy('../Services/
                                                peopleDataService.svc');
  </script>
</head>

<body xmlns:sys="javascript:Sys"
    xmlns:dataview="javascript:Sys.UI.DataView"
    sys:activate="*">

  <ul class="list sys-template"
      sys:attach="dataview"
      dataview:autofetch="true"
      dataview:dataprovider="{{ peopleService }}"
      dataview:fetchoperation="People"
      dataview:fetchparameters="{{ {$orderby: 'Name'} }}"
  >
    <li>
      <span class="name">{{ Name }}</span>
      <span class="value">{{ Address }}</span>
    </li>
  </ul>
</body>
```

ADONETDATACONTEXT

Although you should be familiar with *AdoNetServiceProxy*, ASP.NET AJAX provides a second class for accessing WCF data services: *AdoNetDataContext*. *AdoNetDataContext* is derived from *DataContext*, and it uses the *AdoNetServiceProxy* class for communicating with WCF data services. However, it adds support for identity management, associating entity sets from different fetch operations, hierarchical data, and optimistic concurrency. You can use *AdoNetDataContext* exactly like you use *AdoNetServiceProxy*.

> **MORE INFO** **AdoNetDataContext**
>
> For more information, read "How to Call ADO.NET Web Services" at *http://www.asp.net/ ajaxlibrary/HOW%20TO%20Call%20ADO%20NET%20web%20Services.ashx*.

Objective Summary

- When developing traditional ASP.NET applications, you can bind server controls directly to data sources.

- MVC views are always bound to the object model. You can display data from the object model in several ways, but you should always choose the strongly typed techniques. Use model binders in your controller actions to automatically process data input from the user.

- You can use ASP.NET AJAX to bind client controls to data on the server. Templates allow you to format the day for display with HTML. To allow users to update data on the server with ASP.NET AJAX, use the *DataContext*, *AdoNetServiceProxy*, and *AdoNetDataContext* classes.

Objective Review

Answer the following questions to test your knowledge of the information in this objective. You can find the answers to these questions and explanations of why each answer choice is correct or incorrect in the "Answers" section at the end of this chapter.

1. You are designing an ASP.NET MVC 2 web application that will provide information about products that your company sells to potential customers on the Internet. You create a custom class named *Product* that contains all information about each product. You need to create two pages: one for administrators to use to update product information, and one for end users to view the product information. You must use strong typing in both the action and the view while allowing MVC to automatically process form data. What should you do? (Choose two. Each answer forms part of the complete solution.)

   A. Access the *ViewData* items.

   B. Use strongly typed view model classes.

   C. Use automatic model binding.

   D. Access the *FormCollection* items.

2. You are designing a web application that accesses a separate WCF data service to view and update records in a database. You want to provide a highly responsive user interface that supports identity management and does not rely on the web server to retrieve or submit data. You need to minimize development time. Which approach should you use?

   A. Create a custom web form with HTML controls. Use jQuery to manipulate the contents of the HTML controls.

   B. Create a custom web form, with all server controls contained within an *UpdatePanel* control.

C. Use the *GridView* and *EntityDataSource* server controls.

D. Use ASP.NET AJAX and the *AdoNetDataContext* and *DataView* classes.

3. You are creating a view for an MVC application. You need to create a nonstandard HTML control that should be rendered on the server. You must minimize the amount of client and server resources used as well as your development time. Which approach should you choose?

A. Use the jQuery library to dynamically add the HTML control to the document object model.

B. Create an *HtmlHelper* extension.

C. Create a custom server control.

D. Create a custom Web Part.

THOUGHT EXPERIMENT
Online Banking with Data Binding

In the following thought experiment, you will apply what you've learned about the "Designing Data Presentation and Interaction" objective to predict how a theoretical website architecture will perform. You can find answers to these questions in the "Answers" section at the end of this chapter.

You are a consultant for Woodgrove Bank. You are working with the IT development team to review their design for an MVC Internet application that provides the bank's clients with access to their account details and the ability to edit account properties.

Each customer's account details are stored in a database. Separate tables store the account properties (including the customer's name, address, and service level) and the various account transactions, including charges and payments the customer has made.

The development team's design includes these features:

- Account and Transaction data models based on the associated tables in the underlying database (using the Entity Framework)
- Strongly typed views
- Controller methods that use the default model binder to convert form input into the custom account properties classes
- Two-way data binding to allow customers to add descriptions to individual transactions without requiring a postback

Management wants your opinion on whether the design meets their goals and whether it will protect the database from unauthorized changes. Answer the following questions about the future performance of the application:

1. We have a strongly typed Edit view for our custom *Account* class and an *Edit* method in the *Account* controller. Will the default model binder be sufficient to allow customers to edit their account details?

2. The *Account* class includes properties that the user is allowed to edit, such as the user's address. It also includes properties that users are not allowed to edit, such as their service level. Is there any risk of a user changing his service level? How could you mitigate that risk?

3. Will two-way data binding work to allow customers to add transactions information without requiring a postback to the server?

4. How could you change the design to allow customers to update transaction information without using postbacks?

Objective 3.3: Plan for Data Validation

Applications must validate all user input to protect the security and integrity of the database. The .NET Framework provides data-validation capabilities at many different layers. For example, in an MVC application, you can validate data in the view (as you would for an ASP.NET application), the data model, the model binder, the controller, or the database itself. Within each layer, you can choose from several validation techniques.

This objective provides an overview of data validation in the .NET Framework and describes the concepts you need to understand to choose the best data-validation techniques for different scenarios.

This objective covers how to:

- Design data validation in ASP.NET applications.
- Design data validation in MVC applications.

Designing Data Validation for ASP.NET Applications

ASP.NET includes several validation server controls, each of which provides a specific type of validation on both the client (using JavaScript) and the server (using the .NET Framework):

- **CompareValidator** Compares input to another control, which is useful when you need a user to type her email address or password in two separate fields. You can also compare a value to a constant.

- **CustomValidator** Allows you to write custom server-side code (specified by using the *OnServerValidate* property) and custom client-side JavaScript (specified by using the *ClientValidateFunction* property) to validate user input.

- **RangeValidator** Compares a value to a range of values as defined by the *Minimum Value* and *MaximumValue* properties.

- **RegularExpressionValidator** Compares a value to a regular expression.

- **RequiredFieldValidator** Verifies that the user has entered something into a field. The other validation controls operate only when the user enters data; therefore, you must often use both *RequiredFieldValidator* and another validator together.

Each validation control must be associated with a server control that accepts user input by specifying the *ControlToValidate* property. You can associate multiple validation controls with a single user input control. For example, if you need a user to enter his birth date, you might associate it with *RequiredFieldValidator* and *RangeValidator*. You should provide a useful error message by defining the *ErrorMessage* and *ToolTip* properties for each validator control.

For example, the following sample from an .aspx file verifies that the user entered a value in *TitleTextBox* and that the value matches a regular expression requiring up to 50 characters. If either condition is not met, the webpage displays the contents of the validator control (in this case, an asterisk) and the validator's *ErrorMessage* text is displayed by using a *Validation Summary* server control somewhere on the form.

```
<asp:RequiredFieldValidator ID="TitleRequiredFieldValidator" runat="server"
    ControlToValidate="TitleTextBox" ErrorMessage="Please add a title"
        ToolTip="Please add a title">*</asp:RequiredFieldValidator>
<asp:RegularExpressionValidator ID="ShortTitleRegularExpressionValidator"
    runat="server" ControlToValidate="ShortTitleTextBox"
    ErrorMessage="The Title must be 50 characters or less"
    ToolTip="The Title must be 50 characters or less"
    ValidationExpression="^.{1,50}$">*</asp:RegularExpressionValidator>
Title: <asp:TextBox ID="TitleTextBox" runat="server" MaxLength="50">
```

ASP.NET validation is highly configurable. For example, you can use the *ValidationGroup* property to create validation groups if a single page has multiple virtual forms that need to be separately validated. You can disable the built-in JavaScript client-side validation by setting the *EnableClientScript* property to *false*.

If validation fails, the client validation scripts display a message before the browser submits the form to the server. If a user bypasses the client validation scripts (for example, by disabling JavaScript in her browser) and submits a form with invalid data, ASP.NET will perform server-side validation and render an updated HTML page that includes the invalid data the user entered and the same validation messages that would have appeared if the client supported JavaScript. To avoid processing invalid data in your code-behind file, check the page's *IsValid* property, as the following example shows:

Sample of Visual Basic.NET Code

```
Public Sub SubmitButton_Click(ByVal sender As Object, ByVal e As System.EventArgs) _
Handles Button1.Click
    If Me.IsValid Then
        ' Process user input
    End If
End Sub
```

Sample of C# Code

```
void SubmitButton_Click(object sender, System.EventArgs e)
{
    if (IsValid)
    {
        // Process user input
    }
}
```

> **MORE INFO**   **VALIDATION**
>
> For more information about validation in ASP.NET applications, read "ASP.NET Validation Controls" at *http://msdn.microsoft.com/library/debza5t0.aspx* and "Validating ASP.NET Server Controls" at *http://msdn.microsoft.com/library/aa479013.aspx*.

Designing Data Validation for MVC Applications

In an MVC application, you can perform server validation in several different places. In order of most important to least important, those places are

- **Data Model**   The best place to configure data validation is within the data model. Data annotations make it simple to provide both client-side and server-side data validation.

- **Model Binder**   The default model binder provides some validation automatically, such as adding a model error when type conversion errors occur.

- **Controller**   You can detect validation problems and add errors to the *ModelState* within a controller that receives user input. However, you need to write client-side JavaScript validation code separately, and you have to write separate code for each controller that processed input for a specific data model.

- **Views**   Although views have minimal server-side logic, you can use HTML helpers to embed JavaScript validation in the HTML.

The sections that follow describe how to validate data within the data model, model binder, controller, and view.

Validating Data in the Data Model

With MVC, you can mark object model properties with attributes to provide both client-side (using jQuery) and server-side validation. The *System.ComponentModel.DataAnnotations* namespace provides four built-in validators: *Range*, *RegularExpression*, *Required*, and *StringLength*.

Although the 70-519 exam will focus on the built-in data annotations, you can get several additional validators at *http://dataannotationsextensions.org/* (which are also available via NuGet): *CreditCard*, *Date*, *Digits*, *Email*, *EqualTo*, *FileExtensions*, *Integer*, *Max*, *Min*, *Numeric*, and *Url*.

To use data validations, add the data annotation attribute to the model properties, as the following abbreviated example shows. Note that the *Email* attribute requires installing *DataAnnotationsExtensions* from NuGet, and adding *DataAnnotationsExtensions* to the namespace:

Sample of Visual Basic.NET Code

```vbnet
Public Class Person
    <Required> _
    <StringLength(20)> _
    Public Property Name() As String
    End Property
```

```
    <Range(0, 200)> _
    Public Property Age() As Integer
    End Property

    <Required> _
    <RegularExpression("^(\d{5}-\d{4}|\d{5}|\d{9})$|^([a-zA-Z]\d[a-zA-Z]
                                           \d[a-zA-Z]\d)$")> _
    Public Property Zipcode() As String
    End Property

    <DataType(DataType.EmailAddress)> _
    <Email> _
    Public Property email() As String
    End Property
End Class
```

Sample of C# Code

```
public class Person
{
    [StringLength(30), Required]
    public string Name { get; set; }

    [Range(0,200)]
    public int Age { get; set; }

    [RegularExpression(@"^(\d{5}-\d{4}|\d{5}|\d{9})$|^([a-zA-Z]\d[a-zA-Z]
                                          \d[a-zA-Z]\d)$"), Required]
    public string Zipcode { get; set; }

    [DataType(DataType.EmailAddress)]
    [Email]
    public string email { get; set; }
}
```

Within the view (or a master page), reference the required scripts and call the *Html.EnableClientValidation* HTML helper, as the following example shows:

```
<head runat="server">
    <script src="<%= Url.Content("~/Scripts/MicrosoftAjax.debug.js") %>"
        type="text/javascript"></script>
    <script src="<%= Url.Content("~/Scripts/MicrosoftMvcAjax.debug.js") %>"
        type="text/javascript"></script>
    <script src="<%= Url.Content("~/Scripts/MicrosoftMvcValidation.debug.js") %>"
        type="text/javascript"></script>
    <% Html.EnableClientValidation()%>
</head>
```

MVC 3 changes client validation in several ways. First, it leverages jQuery, jQuery.Validate, and jQuery.Validate.Unobtrusive-Ajax instead of ASP.NET AJAX. Second, you no longer need to manually call *Html.EnableClientValidation*, because it is enabled by default. You can disable this behavior in the Web.config file:

```
<configuration>
    <appSettings>
        <add key="ClientValidationEnabled" value="false"/>
    </appSettings>
</configuration>
```

MVC 3 also provides built-in support for remote validation, which queries a method on a server to determine whether the value in an input field is valid. Remote validation is important when a range or regular expression is insufficient to validate data. For example, you can use the *EmailAttribute* to verify that a new user's email address matches the standard email format. However, you need to contact the web server and query the database to verify that the email address is not already associated with an existing user account. To use remote validation, add the *System.Web.Mvc.Remote* attribute to the property in the data model and specify the action method and controller, as the following example shows:

Sample of Visual Basic.NET Code

```
<DataType(DataType.EmailAddress)> _
<Email> _
<Remote("EmailAvailable", "Person")> _
Public Property email() As String
End Property
```

Sample of C# Code

```
[DataType(DataType.EmailAddress)]
[Email]
[Remote("EmailAvailable", "Person")]
public string email { get; set; }
```

On the server side, the controller's action method must accept a string value to be validated and return a Boolean value based on whether it is valid, as the following example demonstrates:

Sample of Visual Basic.NET Code

```
Public Class PersonController
    Inherits Controller
    Public Function EmailAvailable(email As String) As Boolean
        ' TODO: Insert logic
        Return False
    End Function
End Class
```

Sample of C# Code

```csharp
public class PersonController : Controller
{
    public bool EmailAvailable(string email)
    {
        // TODO: Insert logic
        return false;
    }
}
```

The 70-515 exam was created before the release of MVC 3. Therefore, until the exam is updated, it might focus on MVC 2. Real-world applications should be developed with the latest version of MVC, however.

MORE INFO **MVC VALIDATION**

For a more complex example of remote validation, read "How to: Implement Remote Validation in ASP.NET MVC" at *http://msdn.microsoft.com/library/gg508808.aspx*. For more information about validation in MVC 3, read "Client-side validation in MVC 3" at *http://www.jacopretorius.net/2011/01/client-side-validation-in-mvc-3.html*. For information about creating custom validators, read, "How to: Customize Data Field Validation in the Data Model Using Custom Attributes" at *http://msdn.microsoft.com/library/cc668224.aspx*.

Validating Data in the Model Binder

Model binders, as introduced in Objective 3.2, provide some level of data validation. Even if you have not written code to detect errors and added them to the model state, the default model binders will add errors if it encounters any problems converting form data into the action method's required parameter. For example, if the action method accepts a *Person* object that has the integer property *Person.Age*, and a user submits the value "I like turtles" for the form's *Age* value, the model binder will be unable to convert the string to an integer and will add an error to the model state. You can then detect the validation error in the controller, as described in the following section.

You can create custom model binders if you need to add more powerful validation to the model binder. However, you only need to do this if you cannot add the required validation to the data model.

Validating Data in Controllers

Before you access data provided by a model binder, you should verify that validation succeeded by examining *ModelState.IsValid*. For example, the following sample code from Objective 3.2 has been updated to include basic server-side validation:

Sample of Visual Basic.NET Code

```
Public Function Create(p As Person) As ActionResult
    If ModelState.IsValid Then
        db.People.Add(p)
        db.SaveChanges()
        Return RedirectToAction("Index")
    End If
    Return View(p)
End Function
```

Sample of C# Code

```
public ActionResult Create(Person p)
{
    if (ModelState.IsValid)
    {
        db.People.Add(p);
        db.SaveChanges();
        return RedirectToAction("Index");
    }
    return View(p);
}
```

ModelState.IsValid works by determining whether any errors have been added to the *ModelState* by the data model or model binder. Typically, these are sufficient, and you do not need to add model errors in the controller. You can write custom code to validate form values and call *ModelState.AddModelError* if your code finds any problems.

For example, the following code sample from a *Create* action method demonstrates how to create a *Person* object with some data validation. If the validation fails, MVC returns the user to the Create view. If the validation succeeds, the code adds the user to the *people* collection and redirects the user to the Index view:

Sample of Visual Basic.NET Code

```
If person.Age < 1 OrElse person.Age > 200 Then
    ModelState.AddModelError("Age", "You must provide a valid age.")
End If
If Not ModelState.IsValid Then
    ' Validation failed. Return them to the Create view.
    Return View("Create", person)
End If

' Validation succeeded. Add the new object.
people.Add(person)
Return RedirectToAction("Index")
```

Sample of C# Code

```
if (person.Age < 1 || person.Age > 200)
{
    ModelState.AddModelError("Age", "You must provide a valid age.");
}
```

```
if (!ModelState.IsValid)
{
    // Validation failed. Return them to the Create view.
    return View("Create", person);
}

// Validation succeeded. Add the new object.
people.Add(person);
return RedirectToAction("Index");
```

Validating Data in Views

As shown in the previous example, the correct way to handle errors is to return the current view. When displaying the view, MVC will process any errors in the *ModelState* and display messages to the user with any validation *HtmlHelper* controls you added. The validation *HtmlHelpers* are:

- **Html.ValidationSummary**   Displays a summary message for the entire page. Simply pass the method a *true* value to display a list of fields with errors, based on the keys you provided when you called *ModelState.AddModelError*. Alternatively, you can pass this method a string that will be displayed to the user.

- **Html.ValidationMessage**   Displays a summary message for a specific field. You must specify two parameters: a string key that matches the name of the form field the message should be associated with, and a message to display (as either a string or an *Exception*).

The following section of a view displays an editor field with a validation message. If the model binder or the action method added a model error with a key of "Name" and then displayed the view again, the "Name" field would be listed in the *ValidationSummary* HTML helper, and the message associated with the model error would be shown in the *Validation MessageFor* HTML helper:

```
<%: Html.ValidationSummary(true) %>
<fieldset>
    <div class="editor-field">
        <%: Html.EditorFor(model => model.Name) %>
        <%: Html.ValidationMessageFor(model => model.Name) %>
    </div>
</fieldset>
```

EXAM TIP

If the exam requires validation for security purposes, it must be server-side validation. If the exam requires validation for convenience purposes, or to reduce accidental errors on the user's part, especially if the user indicates that he does not want a message sent to the server, the validation must be client-side validation.

Objective Summary

- ASP.NET provides several validation controls: *CompareValidator*, *CustomValidator*, *RangeValidator*, *RegularExpressionValidator*, and *RequiredFieldValidator*. Simply add the controls to an ASPX page, link them to the control they validate, and provide an error message. Use *CustomValidator* when the other validation controls are insufficient.

- MVC provides several opportunities to validate data. You should apply data annotations to the data model whenever one of the available data annotations fits the format of your data. The default model binder will detect type-casting problems, but you can create a custom model binder to perform more precise data validation. You can use the standard ASP.NET validators within views. Finally, you can validate data within controller actions by adding errors to the model state.

Objective Review

Answer the following questions to test your knowledge of the information in this objective. You can find the answers to these questions and explanations of why each answer choice is correct or incorrect in the "Answers" section at the end of this chapter.

1. You are creating an ASP.NET page that allows users to submit URLs that will be indexed by your intranet's search engine. You need to verify that each URL submitted returns a valid response. You need to perform both client-side and server-side validation when the user clicks a *Button* server control. What should you do?

   A. Use a *CustomValidator* control.

   B. Use a *RegularExpressionValidator* control.

   C. Write a JavaScript function that handles the button's *onClick* event.

   D. Write a JavaScript function that handles the text box's *onChange* event.

2. You are creating an ASP.NET page that prompts users to enter their phone number. You need to perform both client-side and server-side validation to verify that the user entered a phone number and that it matches the format *xxx-xxx-xxxx*. Which controls should you use? (Choose all that apply. Each answer forms part of the complete solution.)

   A. *RegularExpressionValidator*

   B. *RangeValidator*

   C. *RequiredFieldValidator*

   D. *CompareValidator*

3. You are designing the data model for an MVC application. The data model includes a class that represents the user, including an optional age field. If the user does enter her age, you want the application to verify that it is between 0 and 150. Which attribute type should you use?

   A. Remote

   B. Range

   C. Required

   D. RegularExpression

THOUGHT EXPERIMENT
Validating User Account Information

In the following thought experiment, you will apply what you've learned about the "Plan for Data Validation" objective to predict how a theoretical website architecture will perform. You can find answers to these questions in the "Answers" section at the end of this chapter.

You are a developer for Consolidated Messenger, which provides a variety of applications to allow instant messaging between users. You are currently designing a controller and view for an MVC application that allows users to create new accounts.

Users need to provide the following information:

- A user name that no other user is currently using
- A password that must be typed twice and must meet complexity requirements
- An email address that must be in standard email format

You need to validate all information on both the client (for responsiveness) and the server (for security.)

You hold a peer review meeting to get feedback about your design. Answer the following questions about your specific design recommendations:

1. Should you implement validation in the data model, model binder, controller, or view?

2. For validation implemented in the data model, how can you define the error message shown to users when validation fails?

3. How can you validate that the user types the same password twice?

4. How can you validate that the password meets complexity requirements?

5. How can you validate that the email address is in a standard format?

6. How can you validate that no other user is using the same user name on the client?

Chapter Summary

- The Entity Framework has replaced ADO.NET as the preferred database access technology. WCF web services have replaced ASP.NET web services as the preferred technology for providing remote applications access to the Application Logic layer. WCF data services are the best way to expose a database using a web service.

- When developing traditional ASP.NET applications, you can bind server controls directly to data sources. MVC views, however, are always bound to the object model, which provides strong typing. Use model binders in your controller actions to automatically process data input from the user. Use ASP.NET AJAX to bind client JavaScript controls to data on the server. To allow users to update data on the server with ASP.NET AJAX, use the *DataContext*, *AdoNetServiceProxy*, and *AdoNetDataContext* classes.

- ASP.NET provides several validation controls: *CompareValidator, CustomValidator, RangeValidator, RegularExpressionValidator, RequiredFieldValidator*, and *CustomValidator*. MVC provides several opportunities to validate data: use standard ASP.NET validators within views, apply data annotations to the data model, create a custom model binder to perform more precise data validation, and validate data within controller actions by adding errors to the model state.

Answers

Objective 3.1: Review

1. **Correct Answer:** B

   A. **Incorrect:** ASMX pages only support IIS communications using HTTP.

   B. **Correct:** WCF web services provide a great deal of flexibility, and they support using multiple binding types.

   C. **Incorrect:** SQL Server Express Edition does not support the different protocol requirements. Additionally, you should avoid exposing database servers to the public Internet because doing so presents a significant security risk.

   D. **Incorrect:** An Entity Data Model is useful for accessing a database directly from an application. In fact, you might choose to generate an Entity Data Model in the application. However, you will then need to create a WCF web service to allow other clients to access the data across the network.

2. **Correct Answer:** D

   A. **Incorrect:** You could connect to the database by using ADO.NET; however, it would require significantly more programming and would not be object-oriented or strongly typed.

   B. **Incorrect:** WCF data services are useful when you need to create a data access layer for applications connecting across the Internet. In this scenario, the database is on the local network, allowing you to take advantage of the more robust Entity Framework.

   C. **Incorrect:** Although you could access data using an ASP.NET web service, it would be very inefficient. First, you would have to manually code your own data access layer. Then all data access would have to be routed through IIS.

   D. **Correct:** The Entity Framework supports strongly typed, object-oriented classes that represent tables in an underlying database. Visual Studio can automatically generate classes based on an existing database, allowing for rapid application development.

3. **Correct Answer:** B

   A. **Incorrect:** JavaScript clients cannot connect to a database using ADO.NET.

   B. **Correct:** WCF data services are useful when you need to create a data access layer for applications connecting across the Internet. You can create a WCF data services data access layer in only a few minutes.

C. **Incorrect:** Although you could create an ASP.NET web service that provided access to an underlying database, it would require far more programming than using WCF data services.

D. **Incorrect:** The Entity Framework supports strongly typed, object-oriented classes that represent tables in an underlying database. However, JavaScript clients cannot access a database by using the Entity Framework.

Objective 3.1: Thought Experiment

1. Yes.

2. WCF is far more powerful and flexible than ASP.NET web services. With WCF, the developers can offer a variety of bindings and support transactions, queuing, and additional security.

3. Yes. Because the application is built using ASP.NET, exposing methods as ASP.NET web services requires only one additional line of code per method. Adding WCF is straightforward, but it requires creating contracts for the different web services and performing additional configuration for the bindings.

4. Yes.

5. Developers will need to use platforms that support SQL Server connections. Although that's straightforward with a .NET Framework application, it is difficult or impossible using JavaScript. Another challenge would be the network protocol itself: although the City Power & Light firewall has been configured to forward TCP port 1433, clients might be behind firewalls that allow only HTTP communications.

6. This architecture exposes the database directly to requests from the Internet. Database administrators would need to be very confident that the database had been properly configured to protect the privacy and integrity of the database. Ideally, all databases would have that level of protection. Realistically, many developers rely on the applications that access the database to validate data and authorize requests.

7. WCF data services allow requests over HTTP, which allow requests across all common firewalls. Additionally, a wider variety of clients (including JavaScript clients) can easily connect to WCF data services.

Objective 3.2: Review

1. **Correct Answers:** B and C

    A. **Incorrect:** You can use the *ViewData* collection to access data passed to a view using the syntax ViewData["<*Property_Name*>"]. However, this approach is not strongly typed.

    B. **Correct:** By using the generic *ViewPage* and associating it with a custom class, you can use strongly typed view model classes. Though Visual Studio automatically fills in model property names when creating the view, if you typed an incorrect property name, the compiler would detect the error before runtime. Thus, using strongly typed view model classes reduces runtime problems and simplifies troubleshooting.

    C. **Correct:** MVC uses automatic model binding to create strongly typed parameters by matching the names of form values to the names of action parameter properties. If you use strongly typed view model classes, those names automatically match, allowing you to access view data using strong-typing without writing code to process the view data.

    D. **Incorrect:** You can use *FormCollection* to access data passed from a view to an action using the syntax FormCollection["<*Property_Name*>"]. However, this approach is not strongly typed.

2. **Correct Answer:** D

    A. **Incorrect:** jQuery provides a great deal of flexibility, and you could write Java-Script to read and update a table by using a WCF data service. However, the *AdoNetDataContext* and *DataView* classes of ASP.NET AJAX are designed to connect to a WCF data service, and they make it extremely easy to bind data from the data service to HTML controls, thus minimizing development time.

    B. **Incorrect:** *UpdatePanels* submit requests back to the web server. Therefore, using an *UpdatePanel* does not meet your requirements.

    C. **Incorrect:** *GridView* and *EntityDataSource* are server controls. Therefore, updates would require submitting requests to the web server, which does not meet your requirements.

    D. **Correct:** The *AdoNetDataContext* ASP.NET AJAX class is designed to easily connect to a WCF data service. You can display the data by using a *DataView* client control. Together, you can use these classes to a build client-side JavaScript that communicates directly with a WCF data service.

3. **Correct Answer:** B

    A. **Incorrect:** Although you could use jQuery to insert custom HTML into a page after it is rendered, the requirements specify that the control should be rendered on the server.

    B. **Correct:** *HtmlHelper* extensions allow you to create custom HTML methods that render HTML code as strings. They are rendered on the server, but they do not require view state, so they are relatively efficient.

    C. **Incorrect:** Custom server controls provide a great deal of flexibility; however, you can meet the requirements by using an *HtmlHelper* extension, and an *HtmlHelper* extension requires less development time.

    D. **Incorrect:** Custom Web Parts require extra development and consume more client and server resources than an *HtmlHelper* extension.

Objective 3.2: Thought Experiment

1. Yes.

2. Yes. The default model binder will process all input from the form. Therefore, if the user maliciously adds a value for the service level, the default model binder would automatically update the value in the instance of the class representing the user's account. You could mitigate that risk by listing the parameters that the model binder processes by using the *Bind.Include* attribute.

3. No.

4. You could use ASP.NET AJAX and an instance of *AdoNetDataContext* with a *DataView*.

Objective 3.3: Review

1. **Correct Answer:** A

    A. **Correct:** You can create both client-side JavaScript functions and server-side ASP.NET methods to validate a control by using a *CustomValidator*. In this scenario, you would write client-side and server-side code to retrieve the specified URL by using HTTP.

    B. **Incorrect:** The *RegularExpressionValidator* control verifies that a control matches a regular expression. You could use this type of control to validate that the user provided a standard URL that, for example, begins with "http://". However, you cannot use the *RegularExpressionValidator* control to perform custom logic such as retrieving a webpage from another server.

    C. **Incorrect:** If you wrote a JavaScript function, you could validate the URL on the client side. However, it would not provide server-side validation.

    D. **Incorrect:** Refer to the description for answer C.

2. **Correct Answers:** A and C

   A. **Correct:** The *RegularExpressionValidator* control allows you to specify a regular expression, such as ^(\d{3})-(\d{3})-(\d{4})$, that verifies text input matches a pattern.

   B. **Incorrect:** *RangeValidator* is useful for checking that user input for numbers or dates is within a range. However, it cannot be used for text input, such as a phone number with hyphens.

   C. **Correct:** If you were to specify only the *RegularExpressionValidator*, validation would succeed if the user typed nothing in the phone number field. To require the user to enter a value, you must also add the *RequiredFieldValidator*.

   D. **Incorrect:** The *CompareValidator* control compares the values of two controls, or it compares the value of a control to a constant. It cannot be used for pattern matching, however.

3. **Correct Answer:** B

   A. **Incorrect:** You can use the *Remote* attribute to specify a method on the server that validates a value the user entered. Although you could write a separate server method to verify the user's age, it is more efficient to specify the *Range* attribute.

   B. **Correct:** The *Range* attribute is the easiest way to validate a numeric value.

   C. **Incorrect:** You would add the *Required* attribute only if the age was not an optional value.

   D. **Incorrect:** Use the *RegularExpression* attribute when a string value must match a specific pattern. Although it is possible to write a regular expression that matches numeric values between 0 and 150, it is more efficient to use the strongly typed *Range* attribute.

Objective 3.3: Thought Experiment

1. You should implement validation in the data model whenever possible.

2. You can set the validator's *ErrorMessage* property.

3. You can add the *CompareValidator* server control to the view. Because the data model would not have two properties for the password, you cannot implement this type of validation in the data model.

4. You can use the *CustomValidator* server control and write methods on both the client (using JavaScript) and the server (using the .NET Framework) to validate password complexity.

5. For an MVC application, the best approach is to add the *RegularExpressionAttribute* to.the email address property of the data model. In an ASP.NET application, the best approach is to add a *RegularExpressionValidator* server control to the ASPX page.

6. There are several techniques. The simplest approach, however, is to write a server method that checks user name availability. Then, in the data model, specify the method using the *Remote* validator attribute.

CHAPTER 4

Designing Security Architecture and Implementation

All network applications are under constant attack, and those attacks are becoming more effective every day. Although security is never absolute, you can reduce the risk of security being compromised by following best practices when designing an application's architecture.

This objective domain covers how to limit an application's privileges to reduce the cost of a successful attack, how to design authentication and authorization to restrict access to different features of an application, and how to help protect an application from common types of attacks.

Objectives in this chapter:

- Objective 4.1: Plan for operational security
- Objective 4.2: Design an authentication and authorization model
- Objective 4.3: Plan for minimizing attack surfaces

Real World

Each time the news covers a breach of security, I hear my developer friends snicker as if it couldn't happen to them. The fact is that anyone can get hacked. The more you develop your security skills, and the more energy you put into protecting your applications, the more types of attacks you can protect yourself against.

For example, it's entirely possible for a beginning developer to create a functional web application without any thought toward security. However, that application will inevitably be compromised. The attacker won't be an evil genius; it'll be a mindless script that attacks random websites by adding cross-site scripting code to comments or drops databases using SQL injection.

A skilled and patient developer can create applications that are safe from common automated attacks. However, that application might still be vulnerable to social hacking techniques, such as convincing technical support to reset a user's password. In the real world, security is never absolute. As a developer, your goal is always to make it as challenging as possible for attackers to compromise your application.

Objective 4.1: Plan for Operational Security

Every application runs with a specific amount of privileges to the local web server and to remote computers. An application will not work correctly if it lacks privileges that it needs. The opposite, however, is even worse. An application with more privileges than it needs can be abused by an attacker to compromise the web server, other computers across the network, and even the web application user's computers.

This objective describes how to assign the proper permissions to your application by using code access security, process identity, impersonation, and delegation.

This objective covers how to:

- Plan code access security.
- Design process identity.
- Design impersonation and delegation.

Planning Code Access Security

When you think of security, you typically think of role-based security with resource authorization: authenticating users and then limiting their access to resources. For example, you might allow members of the Users group to read a file while allowing members of the Managers group to edit it.

Code access security (CAS) limits your application's access to resources, regardless of which user is logged on. For example, an application might be allowed to read and write text files to a specific folder, or it might be allowed to communicate only on the internal network. To understand the importance of CAS, consider what happened before CAS was available and all applications ran with full administrator privileges: viruses spread between computers with little or no involvement from users.

Today, CAS provides an extra layer of protection from malware and application vulnerabilities. If you were creating a new web browser, you could use CAS to grant the web browser only the minimum privileges it needed to connect to websites using HTTP, display text and images, and run JavaScript. Even if your new web browser had a vulnerability that allowed it to run malicious code from the Internet, CAS would prevent the browser itself from installing software or modifying system files.

> **NOTE CASPOL.EXE**
>
> By default, the Microsoft .NET Framework 4 no longer uses security settings configured with the CasPol.exe tool. Additionally, machine-level security configuration is no longer supported. For more information, read "Security Changes in the .NET Framework 4" at *http://msdn.microsoft.com/library/dd233103.aspx*.

Using Trust Levels

With the .NET Framework, a developer or systems administrator can use trust levels to restrict the CAS privileges the common language runtime (CLR) gives to a web application. Configure trust level by using the <system.web><trust> element of .config files. You can specify a custom trust level with a separate policy file, or you can use one of the .NET Framework's five built-in trust levels. The five built-in trust levels are described in the following list:

- **Full**   The application has all the privileges available to the CLR. This is the default trust level for web applications.

- **High**   The application has the privileges defined in the Web_hightrust.config policy file, located in %windir%\Microsoft.NET\Framework64\v4.0.<*version*>\Config. Applications with a high trust level have few limitations. Microsoft recommends the high trust level for web applications that your organization creates and manages.

- **Medium**   The application has the privileges defined in the Web_mediumtrust.config policy file, which prevents accessing the Event Log and registry. Applications running with medium trust can read and write files in the application directory, but they cannot access other parts of the file system. Microsoft recommends the medium trust level for web applications that you host for other organizations.

- **Low**   The application has the privileges defined in the Web_mediumtrust.config policy file, which allows access to 1 MB of isolated storage and file system read access to only the application directory. Compared to the medium trust level, the low trust level blocks access to DNS, email, databases, web requests, and printers.

- **Minimal**   The application has the privileges defined in the Web_minimaltrust.config policy file, which allow only core .NET Framework functionality.

The lower the trust level, the less damage an attacker can do after successfully compromising your application. To improve security, specify the lowest level of trust that allows your application to run correctly.

To specify a custom trust level, copy one of the existing policy files, modify it to your needs, and then associate the name and policy file using the <system.web><securityPolicy> <trustLevel> element of the application's .config file. Then specify the custom trust level using the <system.web><trust> element.

Using CAS Imperatively

You can use CAS imperatively to verify that the code has sufficient privileges to carry out an action. This allows you to detect insufficient privileges, catch the exception if the privileges are not available, and log the error or provide helpful information to the user.

The following code sample creates an instance of *FileIOPermission*, which represents privileges to read or write files. *FileIOPermission* can also be used without specifying a file name to determine whether the application has any file access privileges.

Sample of Visual Basic.NET Code

```
' Create a permission to read input.txt
Dim fp As New FileIOPermission(FileIOPermissionAccess.Read, "input.txt")

' Add a permission to read and write output.txt
fp.AddPathList(FileIOPermissionAccess.Write Or FileIOPermissionAccess.Read,
               "output.txt")
Try
    ' Verify that those permissions are available. Demand throws an exception if they
    ' are not
    fp.Demand()
Catch s As SecurityException
    ' TODO: Handle the missing file access permissions
End Try
```

Sample of C# Code

```
// Create a permission to read input.txt
FileIOPermission fp = new FileIOPermission(FileIOPermissionAccess.Read, "input.txt");

// Add a permission to read and write output.txt
fp.AddPathList(FileIOPermissionAccess.Write | FileIOPermissionAccess.Read,
               "output.txt");
try
{
    // Verify that those permissions are available. Demand throws an exception if they
    // are not
    fp.Demand();
}
catch (SecurityException s)
{
    // TODO: Handle the missing file access permissions
}
```

Imperative security can impact performance. For each demand you make, the .NET Framework has to walk the stack to verify that every caller has sufficient privileges. Therefore, make demands prior to entering loops.

After you call a permission's *Demand* method, you can call its *Assert* method to improve performance for future demands of the same permission. After calling *Assert*, any future *Demand* requests do not have to walk the entire stack; the stack walk stops at the method that called *Assert*. Therefore, if you call methods that might make demands, you can improve the performance of those methods by creating an instance of the required permission, calling *Demand*, and then calling *Assert*. After you no longer require the permission, call the permission's *RevertAssert* method.

> **MORE INFO** **OPTIMIZING CAS**
>
> For more information about improving the performance of CAS, read "Security Optimizations" at *http://msdn.microsoft.com/library/ett3th5b.aspx*.

Using Application Domains

The CLR runs .NET Framework applications within application domains. Application domains are virtual environments (commonly called *sandboxes*) with separate memory spaces that can be configured with restricted privileges.

When the CLR runs a new application, it either creates a new application domain or adds the application to an existing application domain. As a developer, you can create application domains to run untrusted components with fewer privileges than the current application domain. At a high level, the process requires creating and configuring an instance of *App DomainSetup*, specifying evidence using an instance of an *Evidence* object, and then using those two objects to create a new *AppDomain* instance for the component.

> **MORE INFO** **CONFIGURING APPLICATION DOMAINS**
>
> For details about how to configure an application domain with limited privileges using a configuration file and evidence, read "AppDomainSetup.ConfigurationFile Property" at *http://msdn.microsoft.com/library/system.appdomainsetup.configurationfile.aspx*.

Understanding Process Identity

Hosted web applications run within a process provided by the web server, such as Internet Information Services (IIS). That process is known as the process identity. Besides CAS, application privileges are restricted by their process' role-based security.

> **NOTE** **CAS AND ROLE-BASED SECURITY**
>
> A hosted web application can never have more privileges than the process identity, but the .NET Framework can further restrict privileges by using CAS.

By default, IIS 5 running on Microsoft Windows 2000 Server and Windows XP use the ASP.NET worker process, Aspnet_wp.exe, as the process identity. IIS 6.0 running on Windows Server 2003 provides application pools that use the more limited Network Service account as the default process identity. IIS 7.5 running on Windows Server 2008 R2 creates virtual accounts with similar privileges to the Network Service account. These virtual accounts have better security than using the shared Network Service account because the virtual accounts prevent applications running in different application pools from interfering with each other.

To minimize the risks of your application being exploited to take unexpected actions on the web server (such as displaying the contents of private files), configure a process identity with minimal privileges. To do this, create a new user account, assign it only the minimal set of operating system privileges it requires to run, and then assign that user account as your application pool's identity. Because IIS 5 does not support application pools, you must configure a custom process identity by using the <system.web><identity> element in the Web.config file.

> **MORE INFO** **PROCESS IDENTITY**
>
> For more information about process identity, read "Application Pool Identities" at *http://learn.iis.net/page.aspx/624/application-pool-identities/* and "Configuring ASP.NET Process Identity" at *http://msdn.microsoft.com/library/dwc1xthy.aspx*. For detailed information about the permissions you must configure for a custom process identity, read "ASP.NET Required Access Control Lists (ACLs)" at *http://msdn.microsoft.com/library/kwzs111e.aspx*.

Once you understand your process identity, you can use resource-level security to limit access to resources from your application. Typically, the default permissions assigned to the Network Service account are sufficient; however, you can assign additional permissions if your application requires access to nonstandard resources, or you can remove default permissions to further limit the risks of a successful breach of security.

If you are deploying your application to a single server, you can modify resource-level security settings manually. For example, you can use Windows Explorer to modify NTFS file permissions and grant your application's process identity to save files to a folder. Similarly, you can use the Print Management console to allow your application's process identity to print, or use the Registry Editor to grant your application's process identity the privileges it needs to update a registry setting. If you manually configure security settings, document those settings thoroughly so that systems administrators understand the security implications and so that they can restore the application to a different server.

Any privilege changes you make will affect all applications using the same process identity. For example, if you grant the Network Service account privileges to create files in a directory, all applications using the Network Service account will have those privileges. This can increase security risks (if you grant additional privileges) or cause unexpected security problems (if you remove privileges). Therefore, you should use this technique cautiously and communicate your changes to systems administrators and other developers.

Rather than manually configuring resource-level security settings, you should configure them by using a setup project. This requires the user installing the application to have sufficient privileges to modify the security settings.

MORE INFO   **SETUP PROJECTS**

For more information, read "Setup and Deployment Projects" at *http://msdn.microsoft. com/library/wx3b589t.aspx*.

The Network Service account has limited privileges on the web server and no privileges to remote computers. In the event of a breach of security, this helps protect other computers on your network from being accessed by an attacker. If your application needs to access local resources to which Network Service does not have access, or remote resources that require authentication, you have several choices:

- **Create a privileged service account.**   Create a domain user account with sufficient privileges on both the web server and any remote servers, and then change the process identity of the application pool to the newly created domain user account. To minimize risks in the event of a breach of security, assign the account the minimal privileges your application requires to run.

- **Use impersonation to access resources on the web server.**   When users authenticate with Windows credentials, you can temporarily change your application's process identity to match the browser's. Any resources the application accesses will be accessed with the user's credentials.

- **Use delegation to access resources on remote computers.**   Like impersonation, delegation changes the process identity of the web application to match the browser's. Delegation flows the credentials to remote computers, however.

MORE INFO   **CONNECTING TO A DATABASE**

For detailed instructions showing how to connect to a database using different process identities, read "Accessing SQL Server from a Web Application" at *http://msdn.microsoft. com/en-us/library/ht43wsex.aspx*.

Understanding Impersonation and Delegation

By default, applications use their process identity to access local and remote resources. Impersonation and delegation allow your application to access resources with the user's credentials instead, synchronizing the security context of the browser and the web application. To access resources on the web server as the user, use impersonation. To access resources on remote computers as the user, use delegation.

You might use impersonation and delegation in any of these scenarios:

- Connecting to a database
- Connecting to a web service
- Accessing files
- Performing administrative tasks

If you use Windows authentication, your application has direct access to the user's credentials. If you use client certificate authentication, you need to map the client certificate to a Windows account when processing requests. If you use Forms authentication or a custom authentication method, you need to programmatically obtain a token for the user's Windows credentials.

> **MORE INFO** **PROTOCOL TRANSITION**
>
> For more information, read "How To: Use Protocol Transition and Constrained Delegation in ASP.NET 2.0" at *http://msdn.microsoft.com/library/ff649317.aspx*.

Impersonating Users

Impersonation allows an application to access local resources with the user's credentials. Impersonation is costly and increases security risks, so you should use it minimally. To imperatively impersonate a user within a method, use *System.Security.Principal.Windows ImpersonationContext or ServiceSecurityContext.Current.WindowsIdentity.Impersonate*, as the following example shows:

Sample of Visual Basic.Net Code

```
Using ServiceSecurityContext.Current.WindowsIdentity.Impersonate()
    ' Access resources with the user's credentials
    Return String.Format("Hello, {0}", WindowsIdentity.GetCurrent().Name)
End Using
```

Sample of C# Code

```
using (ServiceSecurityContext.Current.WindowsIdentity.Impersonate())
{
    // Access resources with the user's credentials
    return string.Format("Hello, {0}", WindowsIdentity.GetCurrent().Name);
}
```

To declaratively impersonate a user for an entire service method, decorate the method with *OperationBehaviorAttribute* and set *Impersonation* to *ImpersonationOption.Required*, as the following example shows:

Sample of Visual Basic.Net Code

```
<OperationBehavior(Impersonation := ImpersonationOption.Required)> _
Public Sub MyMethod(input As String)
    ' TODO: Do work as the user
End Sub
```

Sample of C# Code

```
[OperationBehavior(Impersonation = ImpersonationOption.Required)]
public void MyMethod(string input)
{
    // TODO: Do work as the user
}
```

To imperatively impersonate a user for part of a service method, decorate the method with *OperationBehaviorAttribute*. Within the method, create an instance of *WindowsIdentity* and then call the instance's *Impersonate* method, as the following example shows:

Sample of Visual Basic.Net Code

```
<OperationBehavior> _
Public Sub DoWorkAsUser(input As String)
    Dim userContext As WindowsIdentity = ServiceSecurityContext.Current.WindowsIdentity
    If userContext Is Nothing Then
        Throw New InvalidOperationException("The caller cannot be mapped to a
                                    WindowsIdentity")
    End If
    Using userContext.Impersonate()
        ' TODO: Do work as the user
    End Using
End Sub
```

Sample of C# Code

```
[OperationBehavior]

public void DoWorkAsUser(string input)
{
    WindowsIdentity userContext = ServiceSecurityContext.Current.WindowsIdentity;
    if (userContext == null)
    {
        throw new InvalidOperationException("The caller cannot be mapped to a
                                    WindowsIdentity");
    }
    using (userContext.Impersonate())
    {
        // TODO: Do work as the user
    }
}
```

> **MORE INFO** **IMPERSONATION AND DELEGATION**
>
> For more information, read "Impersonation/Delegation" at *http://msdn.microsoft.com/ library/cc949004.aspx* and "Delegation and Impersonation with WCF" at *http://msdn. microsoft.com/library/ms730088.aspx.*

Delegating Credentials

Delegation allows an application to access network resources with the user's credentials. Because delegation increases the rights your application has to network resources, delegation increases security risks. For example, imagine that you created an intranet site that used delegation to access a database by means of the user's credentials, allowing the user to edit his own profiles within the company's directory. An attacker with access to the application code on the web server could then modify the application to access confidential files with a user's privileges.

Delegation is even more powerful than impersonation; as a result, it is disabled by default in Active Directory environments. If you are running your application in IIS in an Active Directory domain, you must enable the web server's domain computer account for delegation. To allow unlimited delegation for a web server, have an Active Directory domain administrator open Active Directory Users And Computers, edit the computer account's properties, view the Delegation tab, and then select Trust Computer For Delegation.

Constrained delegation reduces the security risks of delegation by restricting which resources an application can access during delegation. Instead of selecting Trust Computer For Delegation, select Trust This Computer For Delegation To Specified Services Only, and then specify the services that your application is allowed to access. Figure 4-1 shows a computer that is configured to allow delegation only to access the Spooler service on a specific computer.

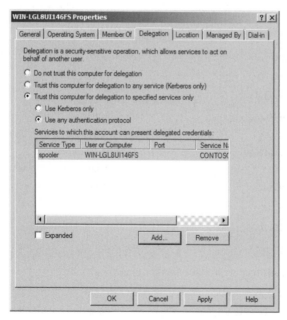

FIGURE 4-1 Use constrained delegation to limit security risks

MORE INFO **CONSTRAINED DELEGATION**

For detailed instructions on enabling constrained delegation, read "Allow a computer to be trusted for delegation for specific services" at *http://technet.microsoft.com/library/cc739764.aspx*.

Objective Summary

- CAS limits the privileges of an application, thereby limiting the potential damage of a successful breach of security. Assign web applications the lowest trust level possible. Within your application, examine the application's CAS before taking actions that require privileges. To enforce CAS for untrusted components, create application domains with limited privileges.

- Web applications run within a process identity, such as the Network Service account. Role-based security limits application privileges based on its process identity.

- Use impersonation when your application needs to access resources on the web server with the user's credentials. Use delegation when your application needs to access remote resources with the user's credentials. You can configure constrained delegation to limit the remote resources an application can access with delegation.

Objective Review

Answer the following questions to test your knowledge of the information in this objective. You can find the answers to these questions and explanations of why each answer choice is correct or incorrect in the "Answers" section at the end of this chapter.

1. You are designing an Model-View-Controller (MVC) application that accesses a database running on a different server. Your organization's security policy states that all database requests must be issued by using the end-users' credentials; the web server's process identity cannot be granted any privileges to the database. Both the web server and the database server participate in the same Active Directory domain. How can you enable database queries while minimizing security risks? (Choose all that apply. Each answer forms part of the complete solution.)

   A. Use delegation to access the database.

   B. Enable constrained delegation for the web server's computer account.

   C. Add the Network Service account to the Domain Admins group.

   D. Change the process identity of the application to the System account.

2. You are designing an ASP.NET application that calls a third-party assembly to generate chart images that it stores in a local folder accessible to web users. You need to minimize the security risks of calling the third-party component. Which approach should you recommend?

    A. Create a local user account with minimal privileges, and configure the account as the third-party assembly's process identity.

    B. Create an Active Directory domain user account with minimal privileges, and configure the account as the third-party assembly's process identity.

    C. Create an application domain with the least privileged trust level, and launch the component within the application domain.

    D. Configure the assembly to impersonate the end-user's credentials.

3. You are designing a public ASP.NET application that allows unauthenticated users to upload files to the Uploads folder. Systems administrators have created a local user account, WebAppUser, and configured the application pool to use it as the process identity. You need to configure NTFS file permissions to allow the application to function correctly while minimizing security risks. What should you do? (Choose all that apply. Each answer forms part of the complete solution.)

    A. Grant WebAppUser Read access to all application files.

    B. Grant WebAppUser Write access to all application files.

    C. Grant WebAppUser Read access to the Uploads folder.

    D. Grant WebAppUser Write access to the Uploads folder.

THOUGHT EXPERIMENT
Role-Based Security

In this thought experiment, you apply what you've learned about the "Plan for Operational Security" objective to predict how a theoretical website architecture will perform. You can find answers to these questions in the "Answers" section at the end of this chapter.

You are a consultant for Humongous Insurance. Humongous Insurance maintains a public web application that customers can use to view and update their account and billing information. The web application retrieves account details from an internal database running on a separate server. A separate web application on the same server allows customer support personnel to manually update additional properties of customer accounts.

To reduce the risk of a breach of security, the IT department has updated their security guidelines as follows:

- All applications must run with minimal privileges.
- All database requests from Internet applications on a customer's behalf will be performed by using a local service account on the web server that has minimal privileges to the database.
- All database requests from internal applications requests must be performed with the employee's user account.

The developers have designed a solution with these features:

- Assigned the public web application the Low trust level
- Assigned the internal web application the Medium trust level
- Created an Active Directory domain service account for the public web application and granted it the minimal privileges it requires to read and update the database
- Granted the web server computer account constrained delegation privileges in the Active Directory so that it can access the database server

Management wants your opinion on the application design. Answer the following questions about the future performance of the application:

1. Will the public website work as expected? If not, what could be done to resolve the problems?
2. Will the internal website work as expected? If not, what could be done to resolve the problems?
3. Is there more they could do to improve security?

Objective 4.2: Design an Authentication and Authorization Model

ASP.NET includes a default authentication and authorization framework: ASP.NET membership. With ASP.NET membership, you can assign users to roles and then assign roles permissions to different aspects of your application. When properly designed, ASP.NET membership provides a reliable access control system that is simple for systems administrators to configure and maintain. If you design an authentication and authorization model without a deep understanding of the technologies, however, you might create an application that is difficult to maintain and can be easily compromised.

This objective provides an overview of the ASP.NET membership framework, how to implement authorization to control access to your application, how to plan role management, how to store passwords, how to use authorization manager, and how to design trusted subsystems.

> **This objective covers how to:**
> - Implement authorization.
> - Plan role management.
> - Store passwords.
> - Use Authorization Manager.
> - Design trusted subsystems.

Using ASP.NET Membership

ASP.NET includes everything you need to create and manage user accounts and assign permissions to those accounts. In fact, standard Microsoft Visual Studio 2010 templates include default pages that allow users to create and manage their own accounts. As a developer, the only thing you must do to configure membership is update the .config file to specify which pages require authentication.

ASP.NET includes two membership providers:

- **SQL Server**   Allows your application to maintain its own user database
- **Windows**   Allows your application to authenticate users with existing local or Active Directory accounts

> *NOTE*   **VISUAL STUDIO 2010 TEMPLATES**
>
> If you create a new ASP.NET MVC 3 project in Visual Studio, you will be prompted to select one of the following templates: Empty, Internet Application, or Intranet Application. If you select Internet Application, the project will be configured to use the SQL Server membership provider. If you select Intranet Application, the project will be configured to use Windows authentication.

Additionally, you can create custom membership providers that use different data stores. For example, you can implement a custom membership provider to use an existing database as the membership provider.

By default, ASP.NET membership stores user information in a local database that it creates automatically; however, you can also configure it to use an existing SQL Server database. You can manage user accounts, roles, and authorization and other security settings by using the Web Site Administration Tool (WSAT), which you can open by selecting ASP.NET Configuration from Visual Studio's Website or Project menu.

EXAM TIP

Remember the differences between membership and personalization: membership stores credentials and role memberships useful for authentication and authorization, while personalization stores user preferences.

Implementing Authorization

Whichever membership provider you choose, authorization works the same way. As the following sections describe, you can declaratively restrict access to entire methods or imperatively restrict access to sections of code.

Authorizing Access with Configuration Files

The simplest way to control access to your application is to use .config files. Although it is possible to use declarative security to protect individual methods, changing permissions requires recompiling the application. For example, the following configuration file allows anonymous access to the default.aspx page while allowing only administrators authenticated through a web form to access the /manage/ subfolder:

```
<location path="/manage/">
    <system.web>
        <authorization>
            <allow roles="Administrators" />
            <deny users="*"/>
        </authorization>
    </system.web>
</location>
```

There's a significant security risk that using MVC routing can bypass location-specific authorization settings. For example, the previous code sample allows only Administrators to access the /manage/ folder. If you created an MVC route that mapped /backdoor/index.aspx to /manage/index.aspx, unauthorized users could access the content by using the /backdoor/ index.aspx. Because pages can be accessed by different URLs, you should protect entire controllers or individual actions using the *AuthorizeAttribute* filter, as described in the next section.

Declaratively Requiring Membership Roles

Use the *Authorize* attribute to control which users can access methods in an MVC application. The following example limits access to the Administrators role and this restriction cannot be bypassed by routing:

Sample of Visual Basic.Net Code

```
<Authorize(Roles := "Administrators")> _
Public Function AdministratorsOnly() As ActionResult
    Return View()
End Function
```

Sample of C# Code

```
[Authorize(Roles = "Administrators")]
public ActionResult AdministratorsOnly()
{
    return View();
}
```

> **MORE INFO** AUTHORIZEATTRIBUTE
>
> For detailed information, read "AuthorizeAttribute Class" at *http://msdn.microsoft.com/ library/system.web.mvc.authorizeattribute.aspx*.

You can use the *PrincipalPermission* attribute in ASP.NET applications to limit entire methods to being run by specific users or roles. The following code sample shows a method that only members of the Administrators role can run. If the current user is not a member of the Administrators role, ASP.NET throws a security exception:

```
<PrincipalPermission(SecurityAction.Demand, Role:="Administrators")> _
Shared Sub Manage()
    ' TODO: Administrator-only tasks
    End Sub
```

Sample of C# Code

```
[PrincipalPermission(SecurityAction.Demand, Role = "Administrators")]
static void Manage()
{
    // TODO: Administrator-only tasks
}
```

Imperatively Requiring Membership Roles

You can use *PrincipalPermission* or *User.IsInRole* to verify the current user's group member-ship within a method. *User.IsInRole* returns a Boolean value indicating whether the user is a member of the specified role, while *PrincipalPermission.Demand* throws an exception if the user is not a member of the specified role.

To use *PrincipalPermission*, your code must follow this process:

1. Set the principal policy to *WindowsPrincipal*.

2. Create an instance of *PrincipalPermission* with the required privileges.

3. Call the *PrincipalPermission.Demand()* method.

4. Run the privileged code.

As with *PrincipalPermissionAttribute*, if the user fails the security check, ASP.NET throws a security exception. The following code sample demonstrates this process:

Sample of Visual Basic.NET Code

```
AppDomain.CurrentDomain.SetPrincipalPolicy(PrincipalPolicy.WindowsPrincipal)
Dim principalPerm As New PrincipalPermission(Nothing, "Administrators")
principalPerm.Demand()
```

Sample of C# Code

```
AppDomain.CurrentDomain.SetPrincipalPolicy(PrincipalPolicy.WindowsPrincipal);
PrincipalPermission principalPerm = new PrincipalPermission(null, "Administrators");
principalPerm.Demand();
```

To verify whether a user other than the current use is a member of a specific role, call *Roles.IsUserInRole*.

Planning Role Management

When planning role management, follow these best practices:

- Use Windows authentication for intranet applications when users have Active Directory domain accounts. This provides single sign-on for users and centralizes account management. If you use Windows authentication, ASP.NET uses roles to represent group memberships.

- If you must create accounts for users separate from their Active Directory domain accounts, work with systems administrators to include the application's role management in their account management process. For example, when a user leaves the organization, systems administrators will need to remove both the user's Active Directory domain account and the application account.

- Never assign privileges to an individual user. Instead, add users to roles, and assign privileges to those roles. If an employee leaves the organization, you only need to remove the user from the role rather than modifying how privileges are assigned.

- Create separate roles for different management tasks. For example, instead of creating roles for just users and administrators of a blog application, create separate roles for readers, writers, editors, content approvers, and website managers. Even though it might require you to add users to multiple roles, having more granular roles simplifies delegating tasks if more flexibility is required in the future.

- Always derive new security classes from existing .NET classes. Microsoft has carefully reviewed and tested the security components of the .NET Framework. This does not mean the .NET Framework does not contain security weaknesses; all code does. However, the .NET Framework's extensive review and testing helps to make them more secure than classes written by individual developers.

> **MORE INFO** **THE RISKS OF CREATING CUSTOM SECURITY CLASSES**
>
> For more information, read "How to Customize ASP.NET MVC Authentication" at *http://blogs.teamb.com/craigstuntz/2009/09/09/38390/*.

Storing Passwords

In recent years, a number of organizations have had security breaches that resulted in user passwords being exposed. The cost of this can be devastating to both the organization and the users. The organization receives bad publicity and loses the confidence of its users. The users risk having their privacy violated, and if they use the same password at different sites (as most users do), they could have many different accounts compromised.

If you create your own membership provider, store only hashes of user passwords. Hashing is a cryptographic technique for creating a unique set of characters that represents the original password. To further improve security, add a secret key to the password prior to hashing.

To authenticate a user with a hashed password, store the hashed version of the password in a database when the user creates her account. When the user authenticates, repeat the hash process on the password the user submits and compare it to the hashed password in the database. If they match, the user provided the correct password.

Unlike encryption, you cannot reverse a hash to determine the original password. Therefore, if an attacker obtains access to your database, he would be unable to decrypt the passwords. As an attacker, the best approach to identifying the original passwords would be an inefficient brute force attack: repeat the hashing process on a password dictionary and identify matching hashes. If you add a secret key prior to hashing the passwords, that approach would be successful only if the attacker also had the secret key.

EXAM TIP

For the exam, know that you should always hash passwords unless you need to retrieve the original passwords from the database. In those circumstances, choose reversible encryption. In the real world, you should use only hashing.

Using Authorization Manager

Recent versions of Windows include the Authorization Manager snap-in, commonly known as AzMan. To run AzMan, open a blank Microsoft Management Console (MMC) console by running mmc.exe. In the File menu, select Add/Remove Snap-in. Follow the prompts that appear to add Authorization Manager.

When Authorization Manager is open, view the options to switch Authorization Manager into Developer mode to create a new Authorization Store. As shown in Figure 4-2, you create roles, tasks, and definitions to configure which actions users and groups can perform within your application. You can use this information within your application to determine whether users have access to perform specific actions. Later, systems administrators can use Authorization Manager to change the permissions without requiring changes to the application code.

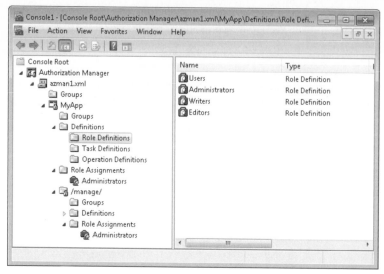

FIGURE 4-2 Use Authorization Manager to create roles and rules for applications

Authorization Manager supports storing information in three different formats:

- Active Directory and Active Directory Application Mode (ADAM)
- Microsoft SQL Server
- XML files

Because Authorization Manager can connect to an Active Directory domain, administrators can assign domain users privileges to specific tasks within an application, similar to the way they might assign privileges to read or write files.

> **NOTE MICROSOFT ENTERPRISE LIBRARY**
>
> Though the exam will probably not cover it, you can use the Security block of the Microsoft Enterprise Library to add more sophisticated role management capabilities to your application. For more information, visit *http://entlib.codeplex.com/*.

Authorization Manager provides separate definitions for roles, tasks, and operations:

- Role definitions define which tasks a given role can perform. For example, the Writers role might have privileges for the Create Blog task, but not the Edit Layout task.
- Task definitions, such as Approve Blog or Delete Blog, are actions that require their own permissions. Systems administrators should be able to understand task definitions without knowledge of the application code. Task definitions contain one or more operations.

- Operations, such as *ReadMetadata* or *PersistChanges*, are the lowest-level privilege and typically map to methods within the application. Operations are building blocks for tasks. Only developers need to understand operations; systems administrators should always assign privileges to tasks.

For the exam, know that you should use Authorization Manager when you need to provide nondevelopers with the ability to configure role-based access to application functions.

> **MORE INFO** **AUTHORIZATION MANAGER**
>
> For general information, read "Windows Authorization Manager" at *http://msdn.microsoft.com/en-us/library/bb897401.aspx.* For information about planning role-based security with Authorization Manager, read "Use Role-Based Security in Your Middle Tier .NET Apps with Authorization Manager" at *http://msdn.microsoft.com/magazine/cc300469.aspx.* For step-by-step instructions showing how to use Authorization Manager with an ASP.NET application, read "How To: Use Authorization Manager (AzMan) with ASP.NET 2.0" at *http://msdn.microsoft.com/en-us/library/ff649313.aspx.*

Designing Trusted Subsystems

There are two approaches to authenticating to back-end systems:

- **Impersonation and delegation** As discussed in Objective 4.1, web servers present the user's credentials to back-end systems. This is the best approach when the back-end systems can authorize individual users—for example, when the back-end systems and the users are in the same Active Directory domain.

- **Trusted subsystems** Web servers present service credentials to back-end systems. This is the best approach when you cannot directly assign user privileges to back-end systems.

Figure 4-3 compares these two architectures. Active Directory domains are used as an example; in practice, any trust boundary can be used, including ASP.NET membership.

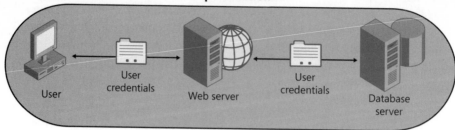

Impersonation

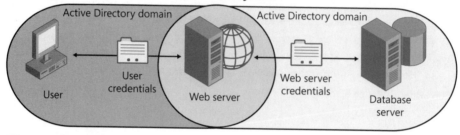

Trusted Subsystem

FIGURE 4-3 Comparing impersonation and trusted subsystems

Impersonation and delegation access back-end resources with the user's credentials. Although this approach is the best design for many applications, it also has several disadvantages:

- Back-end resources must be able to authenticate the user. Typically, this requires the back-end resources to participate in the same Active Directory domain.
- Administrators must grant individual users access to internal resources.
- Impersonation and delegation elevate the web server's privileges, potentially increasing the damage of a successful breach of security.
- The web server must create separate resources, such as database or web service connections, for each user being impersonated.

Trusted subsystems have a significant disadvantage: the application is responsible for controlling access to back-end resources. As a result, the burden of user authentication and resource authorization falls on the application developer, and security vulnerabilities in the application can expose private data to unauthorized users. Trusted subsystems are unable to take advantage of the resource authorization and auditing capabilities that might be built into back-end services.

For example, consider a payroll application with two different roles: users and managers. The presentation and application layers are implemented by using an MVC application, while the data layer is implemented by using a Microsoft SQL Server database server. Users can view their own payroll information, while managers can view or update records.

If the developers implement the payroll application with impersonation and delegation, database administrators can grant users only read access to the database while assigning managers privileges to update the database. Database administrators could audit changes to the database, tracking which manager updated each record. However, the web server and the database server need to participate in the same Active Directory domain. If a user discovered a security vulnerability in the web application that allowed him to submit changes to the database, the database's built-in authorization would reject the change and could record the unauthorized modification attempt.

If the developers implement the payroll application by using trusted subsystems, the web server and the database server do not need to participate in the same Active Directory domain, and the application can use database connection pooling to improve performance. However, database administrators would need to grant the web application's process identity privileges to update the database. Database administrators could audit changes, but the auditing would indicate only that the web application's process identity made a change; it could not track individual users. If a user discovered a security vulnerability in the web application that allowed her to submit changes to the database, the database change would be successful, and the database could not associate the change with the specific user. In this scenario, the web application would be responsible for authorization and auditing.

> **MORE INFO**   **TRUSTED SUBSYSTEMS**
>
> For more information, read "Trusted Subsystem" at *http://msdn.microsoft.com/library/ ff649178.aspx*.

Objective Summary

- ASP.NET membership can store account information in either a SQL Server database or an Active Directory domain. Additionally, you can create a custom membership provider that stores data differently.
- Authorization restricts access to application features. You can implement authorization declaratively, imperatively, and by using configuration files.
- Whenever possible, leverage users' existing accounts in an Active Directory domain. Create roles for different application tasks. Assign privileges to those roles, and then add users to the roles. If you create custom security classes, derive them from existing classes in the .NET Framework.
- Always store hashes of passwords unless you need access to the original password. If you need access to the original password, store the password using reversible encryption.

- Authorization Manager allows systems administrators to assign privileges to different application capabilities without recompiling the application.

- Trusted subsystems grant privileges directly to an application. Impersonation grants privileges to end users and relies on the application to impersonate them.

Objective Review

Answer the following questions to test your knowledge of the information in this objective. You can find the answers to these questions and explanations of why each answer choice is correct or incorrect in the "Answers" section at the end of this chapter.

1. You are designing an ASP.NET application. To fit into existing account management processes, the IT department needs the ability to retrieve users' original passwords. What should you recommend? (Choose two. Each answer forms part of the complete solution.)

    A. Use encrypted passwords.

    B. Use hashed passwords.

    C. Use the built-in SQL membership provider.

    D. Create a custom membership provider.

2. You are designing an ASP.NET application. Within the /administer/ subfolder, you plan to add pages that perform management tasks and should be accessed only by members of the Administrators role. Which approach should you recommend to protect the folder?

    A. Create a custom trust level.

    B. Edit the Web.config file.

    C. Apply the *PrincipalPermission* attribute.

    D. Apply the *Authorize* attribute.

3. You are designing an MVC application. Within the Administer area, you plan to add pages that perform management tasks and should be accessed only by members of the Administrators role. Which approach should you recommend to protect the area?

    A. Configure IIS to block anonymous requests to the folder.

    B. Add the *PrincipalPermission* attribute to each action result.

    C. Add the *Authorize* attribute to each action result.

    D. Edit the Web.config file.

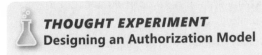

THOUGHT EXPERIMENT
Designing an Authorization Model

In this thought experiment, you apply what you've learned about the "Design an Authentication and Authorization Model" objective to predict how a theoretical website architecture will perform. You can find answers to these questions in the "Answers" section at the end of this chapter.

You are a consultant for Litware, Inc. Management is planning a new internal MVC application that the sales staff will use to track marketing effectiveness and sales efforts. Employees should be able to view and edit their own records, while managers should be able to also view and edit their employees' records. Additionally, management will have access to several additional tools. Users will log on by using their Active Directory domain credentials.

The developers have designed a solution with these features:

- Some views should be used only by members of the Managers role. Developers use *User.IsInRole* to determine whether to display links to those views.

- Some actions have sections of code that can be run only by members of the Managers role. Developers use *User.IsInRole* to determine whether the user can run it.

- Managers and their employees are associated using a table in the database.

- The web application accesses the database as a trusted subsystem.

Management wants your opinion on the application design. Answer the following questions about the future performance of the application:

1. Is hiding the links sufficient to protect the managers-only views? If not, what would you do differently?

2. Is checking *User.IsInRole* sufficient to protect a section of code? If not, what would you do differently?

3. Is using a trusted subsystem the best way to protect records? Why or why not?

Objective 4.3: Plan for Minimizing Attack Surfaces

You can improve the security of your ASP.NET applications by adding multiple layers of protection. One of the most useful techniques is to minimize the attack surface by reducing the opportunities attackers have to exploit vulnerabilities in your application. If your application were a fortress, minimizing the attack surface would involve removing unnecessary doors and windows.

This objective provides an overview of how to handle user input, how to throttle input to protect against denial-of-service attacks, how to filter requests, and how to protect communications with Secure Sockets Layer (SSL).

> **MORE INFO   INPUT VALIDATION**
>
> For information about input validation, refer to Objective 3.3, "Plan for Data Validation."

> **This objective covers how to:**
> - Handle user input.
> - Throttle input.
> - Filter requests.
> - Use SSL.

Handling User Input

Every user is a potential attacker, and every user input is potentially malicious code. To minimize security risks, follow these best practices when handling user input:

- By default, ASP.NET rejects HTML input from browsers to reduce the risk of cross-site scripting (XSS) attacks. If you must accept HTML input from users, filter the user input so that it rejects all input that contains HTML not on an approved list of HTML markup.
- Always HTML-encode user input when displaying it on a webpage to prevent attackers from using your server to render malicious HTML or JavaScript. Malicious scripts regularly add webpage comments containing links and scripts that you should not render as HTML to any user.
- Use *HttpUtility.UrlEncode* to sanitize any URLs submitted with user input.
- Validate the size of user input before storing it to prevent a Denial-of-Service (DoS) attack. An attacker might repeatedly submit large amounts of data in user input, and if you store that user input in a file or database, the input could consume all available space and cause the application to fail.

- If your application accepts file uploads, limit the size of those uploads using *<httpRuntime maxRequestLength>* in the *<system.web>* section of the .config file.

- Limit the number of results returned in SQL queries. For example, never return more than 50 records when a user queries inventory. Attackers might perform a denial-of-service attack by issuing complex queries that consume a large amount of database processing time.

- To reduce the risk of SQL injection attacks, never generate a SQL statement using user input. For example, avoid concatenating user input into a SQL query. Instead, use parameterized queries.

- Never trust information submitted as part of a browser request. Attackers can change HTTP request header fields and modify HTML form values.

- Never rely on client-side scripts to handle user input or perform any security function; they can be easily bypassed.

Throttling Input

One of the most common types of attacks is the DoS attack. To perform a DoS attack, an attacker repeatedly submits a request to your application that uses a significant amount of processor, memory, network, or disk resources. This causes a performance bottleneck on the server, preventing it from responding to requests from legitimate users.

You can mitigate the risk of DoS attacks by intelligently throttling requests. For example, your application could detect more than 20 requests in a second from a single IP address and then stop responding to requests from that IP address until a 30-second cool-down period has passed. To mitigate the risk of a distributed DoS attack, your application could detect similar requests from different IP addresses and disregard them all.

You typically don't need to mitigate denial-of-service attacks for requests that do not consume a significant amount of resources. For example, if a web server can render a web page in only 1/1000th of a second and the page does not contain large images, it would be very difficult for an attacker to successfully perform a DoS attack. Instead, focus your energy on pages that perform processing on the web server, submit complex queries to databases, transmit large files across the network, or store data.

Although there are many ways to implement throttling, one of the most straightforward is to add an object to the Cache when processing a resource-intensive request. Set the Cache key to a unique value that identifies the client, and set the Cache timeout to the request's cool-down period. Before processing a resource-intensive request, check the Cache. If an object exists, provide a descriptive error message to the user.

> **MORE INFO   REQUEST THROTTLING**
>
> For an example of how to implement an MVC action filter that throttles requests, read "Best way to implement request throttling in ASP.NET MVC?" at *http://stackoverflow.com/questions/33969/best-way-to-implement-request-throttling-in-asp-net-mvc*.

You can also implement input throttling at the web server. With IIS 7.0 or 7.5, consider using Dynamic IP restrictions, which are available for download at *http://www.iis.net/download/dynamiciprestrictions*.

Filtering Requests

Request filtering is one of the most effective ways to reduce the risk of attacks against a web application. This section describes four types of filtering: filtering to protect against cross-site scripting attacks, filtering to protect against request forgery attacks, filtering by the source IP address, and custom filtering.

> **MORE INFO   FILTERING BUILT INTO IIS**
>
> IIS can protect against many potentially dangerous requests. For detailed information, read "Use Request Filtering" at *http://learn.iis.net/page.aspx/143/use-request-filtering/*.

Filtering Cross-Site Scripting Attacks

ASP.NET includes basic request filtering that rejects user input containing HTML to reduce the risk of XSS attacks. This drastically reduces the risks of cross-site scripting attacks, even if an application developer is not aware of the risk. For traditional ASP.NET applications, you can override the default request filtering by adding *<%@ Page ValidateRequest="false" %>* to the page directive. For MVC applications, apply the *ValidateInput* attribute to the controller action that accepts the form input and pass it a value of *false*.

You can use the web server to implement additional request filtering. In IIS 6.0, you can use the UrlScan add-on. IIS 7.0 and IIS 7.5 include the Request Filtering security feature, which allows administrators to block requests for specific URLs and file extensions (among other criteria). For detailed information about configuring request filtering in IIS, visit *http://www.iis.net/ConfigReference/system.webServer/security/requestFiltering*.

Especially with MVC applications, you can use routes to implement application-specific request filtering. Simply call *routes.Ignore* from the *RegisterRoutes* method of the application's Global.asax file, and specify a pattern that should be ignored.

Filtering Cross-Site Request Forgery Attacks

Another type of request that you should consider filtering is cross-site request forgery (CSRF) attacks. In a CSRF attack, the attacker hosts a webpage and lures unsuspecting visitors to the page. Typically, the user clicks a link on the attacking page that posts form values to a different site. This post request might add a friend to the user's social network, send a message from the user's account, or add a comment using the user's identity.

To prevent CSRF attacks, verify that the form data submitted to your application is the result of user input typed into a form on your site. The simplest way to do this is to filter HTTP post requests containing a different *Referrer* value. In MVC, you can add the *Html.AntiForgery Token* to the form and decorate the controller action that processes the form values with the *ValidateAntiForgeryToken* attribute.

Filtering by Source IP Address

You can also filter requests based on the source IP address. Source IP address filtering is useful for sites that should be accessed only from the intranet. For example, you might allow a website, or specific pages on a website, to respond only to requests from the 192.168.10.0/24 network.

Typically, administrators implement IP address filtering using the web server. For example, when configuring IIS 7.5 (as shown in Figure 4-4), you can use the IP And Domain Restrictions role service to drop requests from IP addresses that have not been approved. You should not rely solely on source IP address filtering; it can be circumvented by an attacker who takes control of a computer on your local network. Instead, use source IP address filtering as an additional layer of protection on top of traditional authentication.

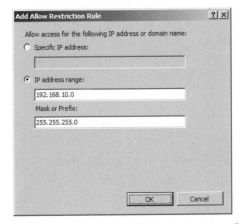

FIGURE 4-4 Use IIS to provide source IP address filtering

Domain restrictions are a closely related, but much less useful, web server security feature. With domain restrictions, the web server performs a reverse DNS lookup for the client's IP address. The web server can then block requests from clients whose hostname is not part of a specified domain. For example, you could allow requests only from clients whose hostnames (as determined by a reverse DNS lookup) are *.contoso.com. Although you should be aware of the capability, avoid using domain restrictions because they require the web server to perform a reverse DNS lookup before responding to a client's first request. This can increase the page load time of the first page by several seconds. Additionally, reverse DNS lookups are not secure and can be circumvented by an attacker who is aware of the request filtering.

If you need to provide an informative error message to users with an invalid source IP address or direct them to a different page, use IIS URL rewriting. You can specify the client IP address as a condition by using {REMOTE_ADDR}, and then process a different webpage, redirect the user, or simply abort processing.

> **MORE INFO** **URL REWRITE**
>
> For more information, read "URL Rewrite" at *http://www.iis.net/download/urlrewrite* and "IIS URL Rewriting and ASP.NET Routing" at *http://learn.iis.net/page.aspx/496/iis-url-rewriting-and-aspnet-routing/*.

Implementing Custom Filtering

Whenever possible, rely on the built-in filtering capabilities of IIS and the .NET Framework. If those filtering features are not flexible enough to detect requests that should be filtered, you can write code to perform custom filtering.

In ASP.NET applications, begin the *Page.Load* (in either content or master pages) to determine whether a request should be filtered. If it should be filtered, use *Server.Transfer* to process a page containing an error message and set *Response.StatusCode* to an error code, such as 401. In MVC applications, you can handle the filtering logic within the controller or create a custom action filter.

> **MORE INFO** **CUSTOM ACTION FILTERS**
>
> For detailed instructions, read "Creating Custom Action Filters" at *http://msdn.microsoft.com/library/dd381609.aspx*.

Using SSL

SSL uses HTTPS to authenticate servers and encrypt both requests and responses. The benefit of server authentication is that it helps reduce the risk of DNS injection attacks that might direct a user to a malicious web server when the user attempts to visit a known hostname, a technique called a man-in-the-middle attack. If the request uses HTTPS and the server does not have a valid certificate for the requested hostname, the user's browser will typically display an error message and warn the user not to visit the site.

The benefit of communications encryption is that it helps prevent attackers with access to network communications from capturing a user's private information. For example, when you log on to a website using Forms authentication, the browser sends the user's user name and password as part of the HTTP request. If the logon request used HTTP instead of HTTPS, an attacker with access to the user's computer, network equipment used in the communications (including wireless access points), or the server could capture the user's credentials.

You should require SSL for the following types of pages:

- Forms that prompt users for a user name, password, credit card number, or any other private information. Even though a blank form might not have any private information, using SSL will prevent the browser from displaying a warning message, and most web browsers highlight that the connection is protected.

- Pages that process private information, if a form posts to a different page.

- Images or other object embedded in SSL-protected pages. Use relative paths that do not specify the domain name to allow webpages to work properly with either HTTP or HTTPS.

Using SSL has several drawbacks:

- To allow browsers to connect to your website without a warning, you must purchase a certificate from a public registrar. For intranet sites in an Active Directory environment, you can configure clients to trust your internal certification authority and then issue private certificates without a fee.

- SSL certificates specify a single hostname. Therefore, you need separate certificates for every hostname that requires SSL. For example, contoso.com, www.contoso.com, and images.contoso.com would each require separate certificates.

- For security reasons, proxy servers and network caches (such as a CDN) never cache content retrieved using SSL. Therefore, using SSL might increase server load and bandwidth, reducing scalability.

- Encrypting web responses uses a small additional amount of the web server's processor time. Typically, this processing overhead is insignificant on all but the busiest websites. To minimize the performance impact, require SSL only for pages that need the additional protection.

- Using SSL requires a website to have a unique IP address. You can use host headers to share a single IP address among multiple sites, but host headers will fail for HTTPS requests.

EXAM TIP

For the exam, remember to use SSL certificates and require HTTPS to mitigate the risk of man-in-the-middle attacks and capturing network traffic.

Objective Summary

- You should treat all user input as potentially malicious. To reduce the threat of malicious user input, you should HTML-encode text input, URL-encode URLs, validate the size of user input, verify file extensions when allowing uploads, and limit the number of results returned by a SQL query.

- DoS attacks overwhelm an application, preventing it from responding to legitimate requests. One way to reduce the risk of DoS attacks is to throttle user input by limiting the number of requests a user or IP address can submit in a specified amount of time.

- You can reduce the risk of security breaches by filtering requests before your application processes them. First, take advantage of the request filtering built into ASP.NET. If you are using IIS as your web server, use IP address filtering and URL rewriting to block or redirect invalid requests. For MVC applications, you can create action filters to perform more complex filtering.

- You can install an SSL certificate on a web server to enable HTTPS communications. HTTPS improves security in two ways: authenticating the web server to reduce the risk of man-in-the-middle attacks and encrypting communications to reduce the risk of data compromises.

Objective Review

Answer the following questions to test your knowledge of the information in this objective. You can find the answers to these questions and explanations of why each answer choice is correct or incorrect in the "Answers" section at the end of this chapter.

1. You are creating an MVC application running on IIS 7.5 that contains a separate area containing management tools. Only administrators on the local network, 10.1.1.0/24, should be allowed to access those pages. Users from other networks should be redirected to a support page on the same site. If the network or support page changes in the future, you would like systems administrators to be able to modify the configuration without recompiling the application. Which approach should you recommend?

   A. Use the IIS URL Rewrite module.

   B. Create a custom action filter.

   C. Use IIS IP address restrictions.

   D. Use Windows Firewall.

2. You are designing an Internet e-commerce application that requires users to enter credit card information to make a purchase. You need to ensure that the credit card information is encrypted when it is transmitted across the network. Which approach should you recommend?

   A. Hash the credit card by using client-side JavaScript.

B. Encrypt the credit card by using client-side JavaScript.

C. Use Internet Protocol Security (IPsec).

D. Require SSL for the page.

3. You are designing an Internet e-commerce application that requires users to enter credit card information to make a purchase. You need to verify that the user's billing address matches the billing address associated with the credit card, which you can retrieve by using a web service. Which approach should you recommend?

A. Handle the Submit button's *onClick* event in JavaScript.

B. Handle the Submit button's *OnClick* event in ASP.NET.

C. Install an SSL certificate on the web server, and require HTTPS for the page.

D. Set the page's *ValidateRequest* attribute to *True*.

THOUGHT EXPERIMENT
Updating a Compromised Web Application

In this thought experiment, you apply what you've learned about the "Plan for Minimizing Attack Surfaces" objective to predict how a theoretical website architecture will perform. You can find answers to these questions in the "Answers" section at the end of this book.

You are a consultant for Coho Winery. Recently, Coho Winery's website was offline for a full week because of repeated breaches of security. After some investigation, the IT department determined the attacks were automated attacks initiated by scripts running on computers around the world that attackers had previously compromised. The successful attacks fell into two categories: SQL inject and cross-site scripting.

Coho Winery would like to update the website so that it cannot be compromised. The developers have designed a solution with these features:

- Replace code that created SQL queries by concatenating user input.
- HTML-encode all user input before displaying it in a webpage.

Management wants your opinion on whether the changes will protect them from future attacks. Answer the following questions about the future performance of the application:

1. Will this improve our security?

2. Will the application be secure against future attacks?

3. What more should we do to protect the application?

Chapter Summary

- Use code access security and the privileges of the application's process identity to assign web applications the fewest privileges required to run. When users authenticate with Active Directory domain credentials, use impersonation and delegation to access network resources with the user's credentials.

- ASP.NET membership can store account information in either a SQL Server database or an Active Directory domain. Whenever possible, leverage users' existing accounts in an Active Directory domain and assign privileges to their roles, which relate directly to Active Directory domain group memberships. When designing a custom membership provider, store hashes of passwords unless you need access to the original password. Use Authorization Manager to allow systems administrators to assign privileges to different application capabilities.

- Reduce the risk of security breaches by filtering requests using the capabilities built-in to IIS and ASP.NET. To reduce the threat of malicious user input, HTML encode text input, URL encode URLs, validate the size of user input, verify file extensions when allowing uploads, and limit the number of results returned by a SQL query. Protect operations that use significant resources by throttling requests. Install an SSL certificate on your web server, and require HTTPS to authenticate the server and encrypt communications.

Answers

Objective 4.1: Review

1. **Correct Answers:** A and B

   A. **Correct:** Delegation issues database requests with the user's credentials, rather than the application's process identity.

   B. **Correct:** Enabling delegation without restriction would allow the application to access any network resource using the user's credentials. If the application was compromised, unconstrained delegation could result in the entire network being compromised. Constrained delegation limits the network resources the web server can access with the user's credentials.

   C. **Incorrect:** The Network Service account (the most common process identity) is a local account and cannot be added to domain groups. Additionally, the Domain Admins group would provide excessive privileges, increasing security risks.

   D. **Incorrect:** The System account would still not have privileges to access the database. Additionally, the System account has unrestricted access to the local computer, increasing security risks.

2. **Correct Answer:** C

   A. **Incorrect:** Although it is technically possible to do this, it is more efficient to use CAS to limit the privileges of a component.

   B. **Incorrect:** Although it is technically possible to do this, it is more efficient to use CAS to limit the privileges of a component. Additionally, Active Directory domain accounts can have access to remote computers.

   C. **Correct:** You can create application domains with a specific trust level and launch components within the application domain. The component will have only the privileges you grant to the trust level. In this scenario, you should configure a custom trust level that grants the component access to create files in the local folder without having other excessive privileges.

   D. **Incorrect:** Although it is technically possible to do this, it would require granting end users access to write files on the web server, which would increase security risks.

3. **Correct Answers:** A and D

   A. **Correct:** An application's process identity must be able to read application files to function correctly.

   B. **Incorrect:** If the application were compromised, having permissions to write the application files would allow the attacker to modify the application's files.

C.   Incorrect: Having only read permissions to the Uploads folder would not allow the application to create new files sent from anonymous users.

D.   Correct: The application's process identity must be able to write files in the Uploads folder to allow it to create new files sent from anonymous users.

Objective 4.1: Thought Experiment

1.   No. To resolve the problems, they would need to run the public web application using the Medium trust level or create a custom trust level based on the Low trust level that also grants database access. Additionally, administrators could not access privileges to the database for a local service account on the web server. To have privileges on multiple computers, the service account would need to be part of the Active Directory domain.

2.   Yes.

3.   They could create custom trust levels that fine-tune the privileges assigned to the applications. Additionally, they could restrict the privileges that the service account has to the web server.

Objective 4.2: Review

1.   **Correct Answers:** A and D

   A.   Correct: If you must be able to retrieve original passwords, encryption provides the best protection possible.

   B.   Incorrect: Hashed passwords are more secure than encrypted passwords. However, you cannot easily reverse hashed passwords.

   C.   Incorrect: The built-in SQL membership provider stores hashes of passwords and prevents you from retrieving the original password.

   D.   Correct: Because the built-in SQL membership provider does not support retrieving users' original passwords, you must create a custom membership provider.

2.   **Correct Answer:** B

   A.   Incorrect: A custom trust level could prevent the application itself from accessing a specific folder, but you cannot use code access security for role-based authorization.

   B.   Correct: Use the *Authorization* element of the Web.config file to restrict access to an entire folder.

   C.   Incorrect: You can use the *PrincipalPermission* attribute to protect individual methods. However, you cannot use it to protect an entire folder.

D. Incorrect: As with the *PrincipalPermission* attribute, you can use the *Authorize* attribute to protect individual methods. The *Authorize* attribute is an MVC class, however.

3. **Correct Answer:** C

A. Incorrect: Although this approach would prevent unauthenticated users from accessing the area, it would not verify that the users are members of the Administrators role.

B. Incorrect: *PrincipalPermission* resembles the *Authorize* attribute, but you should use *Authorize* for MVC applications.

C. Correct: The most secure way to provide authorization for an MVC application is to apply the *Authorize* attribute with the appropriate properties to each action result method.

D. Incorrect: You could edit the *Authorization* element of the Web.config file to force users accessing the Administer area to be members of the Administrators role. However, MVC routing could allow users to access the Administer area using a different path, bypassing the protection offered by the *Authorization* element.

Objective 4.2: Thought Experiment

1. No. The developers should protect any actions with the *Authorize* attribute.

2. Yes. Alternatively, you could call *PrincipalPermission.Demand* and catch an exception if the user is not authorized.

3. Although the trusted subsystem will work properly, it is not the most secure way to access the database. If the design used constrained delegation instead, the web application would access the database with each user's own credentials. This would allow database administrators to configure different authorization for users and managers, adding a layer of security. It would also allow for auditing individual user actions at the database level.

Objective 4.3: Review

1. **Correct Answer:** A

A. Correct: URL Rewrite allows you to specify an IP address range as a condition. If the request originates from an IP address outside the specified range, URL Rewrite can redirect the user to a support page.

B. Incorrect: Although you can create a custom action filter that accomplishes the necessary request filtering, and you can also make it read configuration settings from a file that systems administrators can edit, using URL Rewrite would be easier for both the systems administrators and developers.

C. **Incorrect:** IIS IP address restrictions could block requests from outside the network; however, they cannot easily be used to redirect users to a support page.

D. **Incorrect:** Windows Firewall could be configured to block requests from outside the network; however, you could not configure Windows Firewall to respond to the HTTP request with a support page.

2. **Correct Answer:** D

A. **Incorrect:** Hashing modifies data so that it is unique but cannot easily be reversed. Therefore, if the client hashed the credit card number before sending it to the server, the server would be unable to determine the original credit card number.

B. **Incorrect:** Although it is possible to encrypt information with JavaScript, this would require additional development effort. Additionally, many browsers warn users before submitting data across a connection that is not protected by SSL.

C. **Incorrect:** IPsec can encrypt any type of network communications. However, for IPsec to work, the client and server must be configured ahead of time to communicate with each other. Therefore, IPsec is better suited to intranet applications.

D. **Correct:** SSL encrypts all communications between the client and server. If the SSL certificate is purchased from one of the public certification authorities that browsers accept by default, the encryption will be transparent to end users.

3. **Correct Answer:** B

A. **Incorrect:** JavaScript is capable of contacting a web service and verifying the address. However, client-side scripting is easily bypassed and cannot be trusted for security.

B. **Correct:** Although you could contact the web service from either the client or the server, you can never trust client-side scripts to validate user input. Therefore, you must handle the server control's *OnClick* event.

C. **Incorrect:** SSL certificates authenticate the server and encrypt communications. However, they cannot be used for input validation.

D. **Incorrect:** The *ValidateRequest* attribute enables ASP.NET's built-in protection against cross-site scripting attacks. However, it is not useful for validating the integrity user input.

Objective 4.3: Thought Experiment

1. Yes.

2. No; although the changes will improve security, no application is ever completely secure.

3. Understanding exactly how much Coho Winery should invest in security would require a security cost-benefit analysis. However, there are many straightforward ways to greatly improve an application's security, such as using SSL to encrypt sensitive communications, filtering potentially malicious requests, and throttling input that might result in a DoS.

CHAPTER 5

Preparing for and Investigating Application Issues

Architects design buildings to withstand the shaking caused by earthquakes, car designers plan crumple zones to protect the occupants during a crash, and application designers must create plans for testing, monitoring, and debugging applications. Although these features do not contribute directly to an application's core functionality, they are important because they reduce development time, administrative costs, and downtime.

This chapter describes how to design a testing methodology to verify that a new application meets the design requirements, how to design an exception-handling strategy, how to debug complex issues, and how to design an application for performance monitoring.

Objectives in this chapter:

- Objective 5.1: Choose a testing methodology
- Objective 5.2: Design an exception-handling strategy
- Objective 5.3: Recommend an approach to debugging
- Objective 5.4: Recommend an approach to performance issues

Objective 5.1: Choose a Testing Methodology

Many bugs are impossible to overlook, such as a mistyped variable name that prevents an application from compiling. Other bugs, such as a method that fails to throw an exception for certain types of invalid input, can go undiscovered until a user encounters an error or an attacker finds a way to exploit the bug.

You can identify these subtle but critical bugs by following a testing methodology. A testing methodology is a process for systematically verifying that code does what is expected of it, including rejecting invalid and potentially malicious input. Although following a testing methodology cannot guarantee that you catch all bugs, it can greatly reduce the number of serious bugs and reduce the cost of maintaining an application.

This objective provides an overview of black box and white box testing, code coverage, and how to choose which layer to test.

> **This objective covers how to:**
> - Design a testing methodology.
> - Use code coverage to thoroughly test an application.
> - Test the appropriate layer of an application.

Understanding Testing Methodologies

Although there are many types of testing methodologies, the 70-519 Objective 5.1 explicitly covers two:

- **Black box**   Simulates the user experience by testing required functionality without knowledge of an application's inner workings. For example, black box testing might enter data in web forms and click several links to verify that an application allows new users to create accounts. Creating black box test cases does not require programming skills or examining the source code.

- **White box**   Tests the internal functionality of an application based on likely failure scenarios. White box testing requires programming skills and an internal knowledge of an application's structure. For example, if you knew that the method being tested generated a SQL query based on input, testing could input a SQL injection attack to verify that the method threw an exception.

Creating automated test cases using these methodologies not only detects errors in the first release, it also verifies that errors are not introduced in subsequent releases—a process known as regression testing. Without it, developers tend to test only code they have changed and might not test minor changes at all. Such a process allows new bugs to impact features that worked previously—an event known as a regression.

In addition to regression testing, test plans typically incorporate the following:

- **Acceptance testing**   Verifies that the application does what it is required to do. Acceptance testing is typically performed as part of black box testing.

- **Integration testing**   Verifies that multiple components work together as expected.

- **Range testing**   Tests widely varying input for every parameter and each public method. For example, if a method accepts a first name as a string, black box testing might verify that the method throws an exception for null values, numeric values, HTML metatags, and large blocks of text. If a method accepts a person's age as an integer, black box testing might test every possible numeric value for the integer type (–2,147,483,648 to 2,147,483,647).

- **Security testing**   Verifies that the method rejects known attacks, such as buffer overflows, SQL injection, and cross-site scripting.

- **Stress testing**   Verifies that a method can handle a high number of requests in a limited amount of time. Stress testing might verify that the application degrades gracefully rather than failing completely, that the application performs request throttling as described in Objective 4.3, or that the application properly handles multiple threads.

- **Performance testing**   Measures the response time to a request.

- **Globalization testing**   Inputs text in different languages and numeric values in different formats.

- **Unit testing**   Verifies that individual methods and classes perform as required. Because it requires knowledge of an application's inner workings, unit testing occurs in white box testing but not black box testing.

- **API testing**   Closely resembles unit testing for public classes and methods. Whereas developers are typically responsible for creating their own unit tests and unit tests might test a class' private members, enterprises have a separate quality assurance team to perform API testing, and they test only public members.

> ***MORE INFO***   **TESTING**
>
> **For more information about automating web application testing, explore WatiN (pronounced "What-in") at *http://watin.org/* and Selenium at *http://seleniumhq.org*, both of which automate testing websites.**

Understanding Code Coverage

When creating white box test plans, you must consider how much of the code is being tested—a concept called code coverage. For example, if you are testing a method that includes a *Case* statement, you need to determine whether every branch in the *Case* statement has been tested. The most important coverage criteria are these:

- **Function coverage**   Verifying that each method has been tested (different languages, such as JavaScript, refer to methods as functions).

- **Statement coverage**   Verifying that each line of code is exercised as part of a test.

- **Decision coverage**   Verifying that every branch is tested.

- **Condition coverage**   Verifying that every Boolean value is tested as both true and false.

- **Multiple condition coverage**   Verifying that every possible combination of conditions is tested.

- **Loop coverage**   Verifies that testing runs each loop zero times, once, and multiple times.

- **Race coverage**   Verifying that the application works when running multiple threads at the same time.

Testing the Appropriate Layer

One of the greatest advantages of the Model-View-Controller (MVC) architecture is the developer's ability to test individual layers. The most thorough methodology is to test each layer's functionality. When designing a test case for a specific goal, test the first layer that processes the input.

For example, imagine that you are creating blog software that allows writers to add an article to a website. For an MVC application, a new blog entry might follow this process:

1. MVC generates a view containing a form with a text box control and a button.

2. The blog writer opens her browser, types the blog entry into the text box control, and clicks a button. The browser submits an HTTP POST request containing the new blog to the MVC application.

3. MVC routes the request to an action controller.

4. The action controller performs data validation and then calls a model binder to generate an instance of the Blog model based on the form input.

5. The action controller saves the model instance in a database.

Now imagine that you need to create a test case that verifies the MVC application rejects potentially malicious blog entries containing JavaScript code. You could perform the testing at several layers:

- **Client** Using a tool such as WatiN, you could submit a malicious blog entry and verify that the application returns an error message.

- **Controller** You could call the action controller directly, provide a malicious blog entry, and verify that the controller throws an exception.

- **Model binder** You could call the model binder directly and verify that it throws an exception when presented with a malicious blog entry rather than creating an instance of the model.

- **Data layer** You could attempt to save an instance of the model creating a malicious blog entry and verify that the data layer rejects it.

For white box testing where you are aware of the source code, test a scenario like this as close to the layer performing the validation as possible. Because most developers perform data validation at the controller, you should create tests at that layer. If you performed client-side JavaScript validation, you should also test the client. Similarly, if the design requirements called for validation at the model binder or data layer, you should test those layers.

EXAM TIP

To master this exam objective, you must have a solid understanding of both testing concepts and application architecture. Review Objectives 1.1 and 1.2, and be sure you understand how you would most effeively perform white box testing on components at each different layer.

Objective Summary

- Objective 5.1 covers two testing methodologies: black box and white box. Black box testing verifies application functionality at a high level, without knowledge of an application's inner workings. White box testing uses knowledge of application functionality to test at a lower level.

- Code coverage refers to the portion of an application's code that is tested. Code coverage can be measured by function, statement, decision, condition, multiple condition, loop, and race.

- When performing white box testing, always test the closest entry point to the code you need to verify.

Objective Review

Answer the following questions to test your knowledge of the information in this objective. You can find the answers to these questions and explanations of why each answer choice is correct or incorrect in the "Answers" section at the end of this chapter.

1. You are designing the testing methodology for an MVC application. The application performs server-side data validation in the controllers, performs client-side data validation in the views, implements the application logic in the domain model, and authorizes users in the database itself. You need to create white box test cases that directly verify that the application conforms to the business rules. Which layer should you design the test cases against?

   A. Model

   B. Views

   C. Controllers

   D. Database

2. You are designing the testing methodology for an MVC application. The application performs server-side data validation in the controllers, performs client-side data validation in the views, implements the application logic in the domain model, and authorizes users in the database itself. You need to create black box test cases that verify that the application accepts valid data and rejects invalid data. Which layer should you design the test cases against?

   A. Client browser

   B. Controllers

   C. Model

   D. Database

3. You are designing the testing methodology for an MVC application. The application performs server-side data validation in the controllers, performs client-side data validation in the views, implements the application logic in the domain model, and authorizes users in the database itself. You need to create white box test cases that verify that the application will reject potentially malicious values entered by users for security purposes. Which layer should you design the test cases against?

   A. Model

   B. Views

   C. Controllers

   D. Database

THOUGHT EXPERIMENT
Designing a Testing Methodology

In the following thought experiment, you will apply what you've learned about the "Choose a Testing Methodology" objective to predict how a theoretical website architecture will perform. You can find answers to these questions in the "Answers" section at the end of this chapter.

You are a consultant for Contoso Pharmaceuticals. Contoso is planning a new MVC Web application that exposes several different public web services. Users on the Internet will be able to browse Contoso's products. Partner organizations will be able to connect to the web services to place orders, query about medical interactions, and submit customer service requests.

The quality assurance (QA) team has designed a testing methodology with these attributes:

- Acceptance testing will be performed by using automated tools that simulate web requests and verify that the application returns the expected response.

- Range testing will submit all possible values to every field in the application, and it will verify that the application returns the expected response.

- Globalization testing will request the site in different languages, and it will submit values in varying formats.

- Stress testing will submit a large number of values simultaneously and verify that the application degrades gracefully.

- Security testing will be performed by submitting potentially malicious values and verifying that the application returns the appropriate error message.

  If testing fails, developers are required to resolve any application problems and submit them for retesting before the application can be released.

Management wants your opinion on the design of the testing methodology. Answer the following questions about the future performance of the application:

1. Is the QA team performing both black box and white box testing?

2. When the QA team returns the application to developers because it fails testing, will the developers have the information they need to resolve the problem?

3. Is there 100 percent code coverage? If not, what would you do to improve code coverage?

Objective 5.2: Design an Exception-Handling Strategy

Using an effective exception-handling strategy maximizes code readability, simplifies troubleshooting, and minimizes security risks. This objective provides an overview of configuring exception handling for ASP.NET and MVC applications.

This objective covers how to:

- Design an exception-handling strategy.
- Process unhandled exceptions in ASP.NET.
- Process unhandled exceptions in MVC applications.

Designing an Exception-Handling Strategy

Though a bug in your application might cause an exception, exceptions themselves are not bugs. In fact, a well-designed application intentionally throws exceptions when required resources cannot be found, when users make unauthorized requests, and when the server cannot process additional requests.

Unhandled exceptions, however, should be a rare occurrence. By default, ASP.NET displays an error message to the user, similar to the one shown in Figure 5-1.

FIGURE 5-1 An unhandled exception

Follow these best practices when creating your exception-handling strategies:

- Throw an exception when application logic determines that the application's current flow cannot continue. Do not throw exceptions to return values to calling code.

- Whenever possible, use existing exception classes or derive a new class from an existing subclass. Create a new exception class only if developers will respond differently to information you cannot provide with existing classes.

- Mark exception classes as *Serializable* so that they work properly with remoting and web services.

- Do not expect the calling code to parse the Message field; reserve the Message field for human-readable information.

- Handle the specific exception types whenever the application or user can respond to them, as close as possible to where the exception might be thrown.

- If you catch an exception and then determine that you cannot respond to it, add context information to the exception and rethrow it.

- If you cannot respond to or add context information to an exception, do not catch it. Let the exception propagate.

- Use a *Finally* clause to close any resources that might be open (even when you do not have a *Catch* clause). Alternatively, *Using* blocks are an effective way to ensure the common language runtime (CLR) cleans up resources when an exception occurs.

- If the exception might need troubleshooting (for example, if a database is unavailable or the application cannot create a new file), log an event to the event log with detailed information. IT departments can integrate event logs into their existing real-time monitoring systems. Log *Exception.ToString* instead of *Exception.Message* because *Exception.ToString* includes a full stack trace.

MORE INFO   **HEALTH MONITORING**

You can use ASP.NET Health Monitoring to monitor the status of applications, including occurrences of important events. For more information, refer to Objective 6.4 and visit *http://msdn.microsoft.com/library/bb398933.aspx*.

- Display a friendly, nondetailed message to end users. Never allow users to see source code or stack traces as part of an error message, because every user is a potential attacker, and the more knowledge an attacker has about how your application functions, the more likely he is to successfully compromise it.

MORE INFO   **EXCEPTION-HANDLING STRATEGIES**

For more information, read "Exception Handling Strategies" at *http://tutorials.jenkov.com/exception-handling-strategies/index.html*. Though the article was not written for the .NET Framework, the concepts are universal.

Processing Unhandled Exceptions in ASP.NET

ASP.NET can handle exceptions at several layers. When possible, handle exceptions at the lowest layer possible. From the lowest to the highest layer, ASP.NET exception handling includes the following:

- Catching exceptions within a method
- Catching exceptions at the page level by using *Page_Error* or *Page.ErrorPage*
- Catching exceptions at the application level by using *Application_Error* or the Web. config file

MVC applications support using *Application_Error* and Web.config exactly as traditional ASP.NET applications. The sections that follow discuss each of the ASP.NET exception-handling layers in more detail.

Using *Page_Error*

If ASP.NET encounters an unhandled exception, it raises the *Page.OnError* event. Therefore, to process unhandled exceptions for a specific page, simply implement the *Page_Error* method. To prevent *Application_Error* from also handling the exception, call *Context.ClearError*, as the following example shows:

Sample of Visual Basic.NET Code

```
Sub Page_Error(ByVal src As Object, ByVal args As EventArgs) Handles MyBase.Error
    Dim e As System.Exception = Server.GetLastError()
    Trace.Write("Message", e.Message)
    Response.Write("Sorry, an error was encountered.")
    Context.ClearError()
End Sub
```

Sample of C# Code

```
void Page_Error(Object sender, EventArgs args) {
    Exception e = Server.GetLastError();
    Trace.Write("Message", e.Message);
    Response.Write("Sorry, an error was encountered.");
    Context.ClearError();
}
```

> **NOTE ERROR LOGGING**
>
> Use Error Logging Modules and Handlers (ELMAH), available at *http://code.google.com/p/elmah/*, to simplify logging errors in your web applications.

Using *Page.ErrorPage*

You can send all unhandled exceptions to a different page by setting the *Page.ErrorPage* value. You can set this in the page declaration, as the following example shows:

```
<%@ Page ErrorPage="Errors.aspx" >
```

Alternatively, you can set *Page.ErrorPage* imperatively in code, as this example shows:

Sample of Visual Basic.NET Code

```
If (SomeError) Then
    Me.ErrorPage = "Errors.aspx"
 End If
```

Sample of C# Code

```
if(someError)
    this.ErrorPage = "Errors.aspx";
```

Using *Application_Error*

When both MVC applications and traditional ASP.NET applications encounter an exception that is not handled at the page level, they call the *Application_Error* method in the Global.asax file. *Application_Error* is the perfect place for logging information about errors that occur within a production web application so that you can troubleshoot them later.

This example shows a basic implementation of *Application_Error*. Notice that it calls *Server.ClearError* to prevent ASP.NET from showing the default unhandled exception method.

Sample of Visual Basic.NET Code

```
Private Sub Application_Error(sender As Object, e As EventArgs)
    Dim ex As Exception = Server.GetLastError()
    ' TODO: Log the error
    Server.ClearError()
End Sub
```

Sample of C# Code

```
void Application_Error(object sender, EventArgs e)
{
    Exception ex = Server.GetLastError();
    // TODO: Log the error
    Server.ClearError();
}
```

Application_Error will not catch errors that occur outside of ASP.NET, such as a web server's "file not found" error.

Using the Web.config File

By default, ASP.NET applications show detailed error messages containing a stack trace and source code only (as shown in Figure 5-1) to users logged on directly to the web server. This makes it easier to debug applications during development, when you are likely to be using the local computer as your web server. In production, however, developers rarely log on directly to the web server. Users not logged on to the web server see the general error message shown in Figure 5-2.

FIGURE 5-2 The basic error messages most users see when ASP.NET encounters an unhandled exception

For both MVC applications and traditional ASP.NET applications, you can set the <custom Errors> value in the <configuration><system.web> section of the Web.config file to control who sees detailed error messages. Set the *customErrors mode* attribute to *On* to hide detailed error messages from all users (including those on the local computer) or *Off* to show the error messages to all users (which could reveal sensitive information to an attacker).

If you set it to *Off*, implement error handling in *Application_Error* to avoid showing detailed error messages to remote users. The default value is *RemoteOnly*. If you implement your own exception handling and want to respect the <customErrors> mode, check the *Http Context.Current.IsCustomErrorEnabled* Boolean value.

Specify pages to handle specific HTTP errors by adding the <error> element and specifying the *statusCode* and *redirect* attributes, as the following example shows:

```
<customErrors mode="RemoteOnly" defaultRedirect="AnyOtherErrors.aspx">
    <error statusCode="403" redirect="NoAccessError.aspx"/>
    <error statusCode="404" redirect="NotFoundError.aspx"/>
</customErrors>
```

Processing Unhandled Exceptions in MVC Applications

By default, MVC applications process unhandled exceptions similarly to ASP.NET applications by showing local users a detailed error message and remote users a very general message. Although the default behavior is the same, you must write very different code to override the default behavior.

First, add the *HandleError* attribute to a controller or controller action. This applies a filter that redirects errors to the Error.aspx view, which you need to add to the controller. To process unhandled exceptions for any controller in your application, create an Error.aspx view in the Shared folder. During debugging, set <customErrors mode="On"> to use the *HandleError* filter instead of the standard debugging exception-handling process (which handles the error with Microsoft Visual Studio).

This code sample demonstrates how to apply the attribute in two ways: by redirecting all unhandled exceptions to Error.aspx (the default) and by redirecting *FileIOExceptions* to FileError.aspx. You can apply multiple *HandleError* attributes to a single method; if you specify the *Order* property, the .NET Framework will use the applicable instance with the lowest *Order* value:

Sample of Visual Basic.NET Code

```
<HandleError> _
Public Function Index() As ActionResult

    ...

End Function

<HandleError(View := "FileError", ExceptionType := GetType(FileIOException))> _
Public Function ThrowNotImplemented() As ActionResult

    ...

End Function
```

Sample of C# Code

```
[HandleError]
public ActionResult Index()
{
    ...

}

[HandleError(View = "FileError", ExceptionType = typeof(FileIOException))]
public ActionResult ThrowNotImplemented()
{
    ...

}
```

Alternatively, you can override the *Controller* class' *OnException* method, which MVC calls when an exception occurs within an action.

If you would rather specify a different view to handle errors (such as a custom *Errors* controller), specify it in the Web.config, as this example demonstrates:

```
<customErrors mode="RemoteOnly" defaultRedirect="/Errors/AnyOtherErrors.aspx">
    <error statusCode="403" redirect="/Errors/NoAccessError.aspx"/>
    <error statusCode="404" redirect="/Errors/NotFoundError.aspx"/>
</customErrors>
```

Objective Summary

- You should design an exception-handling strategy that logs unexpected exceptions for administrative analysis and that prevents users from seeing unfriendly error messages.

- You can process unhandled exceptions in several ways. For a single page, use *Page_Error* or *Page.ErrorPage*. For an entire application, use *Application_Error*, and the Web.config file.

- To process unhandled exceptions in MVC applications, use the *HandleError* attribute.

Objective Review

Answer the following questions to test your knowledge of the information in this objective. You can find the answers to these questions and explanations of why each answer choice is correct or incorrect in the "Answers" section at the end of this chapter.

1. You are designing an MVC application. Different developers will be writing different controllers, and each developer needs to be able to implement his or her own code for unhandled exceptions. Which approach should you recommend?

   A. Create a custom *Page* class, implement the *Page_Error* method, and derive your pages from the custom *Page* class.

   B. Configure a custom error page in the Web.config file.

   C. Add code to the *Application_Error* method in the Global.asax file.

   D. Apply the *HandleError* attribute to each controller, and add a view named Error.aspx.

2. You are designing an ASP.NET application. You need to provide an approach for centralized exception management. All unhandled exceptions need to be processed by a single method that provides logging, even if the page developer does not follow your page development guidelines. When unhandled exceptions occur, you want ASP.NET to display the default error message to the user. Which approach should you recommend?

   A. Create a custom *Page* class, implement the *Page_Error* method, and derive your pages from the custom *Page* class.

   B. Configure a custom error page in the Web.config file.

c. Add code to the *Application_Error* method in the Global.asax file.

D. Set the *Page.ErrorPage* property.

3. You are designing an MVC controller action. You need to redirect users to a different view if an unhandled exception occurs. Users need to be sent to different pages, based on the type of the exception. Code readability is a priority. Which approach should you recommend?

A. Add the *HandleError* attribute to the controller.

B. Add multiple *HandleError* attributes to the controller.

c. Surround the action with a single *Try/Catch* block.

D. Surround the action with a *Try* block and multiple *Catch* blocks.

THOUGHT EXPERIMENT
Designing an Exception-Handling Strategy

In the following thought experiment, you will apply what you've learned about the "Design an Exception-Handling Strategy" objective to predict how a theoretical website architecture will perform. You can find answers to these questions in the "Answers" section at the end of this chapter.

You are a consultant for A. Datum Corporation. A. Datum provides data mining services to the public via a public ASP.NET web application. The company is currently designing the next version of the application.

The developers have designed a web application with the following features:

- Every method is enclosed within a *Try/Catch* block.

- Within each method, developers will add nested *Try/Catch/Finally* blocks when code accesses external resources that might not be available, such as a database, the file system, or a web service.

- Each page specifies *Page.ErrorPage* with a value of Error.aspx. The Error.aspx page adds an event to the event log, which is monitored by the A. Datum systems administrators.

Management has the following goals for the application:

- All unexpected errors result in an event being added to the event log.

- Events in the event log must have enough information to allow systems administrators to determine if a resource is offline. If the problem is the result of a bug in the application code, there must be enough information for the developer to identify the code causing the problem.

- When unexpected errors occur, users will be shown the Error.aspx page.

Management wants your opinion on the exception-handling design. Answer the following questions about the future performance of the application:

1. Will all unexpected exceptions result in an event being added to the event log? If so, what would you do to remedy that?

2. What information would you show in the Error.aspx page?

3. What information would you add to the event log?

Objective 5.3: Recommend an Approach to Debugging

The most complex debugging scenarios also tend to be the most time-consuming. For example, debugging a deadlock requires examining how separate processes interact, and debugging a hung application requires creating and analyzing a memory dump. Understanding how to debug these complex issues before a problem occurs can greatly reduce the time you spend debugging.

This objective provides an overview of how to debug deadlocks, memory dumps, assembly binding, and JavaScript. It will also describe how to customize the way the Visual Studio debugger displays values for custom classes.

This objective covers how to:

- Debug complex issues.
- Perform a root-cause analysis.
- Attach to processes.
- Debug JavaScript.
- Control debugger displays.

Debugging Complex Issues

While other exams have covered the fundamentals of debugging, the 70-519 exam focuses on the most complex issues, including debugging deadlocks, analyzing memory dumps, and debugging problems with assembly binding.

Debugging Deadlocks

Deadlocks occur when two threads of an application attempt to access the same resources at the same time. For example, imagine there are two threads, Thread A and Thread B, and they both need to access both File C and File D. Thread A locks File C for writing. Then, Thread B locks File D for writing. Thread A then attempts to lock File D, discovers that the file is already locked, and waits. Thread B attempts to lock File C, discovers that the file is already locked, and waits. Although the file edits might normally take only milliseconds, deadlocks can last until one thread times out or is terminated.

Although the deadlock scenario might sound overly complex, deadlocks are extremely common with databases that require locking multiple tables and rows as part of a single transaction. Debugging deadlocks can be complex, because you have to analyze multiple threads and determine which resources are deadlocked.

Typically, deadlocks do not cause threads to halt indefinitely. Instead, the attempt to access a resource will time-out at some point, and the CLR will throw an exception. However, frequent deadlocks can cause significant performance problems.

You can use Visual Studio to debug deadlocks. First, start the application in debug mode. From the Debug menu, select Windows and choose Threads. This displays the Threads pane (shown in Figure 5-3), which shows active threads and the currently executing line of code. Run the application, trigger the deadlock condition, and examine the Threads window to determine which lines of code are causing the deadlock. To view the currently running line of code for a thread, right-click it, and then select Switch To Thread. You can pause and restart threads by right-clicking them and then selecting Freeze or Thaw.

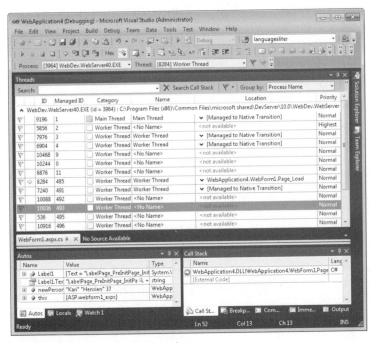

FIGURE 5-3 The Visual Studio Threads pane

Deadlocks can also occur when Internet Information Services (IIS) application pools run out of threads, a common scenario when multiple users issue long-running requests. In this case, you could update the code to be more thread-efficient, or you could simply increase the number of threads available to the application pool. Increasing the threads in the application pool can reduce performance, however. To increase the number of threads, update the <system.web><processModel> settings in the server's Machine.config file. On servers running IIS 7.0 or 7.5, you can increase the number of threads by using <system.web><applicationPool>.

> **MORE INFO   INCREASING APPLICATION POOL THREADS**
>
> For more information, read "applicationPool Element" at *http://msdn.microsoft.com/ library/dd560842.aspx* and "processModel Element" at *http://msdn.microsoft.com/ library/7w2sway1.aspx*.

Debugging Memory Dumps

If you are unable to interactively debug a Web application, you can create a memory dump and then debug the memory dump. During a memory dump, Windows writes a process' entire memory space to a file on the disk. You can then examine the memory dump by using the Debugging Tools For Windows, available at *http://msdn.microsoft.com/windows/hardware/ gg463009.aspx*.

If a serious problem occurs, such as a large memory leak, Windows might stop the IIS process (such as w3wp.exe) and automatically create a memory dump. Alternatively, you can manually initiate a memory dump of the IIS process.

To create a memory dump, use ADPlus, which is available as part of the Debugging Tools For Windows. ADPlus has two modes:

- **Hang**   Troubleshoots processes that stop responding or consume 100 percent of the processor. To troubleshoot hung processes, run ADPlus while the hang is occurring.
- **Crash**   Troubleshoots processes that fail unexpectedly or are stopped by IIS or Windows. To troubleshoot processes that crash, run ADPlus before the hang occurs.

> **MORE INFO   ADPLUS**
>
> For more information, read "How to use ADPlus to troubleshoot hangs and crashes" at *http://support.microsoft.com/kb/286350*.
>
> For 32-bit versions of Windows, you can manually create a memory dump of IIS by using the IIS Debug Diagnostics tool, as described at *http://support.microsoft.com/kb/919790*, or by using Userdump.exe, as described at *http://support.microsoft.com/kb/241215*.

To examine a memory dump, use the DumpChk, WinDbg, or KD tools, which are also available as part of the Debugging Tools For Windows.

Debugging Assembly Binding

Assembly binding is the process the CLR uses to attach to assemblies. In an ASP.NET application, you might bind to assemblies to use a class contained within the assembly or call a static method.

Though assembly binding sounds straightforward, it can become very complex:

- Assemblies can be either private or shared in the Global Assembly Cache (GAC).

- Any given computer might have multiple or different versions and cultures for a single assembly.

- A single assembly might be available both privately and in the GAC, with multiple versions of each available.

- An assembly might be missing entirely, might be the wrong version, or might not be in the folder your application requires it to be in.

The process that the CLR uses to bind to assemblies is predictable but very complex. If the CLR is unable to bind to an assembly, it throws a *TypeLoadException*. To troubleshoot an assembly binding, use the Assembly Binding Log Viewer (Fuslogvw.exe), which is available from the Visual Studio Command Prompt and as part of the Windows SDK.

Performing a Root-Cause Analysis

Often, problems can have many layers, and you might uncover the root cause only after following several layers of failures. A root-cause analysis is the process of finding the true source of a multilayered problem.

For example, consider a web application that occasionally fails. The layers leading to the root cause might be any of the following:

- The application stops processing requests because...
- The application pool runs out of threads because...
- Web requests are taking a very long time to process because...
- The database server is responding very slowly because...
- Someone is generating processor-intensive reports on the database server.

In this scenario, being aware of each additional layer provides other possibilities for solutions. For example, if you knew only that the application pool was running out of threads, you might increase the thread count. That might be enough to reduce the occurrence of the problem, but it would not solve it. If you knew only that web requests were taking a long time to process, you might try upgrading the web server, which would not solve the problem at all. Knowing that the database server is overloaded, you could have a database administrator throttle the processor-intensive reports, or simply move them to a different database server.

> **MORE INFO** **ROOT-CAUSE ANALYSIS**
>
> For more information, read "Finding a Path Through the Storm" at *http://msdn.microsoft.com/library/bb896738.aspx.*

Attaching to Processes

Visual Studio itself never directly runs application code. Typically, it runs web applications in the Visual Studio Development Server, which runs in a separate process. Debugging tasks in Visual Studio—such as catching unhandled exceptions, stepping through breakpoints, and viewing property values—all involve communications between the Visual Studio process and the process running the .NET Framework code. To allow Visual Studio to communicate with another process, Visual Studio must attach to that process.

When you debug an application on your local computer, Visual Studio automatically attaches to the Visual Studio Development Server. If you need to debug a web application running on a remote IIS server, you need to configure the server for remote debugging and then attach to the remote process. If you need to use Visual Studio to debug JavaScript, you need to attach Visual Studio to the browser process, as described in the next section.

> **MORE INFO** **REMOTE DEBUGGING**
>
> For detailed instructions, read "Remote Debugging Setup" at *http://msdn.microsoft.com/library/y7f5zaaa.aspx.*

Debugging JavaScript

JavaScript can be particularly challenging to debug because of the following factors:

- Visual Studio's JavaScript debugging tools are not as robust as the .NET Framework debugging tools.
- For most bugs, you need to attach a debugger to the Internet Explorer process.
- You have to test JavaScript in multiple browsers. If an error occurs only in a single browser, you need to use browser-specific debugging tools.

Because the web browser executes client-side script, you must attach to the Internet Explorer process to debug it with Visual Studio. When Internet Explorer is your default browser, Visual Studio automatically opens Internet Explorer when you debug a web application on your local computer. In that circumstance, client-side script debugging is automatically enabled.

If you need to debug a script running on a remote server, first enable script debugging in Internet Explorer from the Advanced tab of the Internet Options dialog box. Then open the View menu, select Script Debugger, and click Open. You can now choose to open and debug the page by using Visual Studio.

> **MORE INFO** **DEBUGGING CLIENT-SIDE SCRIPT**
>
> For detailed instructions, read "How to: Enable and Start Script Debugging from Internet Explorer" at *http://msdn.microsoft.com/library/z959x58c.aspx*.

For the exam, it's important to understand that you need to attach to Internet Explorer to debug client-side script using Visual Studio. In the real world, most developers prefer to use other debugging tools for client-side scripting. Internet Explorer Developer Tools, a feature of Internet Explorer 8 and 9, and Firebug, an add-on for the Firefox browser, are particularly useful.

Controlling Debugger Displays

One of Visual Studio's most useful debugging features is the ability to pause a running application and examine active values. By default, Visual Studio displays an object instance's *ToString* output in the debugger. If you would rather have Visual Studio display a different value, add the *DebuggerDisplay* attribute (from the *System.Diagnostics* namespace). This code sample demonstrates how to show the *ToString* output child property values for a class. You can also apply *DebuggerDisplay* to individual members.

Sample of Visual Basic.NET Code

```vbnet
<DebuggerDisplay("{FirstName} {LastName} {GetAge()}")> _
Public Class Person
    Private DateOfBirth As DateTime
    Private FirstName As String
    Private LastName As String

    Public Function GetAge() As Integer
        Dim _age As Integer = DateTime.Now.Year - DateOfBirth.Year
        If DateTime.Now < DateOfBirth.AddYears(_age) Then
            _age -= 1
        End If
    Return _age
End Function
End Class
```

Sample of C# Code

```csharp
[DebuggerDisplay("{FirstName} {LastName} {GetAge()}")]
public class Person
{
    DateTime DateOfBirth;
    string FirstName;
    string LastName;

    public int GetAge()
    {
        int _age = DateTime.Now.Year - DateOfBirth.Year;
        if (DateTime.Now < DateOfBirth.AddYears(_age))
            _age--;
        return _age;
    }
}
```

Figure 5-4 shows the default debugging display for the sample *Person* class (which does not have a *ToString* override), and Figure 5-5 shows the effect of applying the *Debugger Display* attribute shown in the previous example.

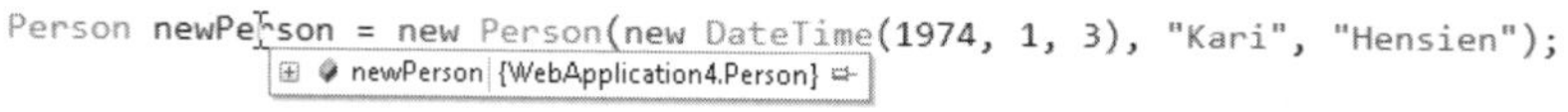

```
Person newPerson = new Person(new DateTime(1974, 1, 3), "Kari", "Hensien");
    ⊞  ● newPerson {WebApplication4.Person} ▣
```

FIGURE 5-4 Debugger preview for a class without *ToString* or *DebuggerDisplay*

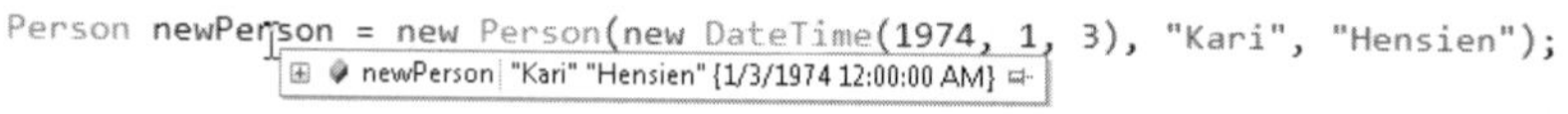

```
Person newPerson = new Person(new DateTime(1974, 1, 3), "Kari", "Hensien");
    ⊞  ● newPerson "Kari" "Hensien" {1/3/1974 12:00:00 AM} ▣
```

FIGURE 5-5 Debugger preview for a class with *DebuggerDisplay*

During debugging, Visual Studio allows you to browse an object's properties' values, including both public and private properties. You can use the *System.Diagnostics.Debugger Browsable* attribute to change the default behavior for individual properties. To use *DebuggerBrowsable*, add the attribute to a class and specify one of the three *Debugger BrowsableState* enumeration values:

- **DebuggerBrowsableState.Collapsed**   Shows the element collapsed by default, but allows developers to expand it. This is the default.

- **DebuggerBrowsableState.Never**   Hides the element during debugging, which cleans up the display for members that developers will never need to see during debugging.

- **DebuggerBrowsableState.RootHidden**   Shows only the child members. For example, applying this attribute to a *DateTime* property displays *DateTime.Year*, *DateTime.Month*, and other child properties. If you apply this to a property, it hides all child members at the same level.

This code sample shows how to use *DebuggerDisplay* to replace the default display for one member and to use *DebuggerBrowsable* to entirely hide a public member. Figure 5-6 shows how Visual Studio displays an instance of the class.

Sample of Visual Basic.NET Code

```
<DebuggerDisplay("{FirstName} {LastName} {DateOfBirth}")> _
Public Class Person
    <DebuggerDisplay("{FirstName} {LastName}")> _
    Private FirstName As String

    <DebuggerBrowsable(DebuggerBrowsableState.Never)> _
    Private LastName As String

    Private DateOfBirth As DateTime
End Class
```

Sample of C# Code

```
public class Person
{
    [DebuggerDisplay("{FirstName} {LastName}")]
    string FirstName;

    [DebuggerBrowsable(DebuggerBrowsableState.Never)]
    string LastName;

    DateTime DateOfBirth;
}

Person newPerson = new Person(new DateTime(1974, 1, 3), "Kari", "Hensien");
```

FIGURE 5-6 Using *DebuggerDisplay* and *DebuggerBrowsable*

If you need to customize a debugger display beyond what *DebuggerDisplay* and *DebuggerBrowsable* allow, use the *DebuggerTypeProxy* attribute. For more information, visit *http://msdn.microsoft.com/library/system.diagnostics.debuggertypeproxyattribute.aspx*.

Objective Summary

- Debug deadlocks by examining separate processes in Visual Studio. Debug crashes and hangs by analyzing the memory dumps. Use the Fuslogvw.exe tool to debug assembly binding.

- Often, the root cause of a problem is hidden many layers beneath the visible symptom. To troubleshoot these layered problems, perform a root-cause analysis. Identifying and resolving the root cause is the best way to solve all interim problems.

- To debug a running application, Visual Studio must attach to the running process. This happens automatically when you run a web application on your local computer. When the web application is running on a remote server, you must attach to the remote instance of IIS. To debug JavaScript, you must attach to Internet Explorer.

- You can use the *DebuggerDisplay*, *DebuggerBrowsable*, and *DebuggerTypeProxy* attributes to customize how the Visual Studio debugger displays instances of custom classes during debugging.

Objective Review

Answer the following questions to test your knowledge of the information in this objective. You can find the answers to these questions and explanations of why each answer choice is correct or incorrect in the "Answers" section at the end of this chapter.

1. You helped develop an MVC e-commerce application that features expandable Java-Script menus. The application is hosted on a remote server running IIS 7.5. Occasionally, the menus fail to expand when the user clicks them, Which approach should you recommend to troubleshoot the problem?

    A. Use the FusLogVw tool.

    B. Use the AdPlus tool.

    C. Attach Visual Studio to the remote IIS process.

    D. Attach Visual Studio to the Internet Explorer process.

2. You helped develop an MVC e-commerce application that features expandable Java-Script menus. The application is hosted on a remote server running IIS 7.5. Occasionally, the application experiences unhandled .NET Framework exceptions, Which approach should you recommend to troubleshoot the problem?

A. Use the FusLogVw tool.

B. Use the AdPlus tool.

C. Attach Visual Studio to the remote IIS process.

D. Attach Visual Studio to the Internet Explorer process.

3. You helped develop an MVC e-commerce application that features expandable Java-Script menus. The application is hosted on a remote server running IIS 7.5. Occasionally, the application hangs. Which approach should you recommend to troubleshoot the problem?

A. Use the FusLogVw tool.

B. Use the AdPlus tool.

C. Attach Visual Studio to the remote IIS process.

D. Attach Visual Studio to the Internet Explorer process.

THOUGHT EXPERIMENT
Debugging Problems in a Production Application

In the following thought experiment, you will apply what you've learned about the "Recommend an Approach to Debugging" objective to predict how a theoretical website architecture will perform. You can find answers to these questions in the "Answers" section at the end of this chapter.

You are a consultant for Wingtip Toys. Wingtip Toys maintains a public web application running on IIS 7.5 that customers can use to browse the company's toy catalog and make online purchases. Since launching the application, Wingtip Toys has experienced several ongoing problems that it did not encounter during the development and testing process.

Currently, the company is experiencing several problems:

- Some users cannot browse an item's photo album. Switching between pictures in the photo album is managed by a client-side JavaScript.

- During times of heavy use, the application might stop responding.

- Periodically, users with a large quantity of items in their shopping cart experience an unhandled exception.

The developers have designed this debugging approach:

- Use Visual Studio to attach to Internet Explorer, and then attempt to re-create the problem with switching between pictures in a photo album.

- Use Visual Studio to attach to IIS and catch an unhandled exception when it occurs.

Management wants your opinion on the debugging approach. Answer the following questions:

1. Will the approach allow us to debug the photo album problem? If not, what might work better?

2. Will the approach allow us to debug the problem of the application not responding? If not, what might work better?

3. Will the approach allow us to debug the shopping cart problem? If not, what might work better?

Objective 5.4: Recommend an Approach to Performance Issues

After deploying an application, administrators need insight into the application's performance. When designing web applications, you must plan to provide performance instrumentation, including performance counters and event tracing, that give administrators insight into your application. This instrumentation can also be useful to developers who need to fine-tune an application's performance in a production environment.

You should also plan to use page and fragment caching to reduce the server-side processing for each page, thereby improving both performance and scalability. This objective provides an overview of performance-monitoring instrumentation and page caching.

MORE INFO **WINDOWS PERFORMANCE ANALYSIS TOOLS**

You can use the Windows Performance Analysis Tools for extremely detailed performance analysis. The tools are installed as part of the Windows SDK. For more information, visit *http://msdn.microsoft.com/performance/cc825801.aspx.*

This objective covers how to:

- Monitor applications.
- Log ASP.NET tracing.
- Cache pages and fragments.

Monitoring Applications

The .NET Framework provides two important techniques for performance monitoring:

- **Performance counters** Numeric measurements of an application's state, such as the number of active users, the number of unprocessed orders, and the number of shopping carts. Administrators can visually monitor performance counters by using the Performance Monitor snap-in, log the data by using Data Collector Sets, or view a snapshot of the current status by using Reports.

- **Event tracing** Messages that provide internal details about the progress of an application. Event Tracing For Windows (ETW) is designed to be turned on only when the information is useful for troubleshooting, thereby minimizing the performance impact. As a developer, you can use event tracing to provide yourself and systems administrators insight into your application's functionality that can be useful for troubleshooting problems. Use the Event Trace Sessions snap-in (in Computer Management\System Tools\Performance\Data Collector Sets) to monitor event tracing, or use the command-line tools: Logman, Tracefmt, Tracelog, and Tracerpt.

Use performance counters in the following situations:

- The data you need to track can be expressed as one or more numbers.

- Administrators need to track performance data over time, such as the number of transactions or the memory consumed.

- Administrators need to track data when the application is functioning correctly.

- Administrators need to be alerted when a metric reaches a specific threshold, such as when the number of unprocessed transactions is over 100, or when the average time to answer a message is more than one hour.

Use event tracing in the following situations:

- Administrators need to be alerted when an event occurs, such as a customer places a high priority order, or the application fails to connect to the database.

- You need to track data that can be expressed only as a string.

- Administrators need to be aware of data only when troubleshooting a problem.

- You want to associate data with different levels of values, such as Verbose, Information, Warning, Error, and Critical.

Applications can both provide and monitor (also known as consume) performance counters and event tracing. Typically, however, applications simply provide data, and administrators use built-in tools to consume them.

In practice, you will often use both performance counters and event tracing together. For example, your application might provide detailed event tracing and a performance counter monitoring the current transaction queue. Administrators could then create a script that logged trace data if the queue exceeded 10, giving the administrators detailed information to help troubleshoot the problem.

Logging Tracing

Many developers use *Trace.Write* and *Trace.Warn* to write messages about the inner workings of an application. Although that information might be useful for troubleshooting, those methods have major drawbacks:

- By default, they're available only through the Trace.axd page, which you must manually go through.

- Trace.axd either automatically removes older trace information or stops logging trace information after a specific number of pages.

- If the application restarts, the tracing information is lost.

To get the most out of tracing, use the Health And Diagnostics\Tracing role service of IIS 7.0 and 7.5. After installing the role service, follow these steps to record tracing for a website:

1. In IIS Manager, select the website. In the Actions pane, click Failed Request Tracing.

2. In the Edit Web Site Failed Request Tracing Settings dialog box, select the Enable check box, as shown in Figure 5-7, and then click OK.

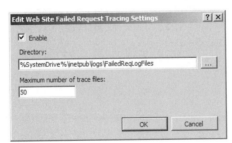

FIGURE 5-7 Enabling Failed Request Tracing for a website.

3. Under IIS, double-click Failed Request Tracing Rules.

4. In the Actions pane, click Add.

5. On the Specify Content To Trace page, select ASP.NET, and then click Next.

6. On the Define Trace Conditions page, specify the conditions under which a request should be traced.

   These can include HTTP status codes (such as 401 for pages that result in authorization failures), pages that take a specific number of seconds to process, and event severity. Click Next.

7. On the Select Trace Providers page, click Finish.

8. Enable tracing for individual pages (by adding *trace="true"* to the Page declaration) or for the entire application (by configuring the <system.web><trace> element of the Web.config file).

   Now, IIS will create XML files containing the event traces for the pages you specified to the folder you specified.

Caching Pages and Fragments

The best way to improve the server performance of an ASP.NET application is to partially or completely eliminate the ASPX rendering process. ASP.NET provides two types of output caching:

- **Page caching** ASP.NET caches an entire page and returns it for subsequent requests for the same page. Page caching caches the entire contents of a page, including any user controls.

- **Fragment caching** ASP.NET caches one or more user controls and inserts the cached output into an ASP.NET page. You can use fragment caching to cache a user control and then insert that cached output into different pages.

To use page caching, call *Response.Cache.SetCacheability* in the code file or use the *OutputCache* directive in the ASPX file. You can add *VaryByParam* to cache different versions of a page based on specific page query parameters. You can use post-cache substitution to replace dynamic portions of the page, such as the time or the user's name. To use post-cache substitution, place the dynamic content within a *Substitution* control or call the *Write Substitution* method in your page code. Both techniques require you to provide a method that ASP.NET will call to dynamically generate the output.

To use fragment caching, create a user control for the content to be cached and add the necessary controls and logic to the user control. Then configure the *PartialCaching* attribute in the class declaration or the *OutputCache* directive in the ASCX file. You can add *VaryBy Param* to cache different versions of a user control separately, based on specific page query parameters.

Whichever caching method you choose, you can use sliding expirations, absolute expirations, and dependencies to control how long the content is cached. Sliding expirations remove content from the cache when it has not been accessed in a specific amount of time. Absolute expiration removes content from the cache at a specific time, such as 20 minutes in the future. Dependencies remove content from the cache when a key, file, database, or other object is updated.

Objective Summary

- Objective 5.4 covers two types of monitoring: performance counters and event tracing. Performance counters are useful for monitoring numeric values revealing how the application is performing, and administrators can monitor it in real time, record it, or be notified when a counter reaches a threshold. Event tracing shows text information about an application's inner workings.

- You can configure ASP.NET applications to log messages generated by the standard *Trace.Write* and *Trace.Warn* methods. This can be useful for monitoring existing applications that use this tracing technique.

- Use caching to reduce the overhead of rendering ASP.NET pages. If you can cache an entire page, use page caching. If you can cache an entire page except for specific parts of it, use page caching with substitution. If you can only cache specific portions of a page, move those portions into user controls and use fragment caching.

Objective Review

Answer the following questions to test your knowledge of the information in this objective. You can find the answers to these questions and explanations of why each answer choice is correct or incorrect in the "Answers" section at the end of this chapter.

1. You are designing an ASP.NET application. One of the pages shows company news, which is read from a database. The news article being viewed is identified as part of the query string, such as http://contoso.com/news.aspx?id=8342. For a given ID, the page is exactly the same, regardless of which user views the page, or when they view it. You expect the page to be extremely busy after company announcements, and need to minimize the server processing time for each page load. Which technology should you recommend?

   A. Use the Application cache.

   B. Create a WCF service that caches database queries.

   C. Use fragment caching.

   D. Use page caching

2. You are designing an update to an MVC application. Systems administrators have requested greater insight into the inner workings of an application to assist them with occasional troubleshooting. For example, they would like to know when the application performs normal tasks, such as connecting to a database, as well as when errors occur, such as when a web service fails to respond. You need to minimize the performance impact. Which technology should you recommend?

   A. Use *Trace.Write* and *Trace.Warn*.

   B. Take advantage of Event Tracing for Windows.

   C. Create and update performance counters.

   D. Store the data in an XML file.

3. You are designing an ASP.NET application. Most of the content on the site is static; however, you will have a section along the side of each page containing dynamically generated, user-specific content. You want to use page caching and update the dynamic content as efficiently as possible. Which technology should you recommend?

   A. Place the content in a user control.

   B. Place the content in a *Placeholder* control.

   C. Place the content in an *UpdatePanel* control.

   D. Place the content in a *Substitution* control.

THOUGHT EXPERIMENT
Improving Insight into Application Performance

In the following thought experiment, you will apply what you've learned about the "Recommend an Approach to Performance Issues" objective to predict how a theoretical website architecture will perform. You can find answers to these questions in the "Answers" section at the end of this chapter.

You are the principal developer for Baldwin Museum of Science. The museum maintains a public web application with information about its exhibits. The application typically works well; however, when a newspaper published an article about one of the exhibits, hundreds of thousands of people visited the site over the weekend, and the application was unavailable for much of it. Systems administrators attempted to identify the cause of the problem, but they were unable to find it. The operating system's built-in performance counters showed normal levels of processor, memory, and disk utilization, and administrators found no related events in the event log.

Management would like to improve their insight into the performance of the application so that they can identify performance bottlenecks if the problem recurs. The developers have designed a solution with these features:

- The application will publish performance counter objects showing the number of unexpected exceptions (which are currently handled at the application layer).
- The application will add events to the event log when failures occur, such as a database server or web service that does not respond.

Management wants your opinion on the application design changes and whether they will meet their requirements. Answer the following questions about the future performance of the application:

1. How will systems administrators use the new error information?
2. Will the changes give enough information for administrators to identify when problems are about to occur? How can you test it?
3. Will the changes give enough information for developers to identify the problem? Why or why not?
4. Will the changes impact the performance of the application?
5. What would you add to the application to ensure systems administrators have the information they need to troubleshoot the problem?

Chapter Summary

- Black box testing verifies application functionality from the perspective of an end user or consuming application, whereas white box testing verifies that individual application components function as expected. The term "code coverage" refers to the portion of an application's code that is tested.

- Exception-handling strategies should log unexpected exceptions and present a friendly message to end users. You can process unhandled exceptions in several ways: *Page_Error* or *Page.ErrorPage* (for a single page) or *Application_Error*, and the Web.config file (for an entire application). Use the *HandleError* attribute to process unhandled exceptions in MVC applications.

- Debug deadlocks by examining separate processes in Visual Studio. Debug crashes and hangs by analyzing the memory dumps. Use the Fuslogvw.exe tool to debug assembly binding. To debug an application on a remote server, attach Visual Studio to that server process. To debug JavaScript, attach Visual Studio to Internet Explorer. Use the *DebuggerDisplay*, *DebuggerBrowsable*, and *DebuggerTypeProxy* attributes to customize how the Visual Studio debugger displays instances of custom classes during debugging.

- Use performance counters for monitoring numeric values, and use event tracing for monitoring messages. If you can cache an entire page, use page caching. If you can cache an entire page except for specific parts of it, use page caching with substitution. If you can cache only specific portions of a page, move those portions into user controls and use fragment caching.

Answers

Objective 5.1: Review

1. **Correct Answer:** A

   A. **Correct:** Because you have knowledge of the inner workings of an application with white box testing, you should create test cases that work as closely as possible to the code being tested. In this case, you need to test business rules, which are implemented as part of the application logic layer in the model.

   B. **Incorrect:** It would be possible to create test cases for business logic at the view level. By submitting data to views and examining the output, you could verify that the application logic was functioning correctly. If you were performing black box testing, you would need to do that because your only option would be to interact with the views. However, this scenario involves white box testing, and you should implement test cases as close to the code you are testing as possible.

   C. **Incorrect:** You should implement white box test cases as close to the code you are testing as possible. In this scenario, the model is closer than the controllers.

   D. **Incorrect:** The database does not implement the business rules. Therefore, you would not be able to test business rules using only the database.

2. **Correct Answer:** A

   A. **Correct:** When creating a black box test case, you do not have knowledge of the application's inner workings. Therefore, the test case must interact with the application as a user would—through the client browser. You can implement such test cases by using tools such as WatiN and Selenium.

   B. **Incorrect:** Although most applications implement data validation within the controller, black box testing does not have knowledge of the inner workings of an application. Therefore, you must perform the testing against the client browser.

   C. **Incorrect:** Some applications perform data validation within the data model itself. However, black box testing does not have knowledge of the inner workings of an application, including the structure and capabilities of the model.

   D. **Incorrect:** Black box testing does not have knowledge of how data is stored. Therefore, you could not communicate with the database.

3. **Correct Answer:** C

   A. **Incorrect:** In this scenario, the model does not perform any data validation.

   B. **Incorrect:** In this scenario, the view performs client-side data validation. However, because the purpose of the test case is to validate security, you must test the server-side data validation, which occurs in the controllers.

C. **Correct:** The controllers perform server-side data validation.

D. **Incorrect:** The database is responsible for authorizing users. However, it does not perform any data validation.

Objective 5.1: Thought Experiment

1. No. The team is performing only black box testing, which assumes no knowledge of the inner workings of the application.

2. Probably not. Black box testing does not indicate in which component an application failure occurred. White box testing would provide more useful information.

3. No, though 100 percent code coverage almost never occurs in the real world. To improve the code coverage, implement white box testing, especially unit tests (which developers can use as they write the code), performance testing, and API testing.

Objective 5.2: Review

1. **Correct Answer:** D

    A. **Incorrect:** This approach would process all unhandled exceptions in the same way, regardless of which controller generated them. Therefore, although it could be used to provide application-level exception handling, it cannot provide controller-level exception handling.

    B. **Incorrect:** Refer to the explanation for Answer A.

    C. **Incorrect:** Refer to the explanation for Answer A.

    D. **Correct:** The other approaches provide centralized exception management; however, they do not provide a technique for each controller to handle its own unhandled exceptions.

2. **Correct Answer:** C

    A. **Incorrect:** This approach requires developers to derive pages from the custom *Page* class.

    B. **Incorrect:** This approach overrides the default error message by showing users a custom error page.

    C. **Correct:** This approach runs the *Application_Error* method each time an unhandled exception occurs, without requiring page developers to follow any guidelines.

    D. **Incorrect:** This approach requires configuring each page.

3. **Correct Answer:** B

    A. **Incorrect:** A single *HandleError* attribute can be configured to only send errors to a single page.

    B. **Correct:** Use multiple *HandleError* attributes to direct users to different pages based on the exception type. Specify the *Order* property to prioritize different exception types.

    C. **Incorrect:** *Try/Catch* blocks reduce code readability.

    D. **Incorrect:** *Try/Catch* blocks reduce code readability.

Objective 5.2: Thought Experiment

1. No. First, they should remove the *Try/Catch* blocks surrounding every method. Exception-handling strategies typically suggest ignoring exceptions that you cannot remedy or add information to; the .NET Framework will pass the exception to the calling code. Second, they should update the Web.config file using <customErrors mode="RemoteOnly" defaultRedirect="Errors.aspx">. This will call Errors.aspx in the event of an unhandled exception. Finally, they should add code to the *Application_ Error* method to perform the event logging.

2. Because end users will see the message, Error.aspx should not show any information about the details of the error. Individual pages should catch errors that the user needs information about, such as insufficient privileges, and provide a useful message to the user.

3. Simply adding *Exception.ToString* should be sufficient, because that contains the exception's message and full stack trace. The message should allow systems administrators to determine if a resource is missing, and the stack trace will allow developers to identify where the error occurred.

Objective 5.3: Review

1. **Correct Answer:** D

    A. **Incorrect:** The FusLogVw tool is useful for examining assembly binding log files. Assembly binding would occur only in server-side code, and the problem described in the scenario is a client-side problem.

    B. **Incorrect:** The AdPlus tool is useful for creating memory dumps. When developing web applications, this is primarily useful for troubleshooting complex server-side problems. However, the problem described in the scenario is a client-side problem.

    C. **Incorrect:** The problem described in the scenario occurs within the client-side JavaScript. IIS runs only server-side code. Therefore, you cannot troubleshoot the problem by using IIS.

D. Correct: The problem is with the JavaScript menu system. Internet Explorer is responsible for running client-side JavaScript code. Therefore, to debug it, you must attach Visual Studio to the Internet Explorer process.

2. **Correct Answer:** C

   A. Incorrect: The FusLogVw tool is useful for examining assembly binding log files. You would use FusLogVw only if you had previously identified the problem as being related to assembly binding.

   B. Incorrect: The AdPlus tool is useful for creating memory dumps. When developing web applications, this is primarily useful for troubleshooting server-side problems that result in crashes or hangs. For less severe problems, including unhandled exceptions, you can simply attach Visual Studio to the remote IIS process.

   C. Correct: The problem described in the scenario occurs within the server-side MVC code on a remote server. To troubleshoot it, you must attach Visual Studio to the remote IIS process.

   D. Incorrect: You would attach to Internet Explorer only to troubleshoot client-side JavaScript code.

3. **Correct Answer:** B

   A. Incorrect: The FusLogVw tool is useful for examining assembly binding log files. You would use FusLogVw only if you had previously identified the problem as being related to assembly binding.

   B. Correct: The AdPlus tool is useful for creating memory dumps. When developing web applications, this is useful for troubleshooting server-side problems that result in crashes or hangs. After you create the memory dump, you can analyze it to better understand resource utilization at the time of the hang.

   C. Incorrect: You cannot troubleshoot hanging server-side applications using Visual Studio, because the application will not be responsive. Instead, you must create a memory dump file and then analyze that.

   D. Incorrect: You would attach to Internet Explorer only to troubleshoot client-side JavaScript code.

Objective 5.3: Thought Experiment

1. Maybe. Different platforms and browsers use different implementations of JavaScript. Therefore, it's possible for one browser to run JavaScript as expected while others experience problems. This approach will work only if the problem occurs in Internet Explorer. If, for example, the problem only occurs when using a non-Microsoft browser, you would need to troubleshoot the problem with that browser's debugging tools.

2. No. A better approach would be to create a memory dump using AdPlus, and then examine that memory dump using a tool such as DumpChk.

3. Yes, this approach should allow the developers to debug an unhandled exception on the remote IIS server.

Objective 5.4: Review

1. **Correct Answer:** D

   A. **Incorrect:** You could improve performance by storing news articles in the Application cache; however, page caching would work well for this scenario and provides better performance.

   B. **Incorrect:** You could improve performance by caching database query results; however, page caching would work well for this scenario and provides better performance.

   C. **Incorrect:** You could improve performance using fragment caching; however, page caching would work well for this scenario and provides better performance.

   D. **Correct:** Page caching stores a copy of an entire rendered page and serves it for subsequent requests without re-rendering the page. Page caching will provide the greatest performance. You will, however, have to specify the *VaryByParam* parameter to ensure each value for the ID query parameter is cached separately.

2. **Correct Answer:** B

   A. **Incorrect:** Standard ASP.NET tracing is not as flexible, nor as efficient, as Event Tracing for Windows.

   B. **Correct:** Event Tracing for Windows is perfect for the described scenario. Administrators can monitor ongoing events, including only the events at the warning level they want to see, with minimal ongoing performance impact to the application.

   C. **Incorrect:** Performance counters allow only for logging numeric data. They cannot easily be used to communicate events such as connecting to a database.

   D. **Incorrect:** Storing data to an XML file would be more difficult for the administrators to monitor. Additionally, it would have a more serious performance impact and require the developers to write more code.

3. **Correct Answer:** D

   A. **Incorrect:** If you place the dynamic content in a user control, you could use fragment caching and cache only the content in the user control. However, if you use page caching, the content in the user control would also be cached.

   B. **Incorrect:** Placeholder controls are useful for dynamically adding controls. However, they do not allow for adding dynamic content to a cached page.

C. **Incorrect:** UpdatePanel controls allow client-side JavaScript to update a page. However, they do not allow for adding dynamic content to a cached page

D. **Correct:** You can add a Substitution control to a cached page and specify a method that will generate HTML that ASP.NET will insert into the cached page at runtime.

Objective 5.4: Thought Experiment

1. They can monitor the performance counter in real time using the Performance Monitor snap-in. They could also create alerts so that they are notified if the performance counter reaches a certain threshold.

2. Maybe. Stress-testing might allow you to reproduce the problem and determine whether the performance counter correlates with impending failure.

3. Maybe. The performance counter will not provide any insight. However, the information in the event logs might be useful, if the problem happens to be related to what is added to the event log.

4. Yes. Adding events to the event log will impact the performance of the application. Whether that impact is noticeable depends on how many events are being added. The impact might even make the problem worse.

5. In this scenario, extensive use of Event Tracing for Windows would be useful. Trace the inner workings of the application at different levels, such as Verbose, Information, Warning, and Error. Administrators and developers can use different tools to consume the traces and get the detailed information they need for future troubleshooting.

CHAPTER 6

Designing a Deployment Strategy

W eb applications are deployed many different times throughout their life cycle. Typically, you deploy them to a staging server for testing, and then to the production environment. Each time you release a new version of the application, you must deploy it to these environments again.

Each environment has different requirements. For example, production environments typically use Internet Information Services (IIS) instead of the Microsoft Visual Studio Development Server, and you should not allow debugging in a production environment.

A good deployment strategy also accommodates an application's growth, known as *scalability*, and its uptime, known as *reliability*. Planning for changes to scalability and reliability requirements in advance can make it much easier to accommodate that growth.

After web applications have been deployed, most organizations rely on a systems administration team to monitor and troubleshoot them. To provide the team with the information it needs, you can use ASP.NET Health Monitoring, which provides flexible tools for logging events and notifying systems administrators of critical situations.

Objectives in this chapter:

- Objective 6.1: Design a deployment process
- Objective 6.2: Design configuration management
- Objective 6.3: Plan for scalability and reliability
- Objective 6.4: Design a health-monitoring strategy

Objective 6.1: Design a Deployment Process

Web applications are rarely just a collection of files; they include connection settings, databases, certificates, and a web server configuration. As a result, deploying a web application is rarely as simple as copying files.

Because updating a web application does not require changing the configuration of client computers, developers tend to update web applications more frequently. Each deployment might involve updating test servers, staging servers, and multiple production servers. Combined, these factors mean web developers can spend a great deal of time deploying applications, so it is important to design an efficient and reliable deployment process.

This objective covers how to:
- Describe deployment methods.
- Prevent applications from being updated.
- Deploy applications as a single assembly.

Understanding Deployment Methods

Today, using web packages is the preferred method for deploying web applications. Some organizations will have an infrastructure in place that might make one of the other deployment techniques simpler, however.

Use XCopy deployment or the Copy Web tool when you make frequent changes to an application and the application does not need to be precompiled. Use the Publish Web Site tool when you need to precompile the website or web application; doing so helps you to avoid storing the source code on the web server and avoid the delay for the first request when the web server dynamically compiles the application. Create a Windows Installer package only when the organization's software deployment techniques require it.

The sections that follow describe each of these deployment methods at a high level.

Creating Web Packages

Web packaging creates a .zip file that contains all the content required to deploy your web application, including the ASPX pages, code files, images, style sheets, JavaScript, databases, IIS configuration settings, security settings, and more. Web packages also include a .cmd file that installs the application on a new web server. Because web packages are simple to deploy, you can create a web package and send it to systems administrators to install on a web server with little risk that configuration problems will occur.

You can create packages in several ways:

- Directly from Visual Studio
- Using the MSBuild tool, available from the Visual Studio command prompt or from within your %windir%\Microsoft.NET\Framework\<*version*>\ folder
- Exporting a website directly from IIS Manager, as described at *http://learn.iis.net/page. aspx/514/export-a-package-through-iis-manager/*

You can use Visual Studio to create deployment packages that automatically configure a web server and copy files to it. In Solution Explorer, right-click your solution, and then click Properties. The properties page includes two tabs for configuring deployment settings: Package/Publish Web (as shown in Figure 6-1) and Package/Publish SQL. The most important settings are accessible by using these tabs; however, other settings can be changed only by directly editing the Visual Studio project file.

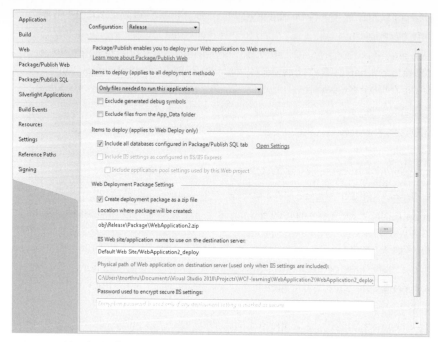

FIGURE 6-1 Use the Package/Publish Web page to configure deployment settings

After creating a web deployment package, you can deploy it to a web server with the Web Deployment tool (also known as Web Deploy or MsDeploy.exe) installed. Web Deploy is available at *http://www.iis.net/download/WebDeploy*. On servers running IIS 6.0, you need to start the Web Deployment Agent Service. On servers running IIS 7.0, you need to start the Web Management Service.

> **MORE INFO** **WEB DEPLOY**
>
> For more information, read "Introducing Web Deploy" at *http://go.microsoft. com/?linkid=9278654*.

After the server is configured, you can install the package in several different ways:

- Run the .cmd file.
- Manually run the Web Deploy tool from the command line, and specify the package to be installed.
- Import the package using the Import Application command IIS Manager.

Deploying Applications with XCopy

The term "XCopy deployment" refers to simply copying all of a web application's files to a web server. XCopy is a tool built into Microsoft Windows that copies files from either a command prompt or a script. Although XCopy is one of the best ways to reliably copy files, you can use any file copy tool to deploy a web application, including Windows Explorer, FTP, and RoboCopy (discussed later).

Because you are simply copying files, an XCopy deployment does not configure the server in any way. Therefore, when using XCopy deployment to a production server you must manually complete the following tasks:

- Configure the web application in IIS.
- Alter the web.config file to disable debugging and prevent users from accessing the trace.axd file.
- Change connection strings to connect to production databases.
- Make any other changes to prepare the application for a production environment.

Although XCopy is the simplest deployment method, it is often more error-prone than other methods. For example, if you forget to disable debugging, you might expose your production application to additional security vulnerabilities.

XCopy is most useful when deploying a simple web application to a large number of servers. After you have prepared the application to be run in a production environment, you can write a script using XCopy that copies the application to all the servers at once.

As an alternative to XCopy, consider the RoboCopy tool, which is included with Windows Vista, Windows 7, and Windows Server 2008. Although it's functionally similar to XCopy, you can use the */Purge* parameter to remove files from the destination that no longer exist at the source. Without that feature, old files that you are no longer maintaining might remain indefinitely on your production web server, perhaps introducing security vulnerabilities.

For web applications, you can also perform an XCopy-style deployment by using the Publish Web tool and selecting File System from the Publish Method list. For websites, use the Copy Web tool, which supports synchronization of changed and removed files.

XCopy deployments are not precompiled. When you copy files to a web server, the web server automatically compiles them the first time a user requests a page—a process that usually takes less than a second. Although the compile time is not typically a problem, relying on the web server to compile the application means that it is possible for compilation to fail because of a missing file or mistyped word.

Publishing Web Applications

Web publishing compiles an application into assemblies and then copies the assemblies to a remote sever without first creating a web package. Because web publishing compiles the application, there is no risk that compilation will fail after deployment. To use web publishing, the web server must be configured to accept Web Deploy requests.

The quickest way to deploy a web application is by using the Publish Web tool, as shown in Figure 6-2.

FIGURE 6-2 Use the Publish Web tool to deploy an application directly to a server

Creating Windows Installer Packages

You can deploy web applications by using a Windows Installer (MSI) package in the same way that Windows applications are traditionally deployed. Deploying with Windows Installer is ideal for enterprise environments that use Active Directory software distribution to deploy applications to web servers.

When you create a Windows Installer package, Visual Studio precompiles the application. To create a Windows Installer package for a web application, add the Web Setup Project template (located within Other Project Types\Setup And Deployment\Visual Studio Installer) to your solution. Then add the web application project output to the setup project, along with any other required components.

When you build a Web Setup Project, it automatically creates a Setup.exe file that administrators can use to manually install the application. After the installation, administrators can easily uninstall the application using the Control Panel.

Preventing Websites and Applications from Being Updated

You can use the ASP.NET Compilation Tool (Aspnet_Compiler.exe) to manually precompile a web application from the Visual Studio 2010 command prompt. In addition to the standard updateable precompilation, You can use the ASP.NET Compilation Tool to perform non-updateable precompilation, which prevents administrators from modifying any file. Non-updateable precompiled applications include separate ASPX pages; however, those pages are used only as placeholders for configuring file permissions; they cannot be updated. To perform a non-updateable precompilation, simply omit the –u parameter.

For ASP.NET websites, you can prevent precompiled sites from being updated by clearing the Allow This Precompiled Site To Be Updateable check box on the MSBuild Options tab of the project property pages dialog box. The same check box is available in the Publish Web Site dialog box.

For ASP.NET web applications, you can manually compile the application with the ASP.NET Compilation Tool or use the Visual Studio 2010 Web Deployment Projects. Although Web Deployment Projects was included with Visual Studio 2005 and Visual Studio 2008, it must be downloaded and installed separately for Visual Studio 2010. After it is installed, you can select Add Web Deployment Project from the Build menu. Edit the new project's properties to clear the Allow This Precompiled Site To Be Updateable check box.

Deploying Applications as a Single Assembly

Another important capability provided by Web Deployment Projects is the ability to compile applications into a single DLL. Figure 6-3 shows the Output Assemblies tab of a Web Deployment Project's property pages. You can select Merge All Outputs To A Single Assembly or choose to create separate assemblies for individual pages, controls, and folders.

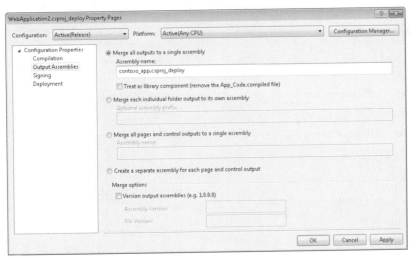

FIGURE 6-3 Compiling an application into a single assembly

The Web Deployment Projects add-on also includes the Aspnet_Merge.exe command-line tool, which you can use to combine the output from Aspnet_Compile.exe into a single assembly.

> **MORE INFO**   **INSTALLING WEB DEPLOYMENT PROJECTS FOR VISUAL STUDIO 2010**
>
> To install Web Deployment Projects, visit *http://www.microsoft.com/download/en/details.aspx?displaylang=en&id=24509*.

Objective Summary

- You can deploy applications in four different ways: creating web packages, using XCopy, publishing the web application, or creating a Windows Installer package. Whenever possible, create a web package.

- To prevent applications from being updated, clear the Allow This Precompiled Site To Be Updateable check box on the MSBuild Options tab of the project property pages dialog box or the Publish Web Site dialog box. If you manually compile the application, omit the *–u* parameter.

- To deploy an application as a single assembly, add a Web Deployment Project to your solution and select Merge All Outputs To A Single Assembly. Alternatively, use the Aspnet_Merge.exe command-line tool.

Objective Review

Answer the following questions to test your knowledge of the information in this objective. You can find the answers to these questions and explanations of why each answer choice is correct or incorrect in the "Answers" section at the end of this chapter.

1. You are planning the deployment of a new ASP.NET web application. The application is going to be deployed to an untrusted web hosting provider, and you must not deploy source code. Also, you must prevent the application from being updated. Which approaches could you recommend? (Choose all that apply. Each answer forms a complete solution.)

    A. Use the Publish Web tool.

    B. Use the ASP.NET Compilation Tool.

    C. Create a web deployment package.

    D. Create a Web Deployment Project.

2. You are planning the deployment of a new ASP.NET web application. You want to deploy the application as a single DLL. Which approach should you recommend?

   A. Use the Publish Web tool.

   B. Use the ASP.NET Compilation Tool.

   C. Create a web deployment package.

   D. Create a Web Deployment Project.

3. You are planning the deployment of a new ASP.NET web application to several servers running IIS 7.5. Because the web servers are protected by firewalls, you need to send the application to systems administrators for installation. You need to deploy a Microsoft SQL Server Express Edition database with the application. Which approach should you recommend?

   A. Use the Publish Web tool.

   B. Use the ASP.NET Compilation Tool.

   C. Create a web deployment package.

   D. Create a Web Deployment Project.

THOUGHT EXPERIMENT
Designing a Deployment Process

In the following thought experiment, you will apply what you've learned about the "Design a Deployment Process" objective to predict how a theoretical website architecture will perform. You can find answers to these questions in the "Answers" section at the end of this chapter.

You are a consultant for Lucerne Publishing. Lucerne consists of 20 smaller publishers with separate offices around the world. Each office has its own IT staff and web hosting infrastructure.

Recently, Lucerne began developing a new ASP.NET web application that includes a SQL Server Express Edition database. Lucerne plans to allow each office to deploy it to its own web hosting environment. The company is currently planning its deployment strategy and would like your opinion on the design.

The developers have designed a deployment strategy with these attributes:

- They will create a staging server on the corporate intranet.

- They will publish the web application and database to the staging server.

- They will grant each office access to the web application's folder on the server's file system.

Answer the following questions about the future performance of the application:

1. Will other offices be able to download the web application?

2. After downloading the web application, will it be easy to copy it to the company's web hosting provider? Why or why not?

3. What approach would you recommend to simplify redeploying the application to different hosting providers?

Objective 6.2: Design Configuration Management

Web applications require both developers and systems administrators to configure many different settings, including settings for connection strings, debugging, and error handling. Although most settings can be defined by using the web.config file, other settings must be configured within IIS. To make matters more complex, most environments require different settings for development, staging, and production.

This objective describes how to plan configuration management for the entire life cycle of an application.

This objective covers how to:

- Describe the configuration hierarchy.
- Use the *ConfigSource* attribute.
- Modify configuration files for different environments.
- Describe the differences between IIS and the Visual Studio Development Server.
- Configure application pools.
- Migrate between different versions of the .NET Framework.

Understanding the Configuration Hierarchy

For many simple applications, the only configuration file you need to modify is the web.config file. The .NET Framework also provides hierarchical configuration, as shown in Figure 6-4.

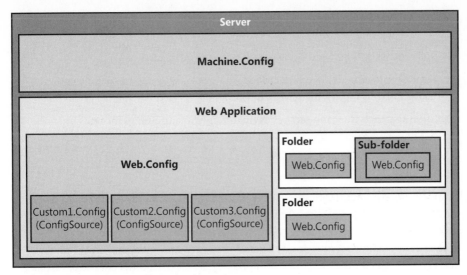

FIGURE 6-4 The ASP.NET configuration hierarchy

The .NET Framework determines an application's configuration by applying settings in the following sequence. Settings applied later can override settings applied earlier.

1. The Machine.Config file, which applies to all applications on a server. Typically, you should not modify this file.

2. The root web.config file, which applies to an entire application.

3. Custom configuration files for specific settings, as defined by the *ConfigSource* attribute (described in the next section).

4. The web.config files contained in application subfolders, which apply only to that folder and any of its subfolders.

Applications inherit the default settings defined in the Machine.config file. Any settings in the web.config file override settings in the Machine.config file. Similarly, subfolders within the application inherit the settings from the root web.config file. However, if a subfolder has any settings defined in its own web.config file, that local file overrides the parent's settings.

> **MORE INFO** **ASP.NET CONFIGURATION AND INHERITANCE**
>
> For more information, read "ASP.NET Configuration Scenarios" at *http://msdn.microsoft.com/library/dtbwsx8s.aspx*.

Using the *ConfigSource* Attribute

Rather than storing all configuration information in the web.config file, you can store individual sections in separate files. You might want to do this for several reasons:

- To delegate privileges to an administrator to modify specific configuration settings without granting rights to the entire web.config file.

- To distribute changes to one section of the file by copying over an entire .config file, without affecting other settings.

- To make it easier for administrators to find specific configuration settings by storing them in separate files.

- To modify configuration settings without restarting the application, which happens automatically when the web.config file is modified. If you want ASP.NET to restart the application when an administrator changes a custom configuration file, set the *RestartOnExternalChanges* property to *true*.

To store settings in a separate file, add the configuration element to the web.config file, but specify only the *configSource* property with the configuration file name, as this example shows:

```
<configuration>
    <system.web>
        <authentication configSource="authentication.config"/>
    </system.web>
</configuration>
```

Modifying Configuration Files for Different Environments

As discussed in Objective 6.1, applications often require different settings for development, staging, and production environments. Configuration transforms are the simplest way to provide support for using different configuration settings in different environments.

For example, most developers need tracing and debugging enabled in a test environment, but these settings can introduce a security vulnerability in a production environment. You can automate modifying these configuration settings by using web.config transformation.

EXAM TIP

You don't need to memorize the transform syntax. Instead, you need to understand the capabilities of transforms and recognize the scenarios in which they would be useful.

When you create a new web application, Visual Studio automatically generates two transform files for you: Web.Debug.config and Web.Release.config. You can access either of these files from Solution Explorer by expanding the web.config file.

To understand how you can use transform files, consider a web application in a development environment that shows detailed error messages. You could use the following transform file to automatically modify the web.config file so that it displays a custom error message to users not logged on to the web server. Notice that the *<customErrors>* element includes the property *xdt:Transform="Replace"*. This indicates that ASP.NET will remove the entire *<customErrors>* element from the web.config file and add the specified element in its place. The *Transform* attribute could also be set to *Insert*, *InsertBefore*, *InsertAfter*, *Remove*, *RemoveAll*, *RemoveAttributes*, and *SetAttributes*.

```
<?xml version="1.0"?>
<configuration xmlns:xdt="http://schemas.microsoft.com/XML-Document-Transform">
  <system.web>
    <customErrors defaultRedirect="MyError.aspx"
      mode="RemoteOnly" xdt:Transform="Replace">
    </customErrors>
  </system.web>
</configuration>
```

Transformations can do more than simply replace configuration elements by name. One of the most flexible capabilities is the *Locator* attribute, which allows you to replace, remove, or update elements that match an expression. For example, the following transform file replaces the *connectionString* and *providerName* attributes of a connection string with a name attribute of *"csName"* or a *providerName* attribute of *"csProvider"*:

```
<?xml version="1.0"?>
<configuration xmlns:xdt="http://schemas.microsoft.com/XML-Document-Transform">
  <connectionStrings>
    <add name="AWLT" connectionString="newConnectionString"
      providerName="newProviderName"
      xdt:Transform="Replace"
      xdt:Locator="Condition(@name=csName'
        or @providerName='csProvider')" />
  </connectionStrings>
</configuration>
```

The following example demonstrates just the *Locator* clause you might use to replace an element using an XPath expression:

```
xdt:Locator="XPath(configuration/connectionStrings[@name='csName'
  or @providerName='System.Data.SqlClient'])" />
```

> **MORE INFO**   **USING TRANSFORMS**
>
> For complete details, read "web.config Transformation Syntax for Web Application Project Deployment" at *http://msdn.microsoft.com/library/dd465326.aspx*.

Comparing IIS to the Visual Studio Development Server

To simplify the testing of a web application, Visual Studio debugs web applications that you create using the Visual Studio Development Server (VSDS). Although it is convenient, the VSDS differs in several important ways from IIS, which hosts most production ASP.NET applications:

- **Hostnames and ports**   VSDS uses nonstandard port numbers (http://localhost:61888), while most IIS servers use the HTTP standard port 80 (http://www.contoso.com). The difference is visible in the browser address bar. This will not cause any problems unless you specify the hostname in paths. For instructions on how to change the port number, read "How to: Specify a Port for the Development Server" at *http://msdn.microsoft. com/library/ms178109.aspx.*

- **Paths**   VSDS might host your application in a subfolder with the application name such as http://localhost:61888/MyApplication/. Most IIS servers host different applications at the root of websites with different hostnames, such as http://myapplication. contoso.com. This difference means that absolute paths that work in VSDS might not work in IIS. To work around this problem, use relative paths (such as ../images/logo.jpg) or code resource paths with a tilde (such as ~/images/logo.jpg).

- **System privileges**   VSDS uses your account privileges, while an ASP.NET application running within IIS has the privileges assigned to the application pool. ASP.NET will throw security exceptions for missing privileges, so test all features with an application running on an IIS server configured identically to the production environment.

- **Database access**   VSDS usually authenticates to databases using your Windows account. When you are running the application in IIS, Windows Integrated authentication will use the application pool account, such as ASPNET or the Network Services account.

- **Resource authorization**   Although VSDS protects all file types using ASP.NET, an IIS server does not process all file types with ASP.NET by default. Therefore, any security settings applied within the application itself, such as requiring forms authentication, apply only to ASP.NET file types, including .aspx, .asmx, and .config. In IIS, application security will not protect images files, JavaScript files, style sheets, and any other file type not associated with ASP.NET.

- **Code access security**   Depending on how administrators have configured it, IIS might assign your application a lower level of trust. If an application feature requires a higher level of trust, ASP.NET will throw a security exception.

Because of these differences, you might consider installing IIS on your local computer instead of using VSDS for development. IIS requires more configuration, but using IIS during development reduces the opportunity for compatibility problems during deployment.

MORE INFO **CONFIGURING IIS**

For more information, read "Walkthrough: Creating a Local IIS Web Site in Visual Studio" at *http://msdn.microsoft.com/library/a1zz9df4.aspx.*

Configuring Application Pools

Application pools, as introduced in Objective 4.1, configure the user and security context for a web application. By placing multiple applications in a single application pool, they have the ability to share resources. By placing applications into separate application pools, you minimize the risk that failing, compromised, or resource-intensive applications will affect other applications.

For the 70-519 exam, you do not need to know step-by-step how to configure application pools. Instead, you should understand the types of configuration changes for which you can use an application pool, including the following:

- Creating a new application pool to minimize the impact of a poorly behaved application on other applications.

- Changing the user account and security context of the web application, which is useful for limiting the privileges an application has and for granting an application access to remote resources.

- Configuring the version of the .NET Framework an application uses. This is important if you need to upgrade an application to .NET 4.0 from an earlier version.

- Choosing between integrated and classic pipeline mode. Classic pipeline mode behaves like IIS 6.0, which uses ISAPI to pass requests only for files with ASP.NET file extensions (such as .aspx) to ASP.NET. All non-ASP.NET files are handled directly by IIS. Integrated pipeline mode sends all file requests to ASP.NET, allowing ASP.NET authorization to apply to non-ASP.NET files (such as static files and images), allows ASP.NET to rewrite URLs, and much more. Integrated pipeline mode typically performs better.

- Changing how often the application restarts, based on a time interval, specific times of day, or memory consumption.

- Changing how long IIS waits for an application to shut down or start up. Applications that cannot start up or shut down within a specified amount of time might not be able to access important resources, such as a database or web service, and the process of starting up or shutting down can unnecessarily consume server resources.

- Configuring processor limits based on the maximum percentage of processor time or which processor cores the application can use.

- On 64-bit servers, choosing whether 32-bit applications are allowed to run.

- Configuring rapid-fail protection, which prevents an application from failing repeatedly in a limited amount of time.

- Configuring how frequently worker processes are pinged to verify they are still responding correctly.

> *NOTE* **CONFIGURING IIS 6.0 APPLICATION POOLS ON IIS 7.0 AND IIS 7.5**
>
> If you create a web application for IIS 6.0 and the installer uses the IIS 6.0 Metabase API to assign or create application pools, you need to enable IIS 6.0 compatibility to use the existing installer on a server running IIS 7.0 or IIS 7.5. In Windows Vista and Windows 7, the Windows Feature is Internet Information Services\Web Management Tools\IIS 6 Management Compatibility\IIS Metabase And IIS 6 Configuration Compatibility. In Windows Server 2008 R2, add the IIS 6 Management Compatibility\IIS 6 Metabase Compatibility role service to the Web Server role.

Migrating Between Different Versions of the .NET Framework

The first time you open a web application created for an earlier version of the .NET Framework in Visual Studio, the Visual Studio Conversion Wizard will prompt you to migrate the application to .NET 4.0. You can make the configuration changes yourself by adjusting several settings in the application's web.config file:

- In the *configSections* section, remove the *system.web.extensions* element.

- In the *system.web* section, remove every <compilation><add> element that refers to an assembly of the .NET Framework.

- Set the target version of the .NET Framework to the <compilation> element, which should resemble <compilation targetFramework="4.0">.

- Optionally, add the *controlRenderingCompatibilityVersion* attribute to the <pages> section, and set it to 3.5. The .NET 4.0 includes several improvements to how controls are rendered to make them compliant with the latest HTML standards. Most web applications will benefit from these improvements; however, if you experience problems with the appearance of some controls, setting *controlRenderingCompatibilityVersion* to 3.5 can fix them.

> *MORE INFO* **UPGRADING A WEB APPLICATION TO .NET 4.0**
>
> For more information, read "How to: Upgrade an ASP.NET Web Application to ASP.NET 4" at *http://msdn.microsoft.com/library/dd483478.aspx*.

Objective Summary

- The .NET Framework configuration hierarchy begins with the machine.config file, which defines default settings. Individual applications each have a web.config file, and folders within an application can have individual web.config files that apply only to that folder and its subfolders.

- If you need to move settings to a separate file, either to prevent the application from automatically restarting when it is edited or to delegate privileges, you can define the *ConfigSource* attribute.

- Use configuration transforms to automatically publish different configuration settings to different environments.

- The Visual Studio Development Server that you use to debug your application during development works differently than IIS, which your application will probably use in the production environment. The most important differences are the hostname and URL, database access, and security.

- Configuration pools, a feature of IIS, control many aspects of an application's behavior. You might have to create a new application pool to isolate an application, run an application with different privileges, or run an application in a different version of the .NET Framework.

- When migrating between different versions of the .NET Framework, there are several configuration settings you might need to change. Most importantly, you might need to set the *controlRenderingCompatibilityVersion* attribute to preserve or update how controls are formatted.

Objective Review

Answer the following questions to test your knowledge of the information in this objective. You can find the answers to these questions and explanations of why each answer choice is correct or incorrect in the "Answers" section at the end of this chapter.

1. You are planning to deploy a new .NET 4.0 web application to a web server running IIS 7.5. Currently, the web server has several .NET 2.0 applications running on it, and those applications have not been tested with the .NET Framework. How can you deploy the new application to minimize the risk of affecting the existing applications?

   A. Add the new application to the existing application pool, but update the application pool to .NET 4.0.

   B. Add the new application to a new application pool.

   C. Configure the application pool to use classic pipeline mode.

   D. Configure the new application with a separate web.config file.

2. You are planning to deploy a new .NET 4.0 web application developed on your local computer to a staging environment for testing. After the quality assurance team approves the application in the staging environment, you need to deploy it to the production environment. The staging and production environments should not display detailed error messages or allow tracing. Additionally, they each require different connection strings than you use on your local computer. You will need to deploy the application multiple times to each environment, and you want to minimize the effort required with each deployment. Which solution do you recommend? (Choose all that apply. Each answer forms part of the complete solution.)

   A. Set the <customError> mode to *RemoteOnly*.

   B. Use the *ConfigSource* attribute to store the connection strings in a separate file.

   C. Edit the Web.Release.config file.

   D. Create a Web.Staging.config transform file.

3. You are planning to deploy a new .NET 4.0 web application. The systems administration management has described that they have a separate group who administers databases and database-related settings, and that this group should be able to change the connection strings for the application but not modify other settings. The new application stores the connection strings in the web.config file. Which solution do you recommend? (Choose all that apply. Each answer forms part of the complete solution.)

   A. Move the setting to a separate .config file.

   B. Create a new transform file for the production environment.

   C. Grant the database administrator read-only privileges to the web.config file and write privileges to the new file.

   D. In the web.config file, specify the new file using the *ConfigSource* attribute.

THOUGHT EXPERIMENT
Designing Configuration Management

I n the following thought experiment, you will apply what you've learned about the "Design Configuration Management" objective to predict how a theoretical website architecture will perform. You can find answers to these questions in the "Answers" section at the end of this chapter.

You are a consultant for Woodgrove Bank. Woodgrove is planning a new public web application. Because the reliability of the application is critical, Woodgrove has created a plan for testing the application in a staging environment prior to deploying it to the production environment. Every month, new features will be copied from the development environment to the staging environment. After testing, the updated application will be copied from the staging environment to the production environment.

The development and staging environments are both hosted on the same server running IIS 7.5. The production environment is on a separate server connected directly to the Internet, also running IIS 7.5.

For testing in the staging environment, the application must connect to an internal database containing sample data. In the production environment, it will connect to an internal database with real customer data. Occasionally, quality assurance (QA) team members need to change the connection string of the staging server to connect it to a different database.

The development team has designed a configuration management methodology with these attributes:

- Developers will create transform files to modify the connection strings when publishing the application to the staging and production environments.
- QA team members will be granted access to modify the web.config file in the staging environment.

Management wants your opinion on the configuration management design. Answer the following questions about the future performance of the application:

1. Will this approach allow us to publish different database configurations to the different environments? Why or why not?

2. In the past, a QA team member accidentally changed an unrelated setting in the web.config file when he was updating the connection string. That mistake cost almost a day of work, because the team thought the problem was caused by the developers. Is there a way we can minimize the risk of QA team members changing settings they do not need to edit?

3. In the past, errors in the code published to the development environment caused failures in the staging environment, again causing the QA team to waste their time attempting to identify an error in the staging environment. Is there a way we can minimize the risk of that happening again?

Objective 6.3: Plan for Scalability and Reliability

Public web applications and intranet applications for large enterprises often need to scale to support thousands of requests per minute. Critical applications such as these also require a high level of reliability. Fortunately, the .NET Framework, IIS, and Microsoft SQL Server are all designed to support both scalability and reliability.

This objective provides an overview of how to scale your application by using performance tuning or by scaling server hardware.

This objective covers how to:

- Scale web applications up and out.
- Describe the benefits of moving an application to the cloud.
- Load test an application to identify bottlenecks and peak capacity.
- Use queuing to provide asynchronous request handling and prioritization.
- Performance-tune an application.

Scaling Web Applications

Scaling up and scaling out are two different ways to meet increased capacity requirements, and they each have their own advantages. Scaling up, which involves upgrading existing servers, keeps the architecture simple and minimizes hardware costs, setup time, and management time. Scaling up limits you to the performance of a single server, however, and becomes increasingly expensive the further you have to scale. Scaling out, which involves adding more servers, provides unlimited scalability and adds failover to keep the application available in the event of a hardware failure. As you scale out, the cost increases are more linear. The additional complexity of scaling out greatly increases setup and maintenance costs, however.

Before studying this section, review "Mapping the Logical Design to the Physical Implementation" in Objective 1.2.

Figure 6-5 illustrates the difference between the two approaches. The subjects that follow describe each in more detail.

Scaling Up

The term *scaling up* refers to upgrading individual servers with faster storage subsystems, more memory, and additional processors. For most applications, scaling up (also known as scaling vertically) is the most cost-effective way to meet capacity requirements, because it does not require any software changes or additional infrastructure.

Note that scaling up does not require all services to run on a single server. You can still use the multiple-server model described in Objective 1.2 by placing the presentation, logic, and data tiers on separate servers. In practice, this typically means separating the web server and database server onto different computers. As your capacity requirements increase, you can upgrade the individual servers, or replace the servers with more powerful hardware.

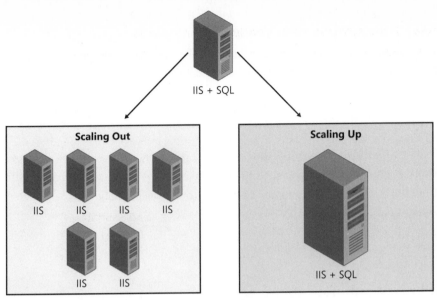

FIGURE 6-5 Growing a website by scaling out or scaling up

Scaling up is a convenient way to handle gradual growth because improvements in technology over time lead to more powerful servers. For example, if you require a single high-end server to meet your current capacity requirements and know that the load on the server will double over the next five years, you can simply plan to replace the server in five years with a future high-end server (which is bound to be several times more powerful than a current high-end server).

Scaling Out

The term *scaling out* refers to adding multiple servers to a single role. In practice, scaling out (also known as scaling horizontally) is most often implemented by deploying multiple web servers and a load-balancing mechanism to distribute requests between the web servers.

Commonly used load-balancing mechanisms include:

- **Round-robin DNS** The easiest, least expensive, and most common load-balancing mechanism. Simply specify multiple IP addresses for the web server hostname, and browsers will connect to any of the listed IP addresses. If the first IP address a browser attempts to connect to does not respond, the browser will try the next IP address in the list until a server responds. Therefore, round-robin DNS also provides for failover if a single server fails.

- **Hardware load balancers** You can purchase load balancers that you connect between the client and the server. Configure the website's hostname with the load balancer's IP address, and configure each web server with a unique, internal IP address. The load balancer will accept all requests from clients and forward them to one of the servers on the internal network. Although load balancers have widely varying features, many load balancers can efficiently balance the load between servers by monitoring the server response time and utilization. Some routers have this capability built in. Hardware load balancers can stop sending requests to a failed server, thus providing failover.

- **Software load balancers**   Many software products, including Microsoft Forefront Threat Management Gateway 2010, use software to perform the same capabilities of hardware load balancers. Software load balancers often integrate more tightly with the operating system and application by monitoring the usage of individual servers and sending requests to the server with the most capacity. Additionally, software load balancers can be managed like servers, which reduces maintenance costs for some organizations.

- **Network load balancing (NLB)**   Windows Server 2008 R2 includes NLB, which is a type of software load balancer that can distribute incoming requests between multiple servers without requiring a separate server.

> **MORE INFO   NETWORK LOAD-BALANCING SOFTWARE**
>
> For more information, read "Overview of Network Load Balancing" at *http://technet. microsoft.com/library/cc725691.aspx* and "Microsoft Forefront TMG – Webserver Load Balancing" at *http://www.isaserver.org/tutorials/microsoft-forefront-tmg-webserver-load-balancing.html.*

Because scaling out uses multiple servers to provide a single service, the service might be able to continue to function if a single server fails. Remember to test the failover mechanism thoroughly and verify that clients with existing connections to the failed server are success-fully redirected to a functioning server. Redundancy also requires that the application be able to meet peak capacity requirements with at least one server failed; therefore, providing redundancy requires you to deploy at least one additional server beyond that required to meet your peak capacity requirements.

When scaling out to increase reliability, strive to eliminate all single points of failure. For example, avoid connecting all web servers to a single network switch. Depending on your redundancy requirements, you might need to deploy your application to multiple data centers in different geographic locations and implement load balancing between those data centers.

The biggest challenge of scaling out is keeping multiple servers synchronized. First, you must ensure that the web application files and settings (including SSL certificates) are syn-chronized. You can use Web Deploy to synchronize two web servers running IIS 6.0, IIS 7.0, or IIS 7.5. If you synchronize between different versions of IIS, always sync from the earlier version to the newer version.

> **MORE INFO**   SYNCHRONIZING WEB SERVERS
>
> For detailed steps, read "Synchronize IIS 6.0 Web Sites" at *http://learn.iis.net/page. aspx/445/synchronize-iis-60-web-sites/* or "Synchronize IIS 7" at *http://learn.iis.net/page. aspx/446/synchronize-iis-7/*. You can automate the process of synchronizing servers by using the Web Farm Framework for IIS 7.0. For more information and to download it, visit *http://www.iis.net/download/WebFarmFramework*.

Second, you might need to ensure that all web servers share session state. As discussed in Objective 1.5, you can do this by storing state information in a SQL Server database or a separate state server. If your plan includes avoiding single points of failure, use clustering to provide redundancy the state server. Synchronizing session state is not always required. You will not need to synchronize session state if any of the following scenarios apply:

- Your application does not rely on session state. Storing session information in client-side cookies and never using the *Session* object helps you to avoid relying on session state.

- Your load-balancing technology ensures server affinity, sending subsequent requests from a single client to the same server in the web farm. Server affinity can slightly decrease the effectiveness of load balancing. Round-robin DNS provides server affinity automatically.

EXAM TIP

Remember that using session state with load-balanced web servers requires either a shared state server or server affinity. Using both together is unnecessary.

As discussed in Objective 1.2, scaling out increases the capacity of your web application, but it often decreases performance. By placing the web server, database server, and state server on separate computers, requests have to traverse the network, which adds milliseconds of latency. In other words, application responsiveness for a single user is typically better for applications that are scaled up rather than scaled out.

> **MORE INFO**   COMPARING COSTS
>
> When comparing the costs of scaling up and scaling out, consider software licenses and electricity costs, as well. For specific examples, read "Scaling Up vs. Scaling Out: Hidden Costs" at *http://www.codinghorror.com/blog/2009/06/scaling-up-vs-scaling-out-hidden-costs.html*.

Moving to the Cloud

One of the most exciting trends in web application development is to move applications into the cloud. The "cloud" refers to a group of networked servers, usually connected to the Internet, that are available to process your application requests.

The traditional web hosting model runs your application on a single web server. If you use a shared hosting model, many other web applications are running on the same server. If you use a dedicated hosting model, only your applications run on that server. Nonetheless, scalability is limited by the performance of that server, and if the server fails, your application fails, too.

The cloud hosting model runs your application on any of many different virtual servers in the hosted cloud. The hosting provider is typically responsible for determining which server or servers run your application. If your application is not busy, your application might be running on only one or two servers. If your application gets busier, the cloud hosting provider can automatically distribute your application to dozens or hundreds of servers, and those servers might be located in different data centers.

Perhaps the greatest advantage of cloud computing is the ability to easily scale down. With a traditional hosting model, you need to deploy enough hardware for your application's peak capacity, even though you might only require that peak capacity one or two times per year. Typically, the hosting provider charges you a flat monthly rate (with varying fees for the bandwidth you use). During quieter times, you pay the same monthly rate and still need to manage the unneeded hardware. With cloud hosting, the cloud hosting provider automatically scales your application down and charges you only for the resources you use.

> **MORE INFO**   **WINDOWS AZURE**
>
> The Microsoft cloud computing network is Windows Azure. For more information, visit *http://www.microsoft.com/windowsazure/*.

Load Testing

Load testing, also known as stress testing, generates a large number of application requests to determine your application's peak capacity. Load testing allows you to determine several pieces of information:

- The maximum number of requests per second to which your application can respond.

- How your application fails at peak capacity: whether it degrades gracefully or simply crashes.

- Your application's performance bottleneck. By using Performance Monitor during load testing, you can identify whether the performance bottleneck is the web server, application server, or database server, and whether that server is bottlenecked by processing capabilities, memory, disk I/O, or network I/O.

Using Queuing

Queuing is an important concept for scalability because it allows requests to be handled at a later time, smoothing out the utilization peaks that most server applications experience. Queuing also allows the application to prioritize requests, processing the most critical requests immediately and processing less important requests when the server has capacity. Essentially, queuing allows an application to asynchronously handle a request at a later time, rather than immediately rejecting it.

Although queuing is not an option for many application scenarios, it works well with scenarios that might take a long time to process, or where a dependent service might not always be available—for example:

- **Credit card processing**   Credit card processing services are notoriously unreliable. Using queuing, an e-commerce application can accept a customer's order and add her credit card information to the queue. If the queue is short and the credit card processing service is responding immediately, the application can confirm the order while she is still online. If the service is offline or there is a long queue, it could confirm the order later or request alternate payment information by sending an email to her.

- **Reporting**   Some reports can take several minutes or even hours to process. In this scenario, the application can add the report request to a queue and email the user when the report is available. Shorter or more important reports can be prioritized so that they are handled first.

You can use Microsoft Message Queuing (MSMQ) and the *System.Messaging* namespace to implement queuing. There are also third-party queuing systems, such as RabbitMQ. Because this exam is design-oriented, you do not need to know how to implement queuing. However, you should understand the types of scenarios where queuing might be useful, and you should be able to suggest queuing to meet requirements for prioritization or asynchronous request handling.

Performance Tuning

You don't always need to upgrade hardware to increase scalability. As a developer, you can increase an application's scalability simply by improving its efficiency. Some of the ways to performance-tune applications include:

- Turn off session state and view state when they are not required.

- Use the fewest server controls possible, and use the simplest server control that meets your needs. For example, do not use a Label control when you could use a Literal control instead. Do not use a Literal control when you do not need to change the contents at runtime; simply add the text directly to the ASPX page. For the greatest performance, create user controls that use *Response.Write* to render HTML and bypass server controls entirely.

- Optimize your database indexes based on actual application usage. One way to do this is to use the SQL Server Profiler, as described at *http://msdn.microsoft.com/library/ ms181091.aspx.*

- Use the Cache object and page and fragment caching, as discussed in Objective 5.4.

- Examine the Trace Information section of the Trace.axd output. Notice which portions of the page processing take the longest, and optimize those sections for performance.

- Use debugging tools to step through sections of code that consume the most resources, and verify that they run as efficiently as possible. Pay particular attention to code that runs within a loop, and move as much code outside of the loop as possible.

Before putting time into performance tuning an application, compare the cost of your development time to the cost of scaling the application up or out. In most cases, it is less expensive to purchase more server hardware to scale an application than it is to pay developers to optimize their code for performance.

Objective Summary

- Web application server hardware can be scaled up or out. When you scale an application up, you upgrade existing servers. When you scale an application out, you add additional servers and distribute the requests between them using load balancing.

- Cloud environments abstract your application from the physical servers that it runs on. They can be more efficient than traditional environments. Additionally, they typically charge only for the capacity that you use, decreasing your costs when your application is below peak capacity.

- Load testing simulates a large number of requests to your web application and determines an applications peak capacity. By using performance monitoring, you can determine your application's bottleneck, allowing you to use performance tuning or hardware upgrades to increase your application's scalability.

- Queuing, using a mechanism such as Microsoft Message Queuing (MSMQ), handles requests asynchronously and allows the application to prioritize requests.

- Though it is often more expensive than upgrading hardware, performance tuning can increase your code's efficiency and scalability.

Objective Review

Answer the following questions to test your knowledge of the information in this objective. You can find the answers to these questions and explanations of why each answer choice is correct or incorrect in the "Answers" section at the end of this chapter.

1. You are planning to scale out a web application to provide increased capacity. Currently, the web application runs on a single web server with a separate database server. The application uses session state to track users throughout their session. How can you add web servers while ensuring session state continues to work as expected? (Choose two. Each answer forms a complete solution.)

    A. Use the InProc session state.

    B. Use a separate session state server.

    C. Configure the load-balancing mechanism for server affinity.

    D. Configure the load-balancing mechanism to distribute requests evenly between the servers.

2. Recently, a web application failed because it received too many requests in a short amount of time. Currently, the web application runs on two servers: a single web server and a single database server. Performance analysis revealed that the web server was at 100 percent processor utilization at the time of the failure. You would like to allow

the web application to handle more requests without increasing your management or software licensing costs. Which approaches would you recommend? (Choose all that apply. Each answer forms part of the complete solution.)

A. Add processors to the web server.

B. Add an additional web server, and then configure round-robin DNS.

C. Use performance-tuning techniques to improve the efficiency of the ASP.NET code.

D. Use the SQL Server Profiler to improve the efficiency of the database indexes.

3. You are responsible for a web application that runs on a single server. You host the server at your local data center, which has a single Internet connection. After a recent application outage, management has decided to eliminate all single points of failure in the application architecture. Which approach should you recommend? (Choose all that apply. Each answer forms part of the complete solution.)

A. Add multiple network adapters to the web server, and then connect them to separate network switches.

B. Deploy the application to a cloud-hosting provider.

C. Deploy a second web server to the same data center, and then use a hardware load balancer.

D. Deploy a second web server to a different data center, and then configure round-robin DNS.

THOUGHT EXPERIMENT
Scaling a Web Application

I n the following thought experiment, you will apply what you've learned about the "Plan for Scalability and Reliability" objective to predict how a theoretical website architecture will perform. You can find answers to these questions in the "Answers" section at the end of this chapter.

You are a consultant for Wingtip Toys. Wingtip Toys is planning a new advertising campaign for its MVC web application at http://www.wingtiptoys.com. They have projected that the application will need to process 100 requests per second at peak utilization. Currently, the web application runs on a single server running Windows Server 2008 R2 and Microsoft SQL Server 2008 R2.

The Wingtip Toys IT department has created the following plan to test and scale its application:

1. Configure the logging of performance data for both IIS and SQL Server.

2. Use Visual Studio from the local network to simulate web requests. Gradually increase the number of requests to 100 requests per second, or increase them until the web server takes longer than two seconds to respond to a request.

3. If the web application fails to serve 100 requests per second, move SQL Server to a separate server and update the web application configuration.

4. Repeat the load test.

5. If the web application again fails to serve 100 requests per second, examine the performance data to identify the bottleneck. If the computer running SQL Server is the bottleneck, add an additional SQL Server computer and configure replication. If the web server is the bottleneck, add an additional web server and configure round-robin DNS.

6. Repeat steps 4 and 5 until the application successfully serves 100 requests per second.

Management wants your opinion on the scalability plan. Answer the following questions:

1. Will this process accurately predict whether the application will stay online? Why or why not?

2. Do you agree that we should move SQL Server to a different physical server if the web application fails the first load test? If not, what would you do instead?

3. Do you agree that we should scale out the web and database servers if they fail the second and subsequent load tests? If not, what would you do instead?

Objective 6.4: Design a Health-Monitoring Strategy

ASP.NET includes health-monitoring capabilities using the *System.Web.Management* namespace. Using built-in health monitoring, you can configure ASP.NET to notify systems administrators when different types of health events occur, such as the application starting and stopping, unhandled exceptions, and failure auditing.

This objective provides an overview of how to design an ASP.NET health-monitoring strategy.

Understanding Health-Monitoring Events

Health monitoring consists of two components: the event and the event provider. ASP.NET raises the health-monitoring events, and the event provider logs the event or directly notifies administrators.

The .NET Framework includes the following health-monitoring event types. Additionally, you can configure custom health-monitoring events.

- **WebBaseEvent**   All events
- **WebHeartbeatEvent**   Heartbeats that occur regularly to indicate the health-monitoring system is functioning
- **WebBaseErrorEvent**   All errors
- **WebErrorEvent**   Configuration errors
- **WebRequestErrorEvent**   Request-processing errors
- **WebAuditEvent**   All audit events, including successful and unsuccessful logon attempts
- **WebFailureAuditEvent** and **WebSuccessAuditEvent**   Either success or failure audits
- **WebAuthenticationFailureAuditEvent** and **WebAuthenticationSuccessAudit Event**   Either successful or unsuccessful authentication attempts
- **WebApplicationLifetimeEvent**   Events such as starting and stopping the application
- **WebRequestEvent**   Occurs when the application handles a request
- **WebViewStateFailureAuditEvent**   View state failures

By deriving a custom class from one of these event classes, you can create custom health-monitoring events to track application-specific events using standard or custom event providers.

Understanding Event Providers

ASP.NET health monitoring can log events or notify systems administrators of events using a variety of provider classes, including the following ones:

- **SimpleMailWebEventProvider** or **TemplatedMailWebEventProvider**   Sends an email

- **EventLogWebEventProvider** Adds an event to the event log (which can then be processed by common monitoring tools)
- **TraceWebEventProvider** Creates a trace message
- **WMIWebEventProvider** Creates a Windows Management Instrumentation (WMI) event

MORE INFO **LISTENING FOR WMI EVENTS**

For more information, read "Walkthrough: Listening for WMI Events in ASP.NET Health Monitoring" at *http://msdn.microsoft.com/library/ms178713.aspx.*

- **SQLWebEventProvider** Saves an event notification to a SQL database (which you must create using aspnet_regsql.exe)

It would be simple to send an email, create a trace message, or perform any of the tasks from the previous list. The advantage of using ASP.NET Health Monitoring is that systems administrators, without knowledge of writing ASP.NET code, can configure the web.config file to process health-monitoring events using whichever approach best integrates with their monitoring system. Even if systems administrators simply want the application to send them an email when events occur, you should leverage ASP.NET Health Monitoring. Later, if systems administrators change to a monitoring system that uses WMI events, they can update the monitoring technique without changing any application code.

Configuring Health Monitoring

Configuring event providers involves defining several elements within the <system.web> <healthMonitoring> section. The default web.config file (located at %windir%\Microsoft.NET\ Framework\v4.0.30319\Config\web.config) includes default values for all of these, simplifying standard configurations:

- **providers** Providers configure which event provider is used and the provider-specific details. For example, you can use the <providers> section to add a *SqlWebEvent-Provider* that uses a specific connection string and buffer mode. The default web. config file includes three standard providers: *EventLogProvider*, *LocalSqlServer*, and *WmiWebEventProvider*.
- **bufferModes** You can use buffers to regulate the flow of events by grouping multiple events together or by limiting the maximum number of events in a specific time period. This can prevent ASP.NET from sending hundreds of email notifications if an event occurs repeatedly, and it can reduce the performance impact of logging by handling a group of events all at once. Critical events that administrators must immediately respond to should not be buffered. Not only does buffering make events easier to manage, it reduces the vulnerability to denial-of-service attacks. The default web. config file includes four standard buffer modes: Logging, Analysis, Notification, and Critical Notification. Each provider can reference a *bufferMode* by name.

- **eventMappings**   Create event mappings to assign names to event sources, such as *System.Web.Management.WebAuditEvent* or *System.Web.Management.WebApplicationLifetimeEvent*. To monitor all events, create an event mapping for *System.Web.Management.WebBaseErrorEvent*. You can use rules to associate an event mapping to a provider.

- **profiles**   Profiles specify the minimum number of events that must occur for an event to be raised to the provider, the minimum interval between two events of the same type, and the maximum number of times events of the same type are raised. The default web.config file includes two standard profiles: Default (which waits one minute between events) and Critical (which does not wait between events).

- **rules**   Rules associate profiles, providers, and event mappings. The default web.config file includes two standard rules: All Errors Default and Failure Audits Default.

Additionally, you can configure the *heartbeatInterval* attribute of the <healthMonitoring> element. The *heartbeatInterval* specifies, in seconds, how often the provider raises the *WebHeartbeatEvent*. Heartbeats are useful for verifying that an event provider is functioning correctly; the consumer can detect a failure if a heartbeat event is not received within a timespan greater than the *heartbeatInterval*.

The following sample of a web.config file demonstrates how to configure a tracing event provider:

```
<healthMonitoring
    enabled="true"
    heartBeatInterval="0">
    <providers>
        <add name="TraceEventProvider"
            type="System.Web.Management.TraceWebEventProvider,
              System.Web"
            buffer="false"
            bufferMode=""
            maxEventLength="4096"
            maxSize="4096"
            maxMessagesPerNotification="1"
        />
    </providers>
    <eventMappings>
        <add name="Request Processing Events"
            type="System.Web.Management.WebRequestEvent, System.Web"
        />
    </eventMappings>
    <profiles>
        <add name="Trace"
            minInstances="1"
            maxLimit="Infinite"
            minInterval="00:00:00"
        />
    </profiles>
```

```
    <rules>
        <add name="Trace Request Processing"
            eventName="Request Processing Events"
            provider="TraceEventProvider"
            profile="Trace"
        />
    </rules>
</healthMonitoring>
```

Designing a Health-Monitoring Strategy

For enterprises with separate development and systems administration staff, designing a health-monitoring strategy is a two-phase process. First, the developers must determine which events within the application might need to be monitored. Second, the systems administration staff must configure health-monitoring providers and integrate them into their existing monitoring system.

As a developer, it is your responsibility to define custom health-monitoring event classes, and to raise those events at the appropriate places in your code. Create a separate class for each event type that the systems administration team might handle in a different way. Do not create custom classes when one of the standard classes will suffice or when your exception-handling strategy is sufficient.

Here are some of the health-monitoring event types that you might want to create:

- Authorization failures when authenticated users attempt to access resources they have not been granted access to

- Attack attempts, such as requests including SQL injection attacks, or repeated requests that might be part of a Denial-of-Service (DoS) attack

- Poor performance of supporting services that cannot be easily monitored by using Performance Monitor, such as an external Web service that takes more than one second to respond

When developers create a thoroughly instrumented application, systems administrators can choose which events are important to monitor and how they monitor them. Application health events must be integrated into their existing monitoring system, such as Microsoft System Center Operations Manager. To systems administrators, an effective health-monitoring strategy must have multiple levels, with these basic characteristics:

- Critical events that require immediate action, such as a database server that is not responding for more than five minutes, result in a notification. Notifications can be sent directly from ASP.NET using an email, or they could be generated by a monitoring system.

- Informational events that require tracking over time, such as a database server that occasionally fails to respond, are logged. ASP.NET can log events to a database, but most large organizations prefer to collect the information in their monitoring system.

- Insignificant events that require no action, such as a user who mistypes her password once, do not result in any notification.

Systems administrators should configure buffering to limit the number of events and reduce the exposure to a DoS attack. For example, systems administrators can configure buffering to ignore up to ten invalid login attempts within a single minute, but to alert systems administrators of a potential ongoing brute-force attack if users attempt more logins.

> **MORE INFO   ASP.NET HEALTH MONITORING**
>
> For more information, read "ASP.NET Health Monitoring Overview" at *http://msdn. microsoft.com/library/bb398933.aspx.*

Objective Summary

- Among other events, ASP.NET automatically raises health-monitoring events when an application starts and stops, when it handles a new request, when unhandled exceptions occur, and when a user attempts to log in either successfully or unsuccessfully.
- ASP.NET includes event providers that send an email, log events to a database, add events to the event log, create a trace message, or create a WMI event.
- Configure health monitoring by creating rules that associate events and event providers. Use buffering to limit when an event provider is called.
- An efficient health-monitoring strategy raises many different, application-specific events, but it calls an event provider only when systems administrators need to be aware of the event. Event providers should communicate with an organization's existing monitoring system.

Objective Review

Answer the following questions to test your knowledge of the information in this objective. You can find the answers to these questions and explanations of why each answer choice is correct or incorrect in the "Answers" section at the end of this chapter.

1. You are designing an ASP.NET application. The systems administration team has requested that their monitoring system be notified each time the application starts. Their monitoring system can read events from the event log. You would like to minimize the amount of code you need to write. Which approach should you recommend?

   A. In *Application_Start*, add an event to the event log.

   B. Create a custom health-monitoring event class, and configure a standard provider.

   C. Use a standard health-monitoring event class, and configure a custom provider.

   D. Use a standard health-monitoring event class and provider.

2. You are designing an ASP.NET application. The systems administration team has a mobile phone that one member of the staff uses to be notified of outages. In the event your application receives more than 100 failed logon attempts in one minute, they would like the application to send a message directly to the on-call mobile phone using a web service on the local network. You would like to minimize the amount of code you need to write. Which approach should you recommend?

   A. Use a standard health-monitoring event class and provider.

   B. Create a custom health-monitoring event class, and configure a standard provider.

   C. Use a standard health-monitoring event class, and configure a custom provider.

   D. Use a custom health-monitoring event class, and configure a custom provider.

3. You are designing an ASP.NET application. The systems administration team has given you a list of events they would like to be able to monitor using ASP.NET health monitoring. Which of the following events will require developing a custom class?

   A. Receiving more than 500 requests in one minute.

   B. An authenticated user attempts to access a restricted portion of the application more than five times in one minute.

   C. A web service takes more than ten seconds to respond more than five times in two minutes.

   D. The application starts more than ten times in one minute.

THOUGHT EXPERIMENT
Designing a Health-Monitoring System

In the following thought experiment, you will apply what you've learned about the "Design a Health-Monitoring Strategy" objective to predict how a theoretical website architecture will perform. You can find answers to these questions in the "Answers" section at the end of this chapter.

You are a consultant for Blue Yonder Airlines. Blue Yonder is updating its existing public MVC web application that it uses to allow customers on the Internet to purchase and manage tickets. As part of the update, the company would like to improve its health-monitoring system so that significant application events are handled by its existing management software, Microsoft Systems Center Operations Manager. Currently, the system monitors the event log of computers and detects significant events.

Blue Yonder would like to monitor the following events:

- Application starts
- Application stops
- Invalid logon attempts
- When the database server fails to respond
- When the application stops responding to outside requests
- When the application returns a page without the company's contact information at the bottom of the page
- Invalid view-state data

The development team has designed a health-monitoring system with these attributes:

- They will use *EventLogWebEventProvider*.
- They will configure rules to monitor *WebHeartbeatEvent*, *WebAuthentication FailureAuditEvent*, and *WebViewStateFailureAuditEvent*.
- They will derive a custom class from *WebErrorEvent* that raises a health-monitoring event if the page output does not include the contact information.

Management wants your opinion on the design of the health-monitoring system. Answer the following questions about the future performance of the application:

1. Will this system meet all of our requirements? If not, what is missing?
2. Currently, they do not plan to use buffering within ASP.NET. Instead, they plan to filter insignificant requests within Operations Manager. Will this have any negative consequences? If so, what will the consequences be, and what would you do different?
3. Are we monitoring any unnecessary events? Which ones?

Chapter Summary

- You can deploy applications in four different ways: creating web packages, using XCopy, publishing the web application, or creating a Windows Installer package. When deploying an application, you can prevent the application from being updated or choose to deploy it as a single assembly to protect the source code from being easily viewed.

- The .NET Framework configuration hierarchy includes several levels: the machine.config file, an application's web.config file, a folder's web.config file, and separate configuration files defined by the *ConfigSource* attribute. Use configuration transforms to automatically publish different configuration settings to different environments. Use configuration pools to isolate an application, run an application with different privileges, or run an application in a different version of the .NET Framework.

- Web application server hardware can be scaled up (by upgrading individual servers) or out (by adding additional servers and load balancing). Hosting your application in a cloud can reduce costs and simplify scalability. To determine your application's capacity and identify performance bottlenecks, use load testing. When you need to prioritize asynchronous requests, use message queuing.

- Using ASP.NET Health Monitoring, you can log important events or notify systems administrators when they need to respond to a situation. Configure health monitoring by creating rules that associate events and event providers, and use buffering to limit when an event provider is called.

Answers

Objective 6.1 Review

1. **Correct Answers:** B and D

    A. **Incorrect:** The Publish Web tool precompiles an application, but it does not provide the option to prevent it from being updated.

    B. **Correct:** By omitting the *–u* parameter, you can use the ASP.NET Compilation Tool to prevent an application from being updated after deployment.

    C. **Incorrect:** Web deployment packages do not provide the option for preventing an application from being updated.

    D. **Correct:** If you install the Web Deployment Projects add-on for Visual Studio 2010, you can deploy applications and prevent them from being updated.

2. **Correct Answer:** D

    A. **Incorrect:** The Publish Web tool precompiles an application, but it does not provide the option to compile it to a single assembly.

    B. **Incorrect:** You cannot use the ASP.NET Compilation Tool to compile an application to a single assembly. However, you could use the Aspnet_Merge.exe tool to combine the output from the ASP.NET Compilation Tool to a single assembly.

    C. **Incorrect:** Web deployment packages do not provide the option for preventing an application from being updated.

    D. **Correct:** If you install the Web Deployment Projects add-on for Visual Studio 2010, you can deploy applications as a single assembly.

3. **Correct Answer:** C

    A. **Incorrect:** The Publish Web tool needs to communicate directly with the web server, which the firewalls described in the scenario prevent.

    B. **Incorrect:** The ASP.NET Compilation Tool compiles an application but does not package a database with it, nor does it provide a system for easily installing the application on a server.

    C. **Correct:** Web deployment packages make web applications easy to install, and they support distributing and installing databases.

    D. **Incorrect:** Web Deployment Projects provide more flexible compilation options, but they do not provide the ability to package databases with an application.

Objective 6.1 Thought Experiment

1. Yes.

2. No. Simply copying the files does not configure the database or other web server settings. Administrators would need to manually configure those aspects of the application when redeploying it.

3. A better approach would be to create web deployment packages. They are simple to install, they provide support for configuring a database, and many hosting providers natively support them.

Objective 6.2 Review

1. **Correct Answer:** B

   A. **Incorrect:** This might work, because some applications written for the .NET Framework 2.0 will run properly with the .NET Framework 4.0. However, it will probably cause compatibility problems. To minimize the compatibility problems, configure a new application pool with the .NET Framework 4.0.

   B. **Correct:** IIS can run different applications using different versions of the .NET Framework. Each application pool can use only a single version of the .NET Framework, however. Therefore, to configure the new application to run alongside the existing applications but use a different version of the .NET Framework, you must create a new application pool.

   C. **Incorrect:** Classic pipeline mode causes an application pool to behave more like earlier versions of IIS. However, classic pipeline mode does not minimize compatibility problems between different versions of the .NET Framework.

   D. **Incorrect:** Every application should have its own web.config file, regardless of the version of the .NET Framework that it uses.

2. **Correct Answers:** C and D

   A. **Incorrect:** *RemoteOnly* is a useful setting for production applications because it shows detailed error messages only to users logged on to the web server. However, this option does not address the requirement for preventing tracing, and it is easily handled using a transform file.

   B. **Incorrect:** You could store the connection strings in a separate file. However, you would need to manually update the connection strings each time you deployed the application—a process that would be both time-consuming and error-prone.

C. **Correct:** The standard web application templates provided by Visual Studio include the Web.Release.config file, which you can use to transform the standard web.config file when publishing a release build of the application to the production environment.

D. **Correct:** Because Visual Studio includes transform files only for Release and Debug, you should create a new transform file for the staging environment.

3. **Correct Answers:** A, C, and D

A. **Correct:** To create separate permissions for specific settings, move the settings from the web.config file to a separate file, use NTFS file permissions to configure access to the file, and use the *ConfigSource* attribute to specify the new file in the web.config file.

B. **Incorrect:** Transform files are useful for deploying different configuration settings to different environments. However, you cannot use them to delegate permissions to specific settings.

C. **Correct:** Refer to the explanation for answer A.

D. **Correct:** Refer to the explanation for answer A.

Objective 6.2 Thought Experiment

1. Yes. Transform files make it simple to change any setting, including connection strings.

2. Yes. Store the connection strings and any other settings the QA team needs to edit in a separate .config file, and grant them access to update only that file.

3. Yes. Create a separate application pool for the development environment, and limit the amount of processor time and memory that it can consume.

Objective 6.3 Review

1. **Correct Answers:** B and C

A. **Incorrect:** When you configure the InProc session state, session state is stored in a single server's memory. Therefore, if a subsequent request from the same user is sent to a different server, the server will not have access to the user's session data and will create a new session for the user.

B. **Correct:** When you configure a shared session state server, all web servers will store and retrieve session state from the server. Therefore, if subsequent requests from a user are sent to two different servers, they will each access the same session state data.

C. **Correct:** When you configure server affinity, all requests from a single user are sent to the same web server. Therefore, you can store session state as InProc. The only time session state will not be available in this scenario is when a server fails and a user's request is redirected to a different server.

D. **Incorrect:** Distributing requests evenly between servers provides for consistent session state only when the servers use a shared state server.

2. **Correct Answers:** A and C

A. **Correct:** Based on the performance analysis, the cause of the failure was probably the limited processing capacity of the web server. Adding processors will increase the maximum processing capacity and the maximum number of requests the web server can handle.

B. **Incorrect:** Although adding a web server would increase the maximum capacity of the web application, it would also increase management and software licensing costs.

C. **Correct:** By making the ASP.NET code more efficient, you can decrease the processing requirements for each request and increase the number of requests each web server can handle.

D. **Incorrect:** This approach would only increase processing capacity if the database server had been overutilized.

3. **Correct Answers:** B and D

A. **Incorrect:** Although it is possible to provide redundant hardware within a single server, this does not eliminate single points of failure. A power outage or failure of other server components would still cause the application to fail.

B. **Correct:** Cloud-hosting providers can provide redundancy for your application.

C. **Incorrect:** Although deploying a second web server and load balancer increases redundancy, it does not eliminate single points of failure. In this scenario, because the data center has only a single Internet connection, failure of that Internet connection would bring the web application offline.

D. **Correct:** By deploying a second web server to a different data center, you would be protected against a failure that might bring the first datacenter offline, such as an extended power outage or a failure of the nonredundant Internet connection. To provide the highest level of redundancy, choose a data center managed by a different hosting provider, with connections to different Internet service providers.

Objective 6.3 Thought Experiment

1. Probably. There is a significant factor that the load test is not testing: Internet bandwidth. Because the load test is connected to the local network, you are not testing whether the web server's connection to the Internet provides sufficient bandwidth. You could estimate the bandwidth requirements by determining the average page size and multiplying it by the number of requests per second. Alternatively, you could use a content delivery network (CDN) to provide images and other large files from a different location on the Internet.

2. No; it might be more cost effective to keep the single-server architecture. Instead of immediately separating SQL Server onto a different physical server, you should examine the performance data to determine the bottleneck. If the bottleneck is the database, it might be worthwhile to attempt to optimize the database indexes and the queries issued by the application. If the bottleneck is the web server, it might be worthwhile to examine the code and verify that the application follows ASP.NET performance best practices. Even if you don't want to spend developer time optimizing the code, you should verify that the web application and the database server are consuming the same resource before separating them onto different servers. For example, if web application performance is limited by processor time and the database is consuming very little processor capacity, separating the two processes onto separate servers would not alleviate the bottleneck; instead, it would increase software licensing and management costs.

3. Maybe. Management should also estimate the costs of scaling the application up; it might be more cost-effective.

Objective 6.4 Review

1. **Correct Answer:** D

    A. **Incorrect:** This approach would work, but it requires writing code, which can be avoided by using ASP.NET health monitoring.

    B. **Incorrect:** Although you could create a custom health-monitoring event class, it is unnecessary because you can use the standard *WebApplicationLifetimeEvent* class.

    C. **Incorrect:** Although you could create a custom provider class, it is unnecessary because you can use the standard *EventLogWebEventProvider* class.

    D. **Correct:** You can meet these requirements with standard ASP.NET health monitoring by mapping *WebApplicationLifetimeEvent* to the *EventLogWebEventProvider*.

2. **Correct Answer:** C

    A. **Incorrect:** No standard providers are capable of contacting a web service. There-fore, you need to create a custom provider.

    B. **Incorrect:** No standard providers are capable of contacting a web service. You need to also create a custom provider.

    C. **Correct:** You can use the *WebAuthenticationFailureAuditEvent* class and configure buffering to call the event provider only when the event occurs more than 100 times in a minute. You will need to create a custom provider to contact the web service, however.

    D. **Incorrect:** You do not need to create a custom health-monitoring event class because you can use the *WebAuthenticationFailureAuditEvent* class and configure buffering to call the event provider only when the event occurs more than 100 times in a minute.

3. **Correct Answer:** C

    A. **Incorrect:** You can accomplish this by buffering the *WebRequestEvent* class.

    B. **Incorrect:** You can accomplish this by buffering the *WebAuthenticationFailure AuditEvent* class.

    C. **Correct:** You cannot accomplish this with any of the built-in classes, so you need to derive a class from the *WebErrorEvent* class.

    D. **Incorrect:** You can accomplish this by buffering the *WebApplicationLifetimeEvent* class.

Objective 6.4 Thought Experiment

1. No. The health-monitoring system cannot determine whether the application is responding to outside requests. Although you could monitor *WebRequestEvent* to verify that the application is responding to requests, a better way to test whether the application is available on the Internet is to use a third-party website monitoring service. Such services regularly send requests to your website and alert you if it is not available.

2. Maybe. ASP.NET would need to add an event to the event log for every request. If the application receives a large number of invalid logon requests, this could significantly impact the performance of the application and might even cause the application to fail. A better choice would be to perform buffering in ASP.NET.

3. Yes. You do not need to monitor *WebHeartbeatEvent* to meet your requirements.

Index

A

acceptance testing, 176

access, authorizing with configuration files, 149

action filters, custom, 164

ActiveXControls property, 70

ADONETDATACONTEXT class, 113

ADONETSERVICEPROXY class, 112

ADO.NET, using, 88

ADPlus, 192

AJAX client control, binding a collection to, 107

API testing, 177

appearance, themes and style sheets for changing, 61

application architecture, designing

   client-side technologies (objective 1.3)

      client-side scripting languages, using, 26–29

      objective review correct answers, 52

      objective review questions, 30

      objective summary, 30

      rich client-side plug-ins, using, 29

      thought experiment, evaluating the impact of rich client features, 32, 53

   division of application logic (objective 1.1)

      client-side vs. server-side processes, 2–5

      long-running processes, planning, 7–10

      objective review correct answers, 49

      objective review questions, 10

      objective summary, 10

      partitioning according to separation of concerns, 5

      thought experiment, moving a site from an intranet to the Internet, 12, 50

   requirements and system topology (objective 1.2)

      baseline needs, evaluating, 21

      interactions between applications, designing, 14–17

      mapping logical design to physical implementation, 17–19

      nonfunctional requirements and cross-cutting concerns, validating, 19–21

      objective review correct answers, 51

      objective review questions, 23

      objective summary, 23

      system topology, designing, 13

      thought experiment, planning for scalability and forward compatibility, 24, 51

   server-side technologies (objective 1.4)

      control types, choosing between, 33–35

      objective review correct answers, 53

      objective review questions, 37

      objective summary, 36

      partial classes and methods, using, 35

      server-side methods, accessing from client code, 35

      thought experiment, evaluating a real-time web application design, 38, 54

   state management (objective 1.5)

      application state, using, 39

      cache object, using, 40

      custom page state persisters, creating, 44

      objective review correct answers, 55

      objective review questions, 46

      objective summary, 45

      session state, using, 42–44

      thought experiment, scaling state management, 47, 56

      user state technologies, evaluating, 40

application domains, configuring, 139

Application_Error method, 185

M

N

O

S

W

X

About the Author

TONY NORTHRUP, MCPD, MCITP, MCSE, and CISSP, is a consultant and author living in Waterford, Connecticut. Tony started C++ and assembly programming long before Windows 1.0 was released, but has focused on Windows development and administration for the last eighteen years. He has about 30 books and several video training courses covering Windows development, networking, and security. Among other titles, Tony is coauthor of the Microsoft Press MCTS Training Kit for exam 70-515 (Web Applications Development with Microsoft .NET Framework 4) and the author of the Microsoft Press MCTS Training Kit for exam 70-536 (Microsoft .NET Framework Application Development Foundation). You can learn more about Tony by friending him on Facebook at *http://facebook.com/tony.northrup*, visiting his personal website at *www.northrup. org*, reading his technical blog at *http://vistaclues.com*, and viewing his photography portfolio at *http://northrupphotography.com*.

For C# Developers

**Microsoft®
Visual C#® 2010
Step by Step**

John Sharp

ISBN 9780735626706

Teach yourself Visual C# 2010—one step at a time.
Ideal for developers with fundamental programming
skills, this practical tutorial delivers hands-on guidance
for creating C# components and Windows–based
applications. CD features practice exercises, code
samples, and a fully searchable eBook.

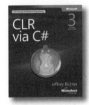

**CLR via C#,
Third Edition**

Jeffrey Richter

ISBN 9780735627048

Dig deep and master the intricacies of the common
language runtime (CLR) and the .NET Framework.
Written by programming expert Jeffrey Richter, this
guide is ideal for developers building any kind of
application—ASP.NET, Windows Forms, Microsoft
SQL Server®, web services, console apps—and
features extensive C# code samples.

**Microsoft
XNA® Game Studio 4.0:
Learn Programming Now!**

Rob Miles

ISBN 9780735651579

Create your own games for Xbox 360®, Windows
Phone 7, or your Windows-based PC—as you learn
the underlying skills for computer programming.
No experience required!

**Programming Windows®
Identity Foundation**

Vittorio Bertocci

ISBN 9780735627185

Take control of access and identity management with
Windows Identity Foundation (WIF). Led by a member
of the WIF engineering team, you'll learn practical,
scenario-based approaches for implementing WIF in
your web applications and services.

**Microsoft® ASP.NET 4
Step by Step**

George Shepherd

ISBN 9780735627017

Ideal for developers with fundamental programming
skills—but new to ASP.NET—who want hands-on
guidance for developing web applications in the
Microsoft Visual Studio® 2010 environment.

**Programming
Microsoft ASP.NET 4**

Dino Esposito

ISBN 9780735643383

Get the definitive guide to programming with
ASP.NET 4 technologies. Led by web development
expert Dino Esposito, you'll gain the essential
insights on design principles, patterns, and tradeoffs—
along with scenario-based guidance for taking your
solutions to the next level.

**Microsoft®
Press**

For Visual Basic Developers

**Microsoft®
Visual Basic® 2010
Step by Step**

Michael Halvorson

ISBN 9780735626690

Teach yourself the essential tools and techniques for Visual Basic 2010—one step at a time. No matter what your skill level, you'll find the practical guidance and examples you need to start building applications for Windows and the web.

Coding Faster: Getting More Productive with Microsoft Visual Studio

Zain Naboulsi and Sara Ford

ISBN 9780735649927

Work smarter and increase your productivity with expert tips and tricks using Visual Studio. You'll find practical advice and shortcuts for the code editor, visual designers, search capabilities, debugger, and other features of the IDE.

Inside the Microsoft Build Engine: Using MSBuild and Team Foundation Build, Second Edition

Sayed Ibrahim Hashimi, William Bartholomew

ISBN 9780735645240

Your practical guide to using, customizing, and extending the build engine in Visual Studio 2010.

Parallel Programming with Microsoft Visual Studio 2010

Donis Marshall

ISBN 9780735640603

The roadmap for developers wanting to maximize their applications for multicore architecture using Visual Studio 2010.

**Microsoft
Visual Basic 2010
Developer's Handbook**

Sarika Calla Purohit and Klaus Löffelmann

ISBN 9780735627055

Learn practical, scenario-based approaches for using Visual Basic 2010 for everything from core Window® and web development to building advanced multithreaded applications.

**Microsoft®
Press**

For Web Developers

**Microsoft® ASP.NET 4
Step by Step**
George Shepherd
ISBN 9780735627017

Ideal for developers with fundamental programming skills—but new to ASP.NET—who want hands-on guidance for developing web applications in the Microsoft Visual Studio® 2010 environment.

**Microsoft Silverlight® 4
Step by Step**
Laurence Moroney
ISBN 9780735638877

Teach yourself essential tools and techniques for Silverlight 4—and begin creating interactive UIs for the web and the latest version of Windows® Phone.

**Programming
Microsoft ASP.NET 4**
Dino Esposito
ISBN 9780735643383

Get the definitive guide to programming with ASP.NET 4 technologies. Led by web development expert Dino Esposito, you'll gain the essential insights on design principles, patterns, and tradeoffs—along with scenario-based guidance for taking your solutions to the next level.

**Microsoft
ASP.NET Internals**
George Shepherd
ISBN 9780735626416

Make web pages more efficient—and speed development—by understanding how ASP.NET works in depth. This book delves into architecture and provides established patterns.

**Programming
Microsoft ASP.NET MVC**
*Covers ASP.NET MVC 2 and
Microsoft Visual Studio 2010*
Dino Esposito
ISBN 9780735627147

Author Dino Esposito leads you through the features, principles, and pillars of the ASP.NET MVC framework, demonstrating how and when to use this model to gain full control of HTML, simplify testing, and design better web sites and experiences.

**Microsoft ASP.NET and
AJAX: Architecting Web
Applications**
Dino Esposito
ISBN 9780735626218

Rethink the way you plan, design, and build web applications. Whether updating legacy sites or architecting RIAs from the ground up—you'll learn pragmatic approaches to AJAX development you can employ today.

**Programming
Microsoft LINQ in
Microsoft .NET Framework 4**
Paolo Pialorsi and Marco Russo
ISBN 9780735640573

The ideal reference for learning how to write queries natively in Microsoft Visual C#® or Microsoft Visual Basic® with LINQ.

What do you think of this book?

We want to hear from you!

To participate in a brief online survey, please visit:

microsoft.com/learning/booksurvey

Tell us how well this book meets your needs—what works effectively, and what we can do better. Your feedback will help us continually improve our books and learning resources for you.

Thank you in advance for your input!